A GRAND OLD FLAG

"The whole inspiration of our life as a nation flows out from the waving folds of this banner."—*Anonymous*

A GRAND OLD FLAG

BY KEVIN KEIM & PETER KEIM

**LONDON, NEW YORK, MUNICH,
MELBOURNE, AND DELHI**

senior editor | ANJA SCHMIDT

designer | JESSICA PARK

art director | DIRK KAUFMAN

managing art editor | MICHELLE BAXTER

dtp coordinator | KATHY FARIAS

production manager | IVOR PARKER

executive managing editor | SHARON LUCAS

Published by DK Publishing
375 Hudson Street, New York, New York 10014

07 08 09 10 10 9 8 7 6 5 4 3 2 1

DK Books are available at special discounts for bulk
purchases for sales promotions, premiums, fund-
raising, or educational use. For details contact DK
Publishing Special Markets, 375 Hudson Street, New
York, New York 10014 or SpecialSales@dk.com.

A catalog record for this book is available from the
Library of Congress.

ISBN 978-0-7566-2847-5
Color reproduction by Colourscan, Singapore
Printed in China by Toppan Printing Co.,
(Shenzen) Ltd.

Discover more at www.dk.com

CONTENTS

PREFACE: *Collecting American Flags*

One of my earliest and most vivid childhood memories is the flag that my grandfather flew at our home in Erie, Pennsylvania, during World War II. Like most of our neighbors, he flew the flag daily, and he taught me to treat the flag with respect. It has always been a proud symbol for our family. Even though my grandfather's flag was an ordinary 48-Star Flag, no different than any of the millions like it that were made, it is one of my most treasured possessions.

For over thirty years I have collected antique Stars and Stripes. A serendipitous discovery launched me on this flag-collecting odyssey. My wife, Patricia, and I loved to collect antique American furniture and spent many weekends, with our children in tow, scouring antique stores, flea markets, and auctions throughout many states. In the summer of 1976, fate led me to a woefully attended flea market set up in a muddy field in rural Kutztown, Pennsylvania, where I encountered a woman selling dishes, glasses, and other unimpressive items for sale, arranged on a card table.

A grocery bag holding what appeared to be an old flag caught my attention. When I asked about its price, she stated, "fifty dollars." From what I could see through the semitransparent bag, one of the white stripes appeared to be stained. Knowing nothing else about the condition of the flag (or anything about antique textiles for that matter), I offered her forty dollars. She accepted.

Only later that day did I open the bag and discover the flag was hand-sewn with thirteen stars. How old was it? Who made it? Where was it made and flown? What was its history?

A few weeks later I purchased a tattered 38-Star Flag at an antique store in Pittsburgh, as well as several books on the history of the flag. I decided to curtail my furniture collecting and instead dedicate my time to building a collection that would tell the story of the Stars and Stripes. Ever since, the search has occupied my time and energy—each flag, instead of making me feel the collection was more complete, propelled me to find even more. I have discovered, pursued, stumbled upon, traded, tracked down, and been given flags as gifts. I have found flags in basements, barns, New York

City auction houses, on the Internet, through dealers, friends, and even in foreign countries. Today, the collection includes well over four hundred flags, dating from every period in our nation's history. Most of these flags were preserved and cared for by Americans from every station in life, reminding us that the flag is for everyone: immigrant or native or descendant of one of the colonists; Army private or Navy admiral; ordinary steelworker or even, in one case, an Italian princess.

As any collector knows, the thrill of the hunt, the unanticipated discovery, or the "eureka" moments, sometimes outshine the pleasure of the actual things we collect.

Carl Keim, my grandfather, was born in 1890 near Mosbach, Germany. He immigrated to the United States when he was about twenty-one years old and settled in Erie, Pennsylvania, where he had a business making cigars in a shop behind his house on Poplar Street. He flew this 48-Star Flag daily during World War II.

For flags, that is especially true, since some flags are particularly rare and difficult to find.

Soon after I began, I realized there was one basic rule for collecting American flags: count the stars. (And to take it one step further, rule two was to count the stripes.) As simple as this rule seems, flags were often described inaccurately because of simple counting errors. Several years ago, for example, I came across a 26-Star Flag for sale. Upon my inquiry, it was indeed confirmed

as having twenty-six stars, representing Michigan, admitted to the Union in 1837, and official until 1845, when Florida became a state. Even though 26-Star Flags are more common than others since they were made for eight years, and even though the seller did not have a photograph of the flag, I purchased it anyway.

The flag arrived and upon my initial inspection, my excitement heightened when I counted, "25, 26, and... 27." Yes, twenty-seven stars, dating to 1845, when Florida was admitted to the Union. Texas was admitted to the Union only ten months later on December 29, 1845, and the 28-Star Flag became official on July 4, 1846. Since this Florida flag was official for such a short period of time, it is extremely difficult to find, and the simple counting error provided an unexpected rare flag for my collection!

Even more memorable than these chance acquisitions are the people and stories that flags represent—they are, in my mind, what make each flag invaluable. Each one is a reminder that flags are far more than pieces of fabric, they are symbols of the most fundamental values we share, windows to people who came before us and whose lives added, through acts of modesty or great valor, to our national heritage.

One 30-Star Flag stands out. In 1995, I was visiting an antique market in Adamstown, Pennsylvania. Walking from booth to booth, I methodically asked the dealers if they had any flags. Seldom did they have anything other than what was on display. But that Sunday I was quite lucky when I stopped to talk to a dealer who featured old toys that were neatly arranged in glass cases. When I asked him the standard question, he said, after a brief pause, "I do have one old flag, but it is in bad shape." He opened one of the toy cases and lifted a small mechanical tin truck, revealing a cardboard box underneath. Written in heavy, script letters on the side of the box were the words "Civil War Flag." (Fortunately the side of the box with the writing faced away from the customers, many of whom were very avid and competitive Civil War collectors!)

Inside the box I found a delicate 30-Star Flag. To my amazement, the history of the flag was written on the inside of the box: "This Flag, my dear Mother was holding, belonged to her Father and laid on the coffin of his friend, Colonel Coyle, a young U.S. Officer of the

This cotton, hand-sewn 30-Star Flag was draped on the coffin of a Civil War colonel. The stripes have turned to a soft red, and the canton has faded to a powder blue.

Civil War, who was shot through the lungs and went to Paris for treatment. I think he died of a hemorrhage in my Father's arms . . . delivered . . . Daughter Dorothy . . . I should thank my beloved cousin, who has always cared for this Flag."

I have attempted to learn more about Colonel Coyle, but my efforts have been unsuccessful. Like many of the millions killed or injured during the Civil War, he left scant footprints. However, each time I display this flag, it resonates powerfully with the great and terrible sacrifices made during that war.

The events of 9/11, of course, deepened and extended the flag's meaning for Americans, including new generations of young Americans. I marked the 50-Star Flag that happened to be flying at our home that day with a special tag. The following year, I began my own simple tradition of flying that same flag on each consecutive September 11th to honor and remember those whose lives changed that day.

As I have traveled the country exhibiting flags from my collection and giving talks on their history, I have been struck by three things. First, very few Americans know much about our flag. Second, they become intensely interested in its history when they begin to listen to stories about the flag. Third, people are eager to display the flag, either to celebrate national holidays or as a daily reminder of the freedoms we enjoy. During exhibitions of flags from my collection, people frequently share stories with me about "their flag." Once a man told me about his 29-Star Flag with an unusual star arrangement and eagerly invited me to his home to see it. I accepted his invitation, and after telling me about the flag, he insisted I add it to my collection, since he wanted it to be enjoyed by people. Each time I include that flag in an exhibition, I am reminded of him and others who are so proud of the American flag.

Thirty years of collecting have resulted in a special opportunity to tell the story of the Stars and Stripes with actual flags. Each individual flag has its own story to tell, representing a particular time in our nation's history. All together, the flags tell a much larger story—one of pride and devotion, and commitment to the ideals that nourish freedom and justice and equality.
—Peter Keim, M.D.

Kevin and Peter Keim stand in front of a garrison-sized, hand-sewn, wool flag with applied linen stars.

Introduction: *A Symbol*

Flags are visual symbols, and few symbols are as universally recognized as the American flag. Despite the widespread familiarity of the flag, however, not many people are familiar with its history. While most Americans can effortlessly recite the *Pledge of Allegiance*, most know little about the origins of the flag itself. The tale of Betsy Ross, for most people, is the beginning and the end of their impression of how the Stars and Stripes came to be.

This is hardly surprising, as one of the facts about the flag is that there are, indeed, very few facts about its origin. Historians have combed through all of our literature, all of our archives, all of our attics, but have found little to illuminate the inspiration for the simple statement, known as the First Flag Resolution, that created the Stars and Stripes.

But from the time the Stars and Stripes was born in Philadelphia on June 14, 1777, its warp and weft have provided the fabric of our nation's story. Extending the metaphor, just as yarns are woven from opposite directions to create fabric, we believe that the Stars and Stripes evolved from the intermingling of two profoundly different messages: one a symbol of subjugation and tyranny, the other a symbol of the splendor of a revolutionary political idea that laid the foundation for the liberty and justice that is the birthright of every American.

This is a story of a collection of actual flags. It is also a story of the Stars and Stripes, its history, meaning, symbolism, and presence in our national experience. It is a deep and rich history, one that intersects with many fascinating spheres of the American story: the founding of the nation's principles, politics, warfare, statehood, territorial expansion, textile production, design, and popular culture.

At their most fundamental level, flags are nothing more than pieces of fabric—wool, cotton, silk, or linen—sewn together to advertise nationhood, or some other political or collective group. They have been used, in some form or another since antiquity, both in the East and the West. But the Stars and Stripes, for the majority of Americans, is something far more than a token of citizenship; it is a deeply meaningful symbol.

WHAT THE FLAG MEANS

When we look at America's history, we begin to understand that the flag's symbolism did not spontaneously capture the average citizen's adoration,

or even attention, when it was first unfurled during the Revolutionary War. Mention of the flag was scarcely made during Revolutionary times, in fact. It was the War of 1812, and especially the Civil War, that permanently implanted the flag in the nation's collective consciousness, making the flag a symbol of freedom, perseverance, liberty, and justice.

Many of the images, both tragic and triumphant, that have cadenced the American experience often include a flag. Washington crossing the Delaware. The bombardment of Fort McHenry. Ellis Island. The Centennial. Pearl Harbor. Iwo Jima. V-J Day celebrations in Times Square. President Kennedy's funeral procession. The Moon landing. The Bicentennial. The 1980 Olympics hockey game. And 9/11. In addition to all of these momentous and poignant events, there are all of the other stories, too many to be told here, of ordinary people and their extraordinary feats of heroism and service.

Those stirring images are today crowded by images of the flag that proliferate everywhere: on car bumpers, T-shirts, television commercials, tattoos, food labels, politicians' lapels, and even on bandanas or underwear. Does the visual abundance of flags, their omnipresence in our cultural landscape, cheapen their meaning? Or does this kind of popularity emphasize a democratic message? Just as society changes, attitudes about how the flag should be used or displayed also change with the times. For generations, using the flag in any kind of advertisement or adorning one's body with the flag was sharply regarded as unacceptable. Even political candidates avoided using the flag as a campaign tool. How one displayed, cared for, and retired a flag was a demonstration of respect, worthy of care and ritual. (Old tattered flags, for instance, were often retired by burning or burial.) Notwithstanding the reverence people felt for the flag, Americans have always been reluctant to support laws prohibiting flag desecration.

NEEDLE AND THREAD

How early American flags were made also reminds us of our nation's humble beginnings. Ironically, many early American flags, even those as late as the Civil War, were made of British wool bunting. America was predominantly a rural, sparsely populated place, with limited capacity for textile production or the wherewithal to start such industries. Sometimes,

flags on the frontier were made of even more modest materials—whatever was available—with patch stars and stitched grommets. Often, spaces were cut out of the blue fabric, so that the white stars on the front "peeked" through to the back, demonstrating an economy of means. Daily survival, to be sure, took precedence over the "fancy" work that flags required. Until the dawn of American industrialism in the mid-19th century, many flags were made at home or by flag makers or seamstresses in small shops. And since sewing was considered "home craft," it is fair to assume that many early flags were made by women. Perhaps that's why the maternal tale of Betsy Ross has so potently and tenaciously adhered to the birth of the flag.

Today, the vast majority of American flags are manufactured. Few of these are even touched by an actual person during the fabrication process. Flags are made with machine-embroidered stars, tightly woven fabric, and chemical dyes, and are stitched together with military, unerring precision. Most are made of synthetic cloth. A profound quality of the old flags presented in this book is the legacy of human touch, of an American's personal care, effort, and attention. The skillful needle stitch, a patch to bind a tear, the thoughtful arrangement of stars, homespun thread—these all remind us that someone expressed their pride by making a flag with their own hands. That flags could be, and were, in fact, made by anyone is emblematic of the idea that it was always a symbol of the American republic, a government responsible to everyone. That ordinary people, most now long forgotten, took the time to sew pieces of red, white, and blue fabric together speaks volumes that the flag is for all people, regardless of station in life, ethnic background, or political persuasion.

And like the nation it represented—absorbing Americans who came from everywhere, with different languages, religious beliefs, and customs—most antique Stars and Stripes were eccentrically unalike. Not until 1912, during the presidency of William Howard Taft, in fact, was there any direction for how, officially, the flag's stars should be laid out. That fact alone provided us with an abundance of wonderful designs, made throughout the history of the Republic according to the judgment, eye, and even whim of the flag maker.

The flag is also symbolic of the very "stitching together" of the Union, state by state, stripe by stripe, and star by star, and this also makes its story the story of

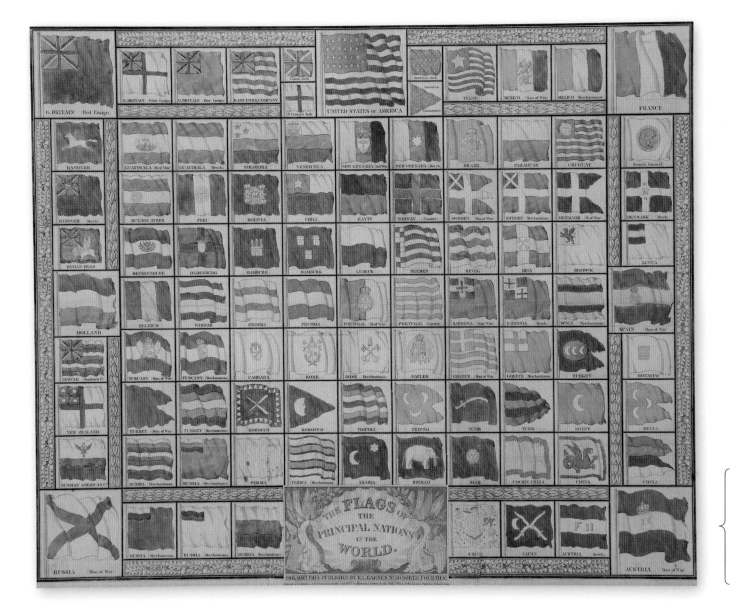

A 19th-century illustration depicts a profusion of designs used by various nations and private trading companies. Stars, crescents, stripes, bars, and crosses were common devices.

America itself. It is difficult as modern-day Americans to imagine the precariousness of 1776 America, to place ourselves in a setting that is profoundly foreign, given our ease of travel, communication, and comfort. That a scattered community of colonists wedged between a domineering colonial power (with awesome naval power to back it up) to the east, and the great, fearsome, wild unknowns to the west (which, for early Americans, began just over the ridge of the Appalachian mountains), managed to create a radically new nation, forged in discussion, debate, philosophy, and science is, in a sense, the loom upon which the Stars and Stripes was woven. Of the countless flags that have been made since 1777,

relatively few authentic ones have survived. Fabric unravels; it disintegrates and fades. The flags in this book, we believe, as tattered and worn as some may be, are precious survivors from our past. Each tells a story. But the story of *A Grand Old Flag*, the origin of the Stars and Stripes, does not, in fact, quite begin with a flag. Instead, it begins with a flag pole.

THE CONTINENTAL COLOURS

On the last day of 1775, Major General William Howe, a British commander, observed through a spy glass a group of men maneuvering an immense ship's mast into place. The activity would have been a familiar sight on

the seafaring New England coast, particularly in Boston where he and his army were besieged, except that the Americans, led by the forty-two-year-old, 6-foot-4 General George Washington, were lifting the mast into the December sky on land, nowhere near a ship. In fact, they were setting it upright on the very top of Prospect Hill across the water from the city. Some say the mast was 76 feet high.

The mast, Howe and his aides realized the next day on New Year's morning 1776, had been set up as a flagpole. Flying at its top was the first flag that represented thirteen united colonies. Known as the Continental Colours, and later the "Grand Union,"

the flag was a field of thirteen alternating red and white stripes, and a British Union Jack in the upper left canton.

The flag was first made and flown in Philadelphia, hoisted it is believed, by the young John Paul Jones on the ship *Alfred* in early December 1775. What the flag meant when Washington raised it himself in Boston was unclear, just as unclear, in fact, as the colonists' goals at the start of the Revolutionary War, before the inking of the Declaration of Independence. Some predicted that the Americans, represented by the stripes, side by side, wished to remain loyal to the Crown, signified by the Union Jack. Others guessed that the Union Jack's diminished size and placement within the thirteen stripes indicated the pursuit of autonomy, recognition as a quasi-independent people, to be treated with the full measure of equality and representation in Parliament. But Howe, who was known to be a lazy, unimaginative commander, hesitant to take risks, interpreted the Continental Colours quite differently, judging it to be a signal of submission to British authority.

The Americans were not willing to submit. Bolstered by a growing army arranged in a great arc around Boston, and reinforced by artillery hauled across Massachusetts from Fort Ticonderoga, Washington had the upper hand, and it was Howe who submitted. On March 17, 1776, the British evacuated to Nova Scotia.

Washington's army entered Boston with this new flag. By April, North Carolina issued a seven-and-a-half dollar note picturing the Continental Colours. And on November 16, the *Andrew Doria*, sent to the West Indies to deliver a copy of the Declaration of Independence, entered the harbor of St. Eustatius flying a Continental Colours. The Dutch governor ordered his men to render a canon salute, the very first time, historian Barbara W. Tuchman wrote, a uniquely American flag was formally recognized by a foreign power. By then, of course, the Declaration made it clear that the Americans' intention was full independence. The Union Jack was no longer an appropriate symbol for the revolutionary struggle. A new flag was needed.

—Kevin Keim

Known variously as the Continental Colours, Great Union, or Grand Union, this flag was used in the early stages of American Revolution. The Grand Union flag shown here was made in 1876 to commemorate the Centennial. Many reproduction flags were made that year in an outpouring of patriotic fervor. A similar reproduction Grand Union Flag was flown over Independence Hall on July 4th, 1876.

How This Book Is Organized

Since states, and hence stars, were introduced at uneven intervals throughout American history, the problem of organizing this book threatened to be a difficult task. Studying flag chronology, however, provided the answer. Since 1818, new flags were authorized on the July 4th following each state's admission, connecting the Stars and Stripes with the propitious events of 1776. Coincidentally, if the Independence Days of 1776, 1826 (Semicentennial), and 1876 (Centennial) are set as milestones, each period of time, before or after each date, produced twelve or thirteen flags!

OFFICIAL AND UNOFFICIAL FLAGS

Historic American Stars and Stripes can be organized into two general categories: official and unofficial flags. Official flags are those that directly resulted from one of three legislations: the first Flag Resolution (1777); the second Flag Act (1795); or the third Flag Act (1818). While the laws of 1777 and 1795 each created a specific flag—the 13-Star and 15-Star, respectively—the 1818 legislation outlined the rule, still in use, that guided how and when each new American flag should be introduced following the admission of states to the Union.

Therefore, while the 13-Star Flag of 1777 can be regarded as official, the 14-Star Flag was never officially mandated. Not until 1795 did the Continental Congress officially add one star each for the 14th and 15th states, Vermont and Kentucky. The 14-Star Flag, therefore, is known as an unofficial flag, and the 15-Star Flag as an

official flag. Nevertheless, both official and unofficial flags are considered legal flags of the United States and are accorded the same respect as a current 50-Star Flag.

OFFICIAL		UNOFFICIAL	
13-Star	33-Star	14-Star	39-Star
15-Star	34-Star	16-Star	40-Star
20-Star	35-Star	17-Star	41-Star
21-Star	36-Star	18-Star	42-Star
23-Star	37-Star	19-Star	47-Star
24-Star	38-Star	22-Star	
25-Star	43-Star		
26-Star	44-Star	Note: Although	
27-Star	45-Star	very rare, Stars and	
28-Star	46-Star	Stripes made with	
29-Star	48-Star	less than 13 stars	
30-Star	49-Star	are regarded as	
31-Star	50-Star	unofficial flags.	
32-Star			

(Once a Stars and Stripes is made, it is permanently regarded as a flag, even though it may be "out of date.") In all, there have been twenty-seven official flags and eleven unofficial flags.

Why would people make flags that were unofficial? In some cases, the flag maker may have wanted to express pride in his or her home territory achieving statehood. A 17-Star Flag would have had special meaning for an Ohioan, for instance, in 1803. It was also not uncommon that the flag maker was simply

unaware of the accurate number of states in the Union. In other cases, stars were added to existing flags as new states were admitted, anticipating the changes that would customarily have been made on upcoming July 4th Independence holidays.

STITCHING TOGETHER A NATION

The Stars and Stripes is one of the few national flags that officially changes as the nation grows, making each flag a textile milestone representing a moment in our history. The history of territorial expansion and statehood is a complex puzzle of geography, politics, warfare, and chronology. This book's maps are intended to represent the extent of the political nation at the time of each state's entry into the Union, focusing on the outlines of states and territories.

Sovereign nations (Britain, Spain, France, the Netherlands, Mexico, Canada, and Russia to name a few), native tribes and confederations of tribes, families and estates, trading and property companies, states and commonwealths, colonies, the federal government and military, and religious communities were all players in the drawn-out struggle over American land and territory. While surges across the land epitomized optimism and the American Dream, conflicts over territory were at the center of some of the most bitter, most vexing political struggles that confronted the nation.

Indian Removal, Manifest Destiny, Free Soil, water and mineral policy, railroad monopolies, religious tolerance, and imperialism all challenged the strength of the Constitution, and, in the case of the westward expansion of slavery, the fabric of the Union itself. Wars with other nations, with natives, and even armed battles between states also shaped the map we know today.

While each star on the flag represents a new state, many of the stars also signify grave injustices borne by Native American peoples, whose world views and nomadic patterns, evolved over generations, clashed with the agrarian mindset of the early republic, new patterns of settlement, and the surges of the Industrial Revolution itself. Forging states meant, time and time again, grave injustices for natives, including savage bloodletting, forced relocations to unfamiliar, destitute, and infertile reservations, or outright extirpation.

Cartographers, constantly attempting to reconcile America's unfamiliar land and waterways with such complex tangles of change, made the business of mapping in small part painstaking surveying, and in large measure experienced guess work. In fact, some boundaries are still disputed today. Only recently for instance, did the Supreme Court rule on a dispute between New York and New Jersey over Ellis Island.

HUNTING INDIANS IN FLORIDA WITH BLOOD HOUNDS.

{ **Future president Zachary Taylor**, a general in the second Seminole War, leads a charge under a 24-Star Flag, with a pack of bloodhounds used to hunt and kill the natives, including women and children.

Fly: 79"

FLAG TERMINOLOGY

The overall scale of antique flags, and the proportional relationships between the devices and the field, are dramatically diverse. Since modern flags are made with standard dimensions and sizes, many historic flags seem oddly proportioned or misshaped. Some antique Stars and Stripes, in fact, are nearly square in shape. Interesting variations include differences in the relative proportions of the canton to the field; the size, shape, arrangement, and radial orientation of the stars relative to the canton; the spacing between the stars; the proportion of a stripe's length compared to its width; or the overall proportions between the hoist and the fly.

A Canton is typically one quarter the size of a flag, upon which devices are typically arranged. (The word *canton* derives from the Old French for "corner," denoting a corner of a shield or flag, or even a "corner" of a country, such as those found in Switzerland today.) Medieval flags were often divided into four cantons, one in each corner. The U.S. flag has one blue canton. It is always situated, when a flag is oriented horizontally or vertically, in the upper left corner of the field. Because the stars and canton on the U.S. flag represent political unity, they are sometimes collectively referred to as the Union.

Sleeves, an alternative to grommets, are tunnels of cloth along the hoist end of the flag, through which the halyard was passed for displaying the flag. Sleeves were often reinforced with leather on their ends.

Grommets are rings through which halyards are led to attach the flag to a pole or staff. (Some older American flags had stitched holes instead of grommets.)

Halyards are ropes or lines used to hoist and secure flag

Hoist: 51"

The Fly is the horizontal dimension, or the length of a flag.

The Hoist is the vertical dimension, or height of a flag. At the hoist end, a strip of canvas or reinforced cotton was attached to withstand the attachment of the rope and the weight of the flag in the wind. It is referred to as the "Hoist Strip."

Devices are the graphic elements of a flag. The American flag's devices are the stars and stripes. Other flags, such as those for individual states, may have devices of mottoes, insignias, or other forms of heraldry. The Field is the overall surface of a flag, typically regarded as the background for the devices.

The Obverse is the front of a flag, the side of the flag seen when the hoist is on the observer's left.

The Reverse is the other side of the flag, opposite the obverse.

A 13-Star Flag demonstrates how the size of a star relative to its canton, and the rotational position of the stars relative to one another, can shape the flag's character. While the grid of nine stars points upward, simply rotating the four inner stars brings the flag alive, suggesting a medallion.

In CONGRESS, July 4, 1776.

A DECLARATION

BY THE REPRESENTATIVES OF THE

UNITED STATES OF AMERICA,

IN GENERAL CONGRESS ASSEMBLED.

WHEN in the Course of human Events, it becomes neceſſary for one People to diſſolve the Political Bands which have connected them with another, and to aſſume among the Powers of the Earth, the ſeparate and equal Station to which the Laws of Nature and of Nature's God entitle them, a decent Reſpect to the Opinions of Mankind requires that they ſhould declare the cauſes which impel them to the Separation.

WE hold theſe Truths to be ſelf-evident, that all Men are created equal, that they are endowed by their Creator with certain unalienable Rights, that among theſe are Life, Liberty, and the Purſuit of Happineſs—That to ſecure theſe Rights, Governments are inſtituted among Men, deriving their juſt Powers from the Conſent of the Governed, that whenever any Form of Government becomes deſtructive of theſe Ends, it is the Right of the People to alter or to aboliſh it, and to inſtitute new Government, laying its Foundation on ſuch Principles, and organizing its Powers in ſuch Form, as to them ſhall ſeem moſt likely to effect their Safety and Happineſs. Prudence, indeed, will dictate that Governments long eſtabliſhed ſhould not be changed for light and tranſient Cauſes; and accordingly all Experience hath ſhewn, that Mankind are more diſpoſed to ſuffer, while Evils are ſufferable, than to right themſelves by aboliſhing the Forms to which they are accuſtomed. But when a long Train of Abuſes and Uſurpations, purſuing invariably the ſame Object, evinces a Deſign to reduce them under abſolute Deſpotiſm, it is their Right, it is their Duty, to throw off ſuch Government, and to provide new Guards for their future Security. Such has been the patient Sufferance of theſe Colonies; and ſuch is now the Neceſſity which conſtrains them to alter their former Syſtems of Government. The Hiſtory of the preſent King of Great-Britain is a Hiſtory of repeated Injuries and Uſurpations, all having in direct Object the Eſtabliſhment of an abſolute Tyranny over theſe States. To prove this, let Facts be ſubmitted to a candid World.

HE has refuſed his Aſſent to Laws, the moſt wholeſome and neceſſary for the public Good.

HE has forbidden his Governors to paſs Laws of immediate and preſſing Importance, unleſs ſuſpended in their Operation till his Aſſent ſhould be obtained; and when ſo ſuſpended, he has utterly neglected to attend to them.

HE has refuſed to paſs other Laws for the Accommodation of large Diſtricts of People, unleſs thoſe People would relinquiſh the Right of Repreſentation in the Legiſlature, a Right ineſtimable to them, and formidable to Tyrants only.

HE has called together Legiſlative Bodies at Places unuſual, uncomfortable, and diſtant from the Depoſitory of their public Records, for the ſole Purpoſe of fatiguing them into Compliance with his Meaſures.

HE has diſſolved Repreſentative Houſes repeatedly, for oppoſing with manly Firmneſs his Invaſions on the Rights of the People.

HE has refuſed for a long Time, after ſuch Diſſolutions, to cauſe others to be elected; whereby the Legiſlative Powers, incapable of Annihilation, have returned to the People at large for their exerciſe; the State remaining in the mean time expoſed to all the Dangers of Invaſion from without, and Convulſions within.

HE has endeavoured to prevent the Population of theſe States; for that Purpoſe obſtructing the Laws for Naturalization of Foreigners; refuſing to paſs others to encourage their Migrations hither, and raiſing the Conditions of new Appropriations of Lands.

HE has obſtructed the Adminiſtration of Juſtice, by refuſing his Aſſent to Laws for eſtabliſhing Judiciary Powers.

HE has made Judges dependent on his Will alone, for the Tenure of their Offices, and the Amount and Payment of their Salaries.

HE has erected a Multitude of new Offices, and ſent hither Swarms of Officers to harraſs our People, and eat out their Subſtance.

HE has kept among us, in Times of Peace, Standing Armies, without the Conſent of our Legiſlatures.

HE has affected to render the Military independent of and ſuperior to the Civil Power.

HE has combined with others to ſubject us to a Juriſdiction foreign to our Conſtitution, and unacknowledged by our Laws; giving his Aſſent to their Acts of pretended Legiſlation:

FOR quartering large Bodies of Armed Troops among us:

FOR protecting them, by a mock Trial, from Puniſhment for any Murders which they ſhould commit on the Inhabitants of theſe States:

FOR cutting off our Trade with all Parts of the World:

FOR impoſing Taxes on us without our Conſent:

FOR depriving us, in many Caſes, of the Benefits of Trial by Jury:

FOR tranſporting us beyond Seas to be tried for pretended Offences:

FOR aboliſhing the free Syſtem of Engliſh Laws in a neighbouring Province, eſtabliſhing therein an arbitrary Government, and enlarging its Boundaries, ſo as to render it at once an Example and fit Inſtrument for introducing the ſame abſolute Rule into theſe Colonies:

FOR taking away our Charters, aboliſhing our moſt valuable Laws, and altering fundamentally the Forms of our Governments:

FOR ſuſpending our own Legiſlatures, and declaring themſelves inveſted with Power to legiſlate for us in all Caſes whatſoever.

HE has abdicated Government here, by declaring us out of his Protection and waging War againſt us.

HE has plundered our Seas, ravaged our Coaſts, burnt our Towns, and deſtroyed the Lives of our People.

HE is, at this Time, tranſporting large Armies of foreign Mercenaries to compleat the Works of Death, Deſolation, and Tyranny, already begun with circumſtances of Cruelty and Perfidy, ſcarcely paralleled in the moſt barbarous Ages, and totally unworthy the Head of a civilized Nation.

HE has conſtrained our fellow Citizens taken Captive on the high Seas to bear Arms againſt their Country, to become the Executioners of their Friends and Brethren, or to fall themſelves by their Hands.

HE has excited domeſtic Inſurrections amongſt us, and has endeavoured to bring on the Inhabitants of our Frontiers, the mercileſs Indian Savages, whoſe known Rule of Warfare, is an undiſtinguiſhed Deſtruction, of all Ages, Sexes and Conditions.

IN every ſtage of theſe Oppreſſions we have Petitioned for Redreſs in the moſt humble Terms: Our repeated Petitions have been anſwered only by repeated Injury. A Prince, whoſe Character is thus marked by every act which may define a Tyrant, is unfit to be the Ruler of a free People.

NOR have we been wanting in Attentions to our Britiſh Brethren. We have warned them from Time to Time of Attempts by their Legiſlature to extend an unwarrantable Juriſdiction over us. We have reminded them of the Circumſtances of our Emigration and Settlement here. We have appealed to their native Juſtice and Magnanimity, and we have conjured them by the Ties of common Kindred to diſavow theſe Uſurpations, which, would inevitably interrupt our Connections and Correſpondence. They too have been deaf to the Voice of Juſtice and of Conſanguinity. We muſt, therefore, acquieſce in the Neceſſity, which denounces our Separation, and hold them, as we hold the reſt of Mankind, Enemies in War, in Peace, Friends.

WE, therefore, the Repreſentatives of the UNITED STATES OF AMERICA, in GENERAL CONGRESS, Aſſembled, appealing to the Supreme Judge of the World for the Rectitude of our Intentions, do, in the Name, and by Authority of the good People of theſe Colonies, ſolemnly Publiſh and Declare, That theſe United Colonies are, and of Right ought to be, FREE AND INDEPENDENT STATES; that they are abſolved from all Allegiance to the Britiſh Crown, and that all political Connection between them and the State of Great-Britain, is and ought to be totally diſſolved; and that as FREE AND INDEPENDENT STATES, they have full Power to levy War, conclude Peace, contract Alliances, eſtabliſh Commerce, and to do all other Acts and Things which INDEPENDENT STATES may of right do. And for the ſupport of this Declaration, with a firm Reliance on the Protection of divine Providence, we mutually pledge to each other our Lives, our Fortunes, and our ſacred Honor.

Signed by ORDER *and in* BEHALF *of the* CONGRESS,

JOHN HANCOCK, PRESIDENT.

ATTEST.

CHARLES THOMSON, SECRETARY.

PHILADELPHIA: PRINTED BY JOHN DUNLAP.

The Dunlap Broadside was the first printed edition of the Declaration of Independence. A broadside was simply a sheet of paper printed on one side. (The famous hand-lettered parchment copy bearing hand signatures was prepared later in the summer.) Twenty-five copies of the Dunlap Broadside survive today. Sixteen are owned by institutions; two by the British Public Record Office; and seven are privately owned.

PART ONE: *1776–1825*

THE 13-STAR FLAG TO THE 24-STAR FLAG

Philadelphia was, in 1776, nearly a century old. America's most important, most cosmopolitan, most tolerant, most learned city, it had a population of a bit over thirty thousand—hardly a city by modern standards, but double the size at the time of Charleston or Boston; ten thousand souls larger even than New York City. Largely because of the energy of its most famous citizen, Benjamin Franklin, the city boasted colonial America's first hospital, first lending library, first fire department, and first secular, liberal arts college. Georgian, red brick architecture composed handsome streets, most paved with cobbles, and distinguishing Philadelphia again, the first to be systematically lit with lamps. But with only candles and whale oil lamps flickering in the lanterns and windows, the principle quality of Philadelphia at night was darkness. The absence of light made the multitude of stars cresting through the Milky Way an ever-present, familiar yet transporting sight.

By 1776, Philadelphia had become the unofficial capital of the tentative and fragile confederation of colonies. The Pennsylvania State House sheltered the Continental Congress, whose delegates, struggling to organize themselves, squelch squabbles, and prosecute a war, also had to cope with acute shortages of money, weapons, ammunition, gunpowder—and soldiers. Since the vast majority of Americans lived beyond the cities, drawing their livelihood from the land or sea, recruiting boys and men was a considerable challenge.

Rebecca Flower and William Young typify a Philadelphia couple, and the grim litany of hardships common to early American families. Married in 1762, their first son was born a year later. Twin boys came in 1765; only one survived. Hannah was born in 1767. Benjamin followed in 1769, and despite living only thirty-three years, he distinguished himself by becoming a physician. Another set of twins were born in 1769, but

both died in childbirth. An eighth child, Charles, was born in 1771 and lived only thirteen months. Rebecca, the ninth child, lived for three years, from 1773 to 1777. Yet another daughter, named Rebecca in memory of the first, was born in 1778 and died an infant. Mary, born on February 12, 1776, lived to be an adult. But when she was two, her father died as the family took refuge in the countryside during the British occupation of Philadelphia. At nineteen, John Pickersgill wed Mary. Of their four daughters, only one lived beyond her first year. And eight years into their marriage John died, leaving Mary to care for their daughter and her widowed mother. To support themselves, Rebecca and Mary made flags.

Seventeen seventy-six proved to be a year of foreboding yet optimism. Just before the new year, in 1775, the Continental Congress had dispatched George Washington to take command of the Continental Army in Boston where he raised the first uniquely American flag on Prospect Hill. Robert Bell, a printer, published, on January 15, Thomas Paine's pamphlet, *Common Sense*.

That August, Washington narrowly escaped defeat when he managed to evacuate his 9,500 soldiers to New York. In September, Philadelphia fell to the British, who burned many of its buildings. On September 9, Americans shed the word colony from their identity. "All continental commissions," Congress resolved, "should be made to read 'United States,' where heretofore the words 'United Colonies' had been used."

By November, the Continental Army had fled to Pennsylvania. But on Christmas night, Washington led his men, under the password "Victory or Death," across the Delaware where Hessian mercenaries were solidly defeated in a surprise early morning attack. Seventeen seventy-six closed with a renewed sense of hope.

The fulcrum against which all of these events received their energy was the issue of the Declaration

of Independence. On June 7, Richard Henry Lee, a delegate from Virginia, officially proposed that Congress invoke complete separation from Britain. His fellow Virginian, Thomas Jefferson, took to his rented rooms in Market Street where he wrote a draft Declaration. After many revisions, the Congress on July 2 approved a final draft. On Thursday morning, July 4, John Dunlap set the type for a print run of two hundred broadside copies of the document. By nightfall, the Declaration of Independence was ready to be distributed to members of Congress, governors, military leaders, and foreign powers.

The first public reading was held in Philadelphia on July 8. With the British fleet assembling in New York's harbor, Washington ordered that the Declaration of Independence be read aloud to his soldiers on July 9, under the same Continental Colours he had unfurled in Boston earlier in January. Rowdy citizens celebrated by toppling a statue of King George III at the foot of Broadway. Twenty days later, a broadside copy made its way across the Atlantic to the King's ministers in London.

Correctly predicting that this was a momentous event destined to be remembered, but incorrectly guessing the actual day that Americans would designate as their day of independence, John Adams wrote home to his wife Abigail, "The Second Day of July, 1776, will be the most memorable Epocha in the History of America. I am apt to believe it will be celebrated by succeeding Generations as the great anniversary Festival. It ought to be commemorated as the Day of Deliverance, by solemn Acts of Devotion to God Almighty. It ought to be solemnized with Pomp and Parade, with Shows, Games, Sports, Guns, Bells, Bonfires, and Illuminations, from one End of this Continent to the other, from this Time forward and forevermore."

AMERICAN SYMBOLS BEFORE THE STARS AND STRIPES

Freemasonry was a secret fraternal organization established in London in 1717. Its rituals were based on quasi-mystical studies of ancient structures, building techniques and, eventually, Enlightenment themes of harmony, balance, and truth. The Freemason code was virtually a pictographic encyclopedia: keys, hammers, trowels, draughting instruments, suns, spheres, moons, stars, telescopes, arches, bridges, structures, columns, keystones, beehives, Noah's arks, skulls and crossbones, caskets, clocks, geometric proofs, doves, owls, and hawks. Members wore buttons, medallions, and sashes to designate rank, and each designed his own masonic apron with special, personal symbols. Freemasonry became an important social mechanism in early America, boasting George Washington, Benjamin Franklin, Paul Revere, and Thomas Jefferson among its members. Some of its symbols figured prominently in American devices, particularly the "all-seeing eye" and the pyramid. For instance, the Great Seal (see page 26) incorporates a pyramid of thirteen layers, twelve stepped levels, and the eye, its apex. A Freemasonry ceremonial chair, crafted by Benjamin Bucktrout in 1770, is covered in such symbols.

Many symbols of unity, determination, self-reliance, and liberty were important precedents for the Stars and Stripes. Symbols infused religion, politics, military and maritime life, enterprise, and the decorative arts. Natives and colonists alike were ever watchful for naturally occurring symbols in the skies and waterways, and in the appearance and movement of animals. Religious, mythological, and astrological superstitions added to the mix; almanacs were full of premonitions, warnings, prophecies, and omens. Colonial currency and coins literally "circulated" symbols from city to city, colony to colony, filling purses and pockets with provocative mottoes and images.

Ordinary shop signs were often symbolic pictograms. With a significantly large illiterate population, or places brimming with overlapping English, German, French, Spanish, Dutch, and native tongues, a simple painting or wood carving of a rooster, wig, shoe, barrel, or pig efficiently communicated trades or crafts. Secret societies such as the Freemasons developed complex codes and languages based on symbols. Native Americans interpreted events and natural phenomena in deeply symbolic ways. Punishment had its own grim lexicon of symbols, meant to shame and deter. Criminals and sinners could be branded directly on the skin or forced to wear letters to identify their transgression, immortalized by Nathaniel Hawthorne as a scarlet "A" on Hester Prynne's bodice.

Symbols also represented colonies, cities, governmental authorities, and eventually political ideas and movements. Long before the official appearance of the Stars and Stripes in 1777, many of these symbols appeared on flags throughout America, representing individual colonies, and their political, ethnic, and religious distinctions. There were also a variety of flags flown by military and naval units, trading companies, merchant fleets, secret societies, churches, families,

and plantations. In fact, there were so many different symbols, people were often unclear about what each represented. Rattlesnakes, beavers, bears, birds, crosses, palmetto trees, pine trees, oak trees, acorns, swords, arrows, shields, the sun, stars, crescent moons, beehives, stripes, and a whole variety of emblems, heralds, and mottoes appeared on colonial flags and banners.

Eventually several symbols began to stand apart from the others, identifying America in a larger sense, leading to the emergence of the Stars and Stripes as a national symbol.

THE PINE TREE

{ **Admiral Esek Hopkins** with a rattlesnake flag and a pine tree flag over his shoulders.

One of the most common flags in early America, especially in the Massachusetts Bay Colony, was a simple white banner with a solitary pine tree. Not only was the tree an abundant feature of the New England landscape, and a commodity of economic and strategic importance, it also symbolized the New Englanders' self-reliance and moral rectitude, often emphasized by the addition of the motto "An Appeal to God." In fact, the oldest documented flag known to have flown in the Americas that has survived to this day is such a pine tree banner dating from 1629.

LIBERTY CAPS, LIBERTY TREES, AND LIBERTY POLES

When British taxes provoked colonists, people resorted to the power of symbols. Most common was a small peaked hat, known as a Liberty Cap, of Roman origins and worn by freed Roman slaves as a symbol and mark of liberation. Colonists often depicted one capping the end of a spear, representing the "common man" in the Revolutionary ranks, the yeoman's humble head wear as opposed to the hereditary crown or authoritative bishops' mitre. (Decades later, the Liberty Cap was revived as a symbol for freed American slaves.)

Liberty Poles (or Posts) and Liberty Trees also played a key role in Revolutionary symbolism and ritual. Liberty Poles were totems or masts erected in town squares, streets, or parks, where citizens could post (often anonymously) grievances or insults aimed at authorities. Many cities and towns designated a venerable oak, elm, or hickory as a "Liberty Tree" not only related to the Pine Tree symbolism, but also representative of a place in the public domain where people could gather, listen to speeches, and organize rallies, separate from the implied regulation of the meeting hall or legislative assembly.

As Liberty Trees and Liberty Poles became more popular, spreading throughout the colonies, they fortified the will of the Americans and tested the will of the British authorities. Orders to chop down each tree or pole only resulted in another appearing in a different location. If that was chopped down, yet another might be set up, but this tree sheathed in metal armor to frustrate British attempts at removal. The November 28, 1765, *Boston News-Letter* reported that "We hear from Windham in the Colony of Connecticut, that a Post is set up in the centre of that Town, called LIBERTY, which is Decorated with various Inscriptions, importing that it shall be Death to any Person who shall presume to make Use of Stamped Paper." Several years later, in New York

The Statue of Liberty was dedicated on October 28, 1886. Organizers had hoped to have it completed for the 1876 Centennial celebrations, but fund-raising shortfalls hampered the project until Joseph Pulitzer used his newspapers to encourage Americans to contribute money for its completion. Frédéric Auguste Bartholdi designed the statue, Gustave Eiffel the interior framework, and Richard Morris Hunt the base.

City, the British cut down another pole and a skirmish erupted. One American was killed. Some historians consider this, the "Battle of Golden Hill," to have been the first battle of the Revolution.

THE GODDESS OF LIBERTY AND INDIAN PRINCESS

Images of Indian princesses and mythical goddesses also represented early America. Typically, if such an Indian princess was drawn by American hands, it represented fertility, abundance, and wilderness self-reliance that native women epitomized. If the female issued from British propaganda, however, it was more likely a derogatory symbol, a symbol of savagery and ignorance, always inferior to the civilized, matronly Britannia.

As the movement for Liberty strengthened, the more mythological goddesses of Greek and Roman origin emerged. Their purity and idealistic resolve were meant to epitomize the fundamental integrity of the new political philosophy.

Thomas Crawford's *Statue of Freedom*, an amalgam of classical and Indian symbolism, crowns the dome of the U.S. Capitol. For many years, people thought that the statue was a Native American figure because of the eagle feathers on her helmet. Others have mistaken her for Athena, the Greek goddess of wisdom and war. Crawford actually created her as an allegorical figure of "freedom triumphant in war and peace." Shortly after its completion, the

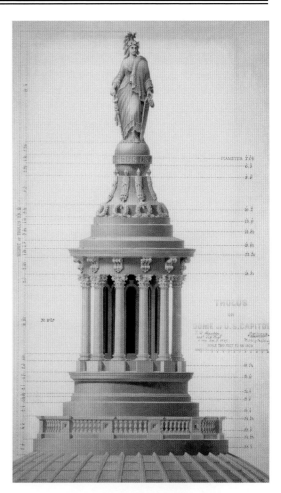

In an early version of the *Statue of Freedom*, the figure wore a liberty cap, but this was changed to a Roman helmet because Southern legislators objected to the anti-slavery message.

Capitol was destroyed by the British in the War of 1812. Reconstruction was started in 1815 and completed in 1830, in the midst of the Civil War; the completion signified the government's commitment to preserving the Union.

In 1863, construction of the dome was advanced enough that the statue could be installed. Made of 15 thousand pounds of bronze and platinum, the 20-foot statue had to be hoisted piece by piece to the top of the dome. On December 2, 1863, the completed statue was saluted with thirty-five guns, the number of stars President Abraham Lincoln insisted remain on the American flag, despite rebellion and secession.

RATTLESNAKES

Colonists taming the land were intimately familiar with the danger of a rattlesnake bite, and it became a potent symbol of American resistance and temperament, not only during the Colonial era but throughout American history. As troubles with Britain worsened and even alienated the once loyal Franklin, he suggested, with his trademark wit, sending rattlesnakes (indigenous to the New World) to infest England as a rebuke to the British policy of banishing criminals to the colonies. They should "be distributed," Franklin instructed, "in St. James's Park, Spring Garden, and other places of pleasure, and particularly in noblemen's gardens." In 1774, Paul Revere incorporated a rattlesnake, hissing at a British griffin, on the masthead of Isaiah Thomas' provocative newspaper, *The Massachusetts Spy.*

Eventually, the rattlesnake made its way onto American flags. The most famous is the Gadsden Flag, which featured a bright yellow field with the slogan "Don't Tread on Me" near a coiled rattler. Another version featured a straighter serpent and motto overlaid on a field of thirteen red and white stripes, a flag that became the first official Navy Jack.

Claims by historians that rattlesnakes were chosen as an especially apt colonial symbol because they had thirteen rattles are incorrect: the number of rattles varies from serpent to serpent, depending on species, age, and molting stages. "[H]aving frequently seen the rattlesnake," Benjamin Franklin again wrote, "I recollected that her eye exceeded in brightness that of any other animal, and that she had no eyelids. She may therefore be esteemed an emblem of vigilance. She never begins an attack, nor, when once engaged, ever surrenders. She is therefore an emblem of magnanimity and true courage. Was I wrong, sirs, in thinking this a strong picture of the temper and conduct of America?"

The rattlesnake persisted as an American symbol, its meaning adapting to circumstance. When hostilities boiled over following Abraham Lincoln's election, Southerners adopted the rattlesnake as an emblem of Southern opposition. In the North, however, radical Democrats who favored truce or separation were deemed copperheads, since those snakes struck without warning.

In his September 11, 1941, radio address, President Franklin D. Roosevelt used the rattlesnake in describing the Fascist threat: "These Nazi submarines and raiders, are the rattlesnakes of the Atlantic. They are a menace to the free pathways of the high seas. They are a challenge to our sovereignty. They hammer at our most precious rights when they attack ships of the American Flag—symbols of our independence, freedom, our very life."

After the attacks of September 11, Secretary of the Navy Gordon R. England ordered the don't-tread-on-me rattlesnake flag to be flown on all naval vessels.

At the center of a Savannah rally in Johnson Square, mobs hung a rattlesnake flag emblazoned with the words "Our Motto: Southern Rights, Equality of the States, Don't Tread on Me."

This portrait of George Washington, as engraved by Noël Pruneau in the late 1770s, features several symbols. The portrait of Washington is held up by a Liberty Pole topped with a Liberty Cap and a rattlesnake. Below are two flags, one with thirteen stars and the other with red and white stripes.

Conservation of the Bald Eagle

★ ★

The bald eagle (*Haliaeetus leucocephalus*) is the only species of eagle unique to North America. During colonial times, it would have been a common sight just about everywhere, as its range spanned virtually the entire continent. Ornithologists estimate there were as many as two hundred fifty thousand bald eagles at the time of the Declaration of Independence. Tragically, however, eagles and many other birds were regarded as both agricultural nuisances and valuable commodities, kept aloft by feathers profitable for hunters, traders, and milliners. (The Audubon Society was in fact established by a group of Boston ladies in 1896 who pressed women not to purchase feathered hats.)

Because of dwindling bald eagle populations, Congress passed a law in 1940 that criminalized killing, trapping, or trafficking of the birds. But that law could not protect the raptors (and countless other species, for that matter) from a more insidious threat, DDT. After this chemical's insecticidal properties were revealed by the Swiss chemist Paul Mueller (who was employed in a dye laboratory and was, in fact, awarded the Nobel Prize for his discovery), it was sprayed without restraint in the 1950s and 1960s. It decimated bird populations everywhere it landed, poisoning animal tissues and spreading through the food chain.

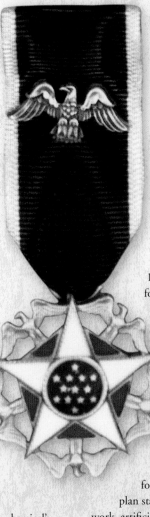

President Harry Truman established the Presidential Medal of Freedom in 1945 to recognize service in World War II. President John F. Kennedy revived the tradition in 1963 as an award to men and women who have significantly contributed to "the security or national interests of the United States, world peace, cultural or other significant public or private endeavors."

By the time Rachel Carson published *Silent Spring* in 1962, the bald eagle population was diminishing precipitously, and by 1967, it had cratered to fewer than four hundred forty breeding pairs. Her book, condemned by the chemical industry as "hysterical," clearly documented DDT's toxic legacy. Carson died in 1964, and it was not until 1972 that the Environmental Protection Agency finally banned DDT. In 1967, the bald eagle was declared an endangered species, and when the Endangered Species Act gained the force of law in 1973, an urgent recovery plan started. Through focused scientific work, artificial incubation, and collaboration nationwide, the number of breeding pairs in the continental United States now amounts to roughly eight thousand. In 1980, President Jimmy Carter awarded posthumously the Presidential Medal of Freedom to Rachel Carson. These medals are decorated with the bald eagle, which her book helped to save.

Meant to hang vertically, this 1870 silk banner features all of the components of the stars and stripes, but with the canton at the top, thirteen descending vertical stripes, and a swallowtail end fringed in silk tassels. The medallion is composed of thirteen stars and a bald eagle placed in the center, all embroidered with gold thread and decorated with sequins.

THE BALD EAGLE

Long considered sacred to native Americans, the bald eagle (sometimes called an "American eagle" or "white-headed eagle") began to appear as a political symbol in the 18th century. The raptors were known throughout the colonies, given their extensive range and population at the time (see sidebar on page 23).

Some historians point to the German use of an imperial eagle as an influence; others suggest an even more antique Roman precedent. Avian heraldic symbols intersected with a rising interest in the natural history of the continent, and in particular, the development of American ornithology, inspiring the selection of an *American* bird as symbol of the land. William Bartram (1739–1823) was the son of an English-born naturalist John Bartram. Just before the outbreak of the Revolutionary War, the younger Bartram solitarily explored the dense forests and wetlands of the Appalachians and southeast, where he compiled hundreds of discoveries. When published, his accounts revealed just how abundant were the continent's unique flora and fauna. (Bartram, for instance, discovered the Venus Flytrap, and a flowering tree that he named *Franklinia alatamatha*, now extinct in the wild, but preserved as cultivated specimens.) "The Bald Eagle," Bartram wrote, "is likewise a large, strong, and

A German print based on John Faber the Younger's portrait of Tomo Chachi Mico, the leader of the Creeks in the Georgia Colony. He traveled to London where they met King George. The boy is depicted with a bald eagle.

very active bird, but an execrable tyrant: he supports his assumed dignity and grandeur by rapine and violence, extorting unreasonable tribute and subsidy from all the feathered nations." In addition to the Bartrams, the painter Charles Wilson Peale took great interest in America's symbolism. Not only did he incorporate eagles into many of his paintings, but he kept a live bald eagle as a pet in his Philadelphia Museum. (Peale, a self-taught taxidermist, preserved and stuffed the eagle after it died; the specimen is now in Harvard University's ornithological collection.)

New York was the first to adopt an eagle as an official symbol, including it as a device on its state seal and flag, created on March 16, 1778. The Latin motto *Excelsior*, "higher," was included in the seal, perhaps in reference to the eagle's lofty domain. The bald eagle appeared as an official emblem of the United States in 1782 as a minor part of the Great Seal design, but later became the central feature of the Great Seal's final design, still used today (see pages 26–27).

Once established as a national emblem, the bald eagle was enthusiastically accepted and began appearing everywhere, particularly in connection to the beloved George Washington. On June 19, 1783, Peter L'Enfant (see page 28) designed an eagle medallion for the Society of Cincinnati. A diamond encrusted version, made in France and presented to Washington (the society's first president), is still worn by newly appointed presidents of the Society. People welcomed Washington's visits to colonial cities and towns by painting soap eagles on windows and back-lighting them with candles. The 1792 Coinage Act required an eagle be impressed on all federally minted coins. (When the federal mint began producing coins, Washington rebuffed suggestions to add his own likeness, believing that such tribute was too similar to the British tradition of monarch's profiles gracing coins. It was not until 1900 that coins began to feature portraits of presidents and prominent figures.)

Benjamin Franklin, however, voiced his objections to the adoption of the bald eagle as a national symbol in a 1782 letter, salted with his tongue-in-cheek wit. "For my own part," he wrote to his daughter, "I wish the Bald Eagle had not been chosen as the representative of our country; he is a bird of bad moral character; he does not get his living honestly; you may have seen him perched on some dead tree, where, too lazy to fish for himself, he watches the labor of the fishing-hawk; and, when that diligent bird has at length taken a fish, and is bearing it to his nest for the support of his mate and young ones, the Bald Eagle pursues him, and takes it from him. With all this injustice he is never in good case; but, like those among men who live by sharping and robbing, he is generally poor, and often very lousy. Besides, he is a rank coward; the little kingbird, not bigger than a sparrow, attacks him boldly and drives him out of the district."

Later, Franklin promoted another bird to represent America: "I am . . . not displeased that the figure is not known as a Bald Eagle, but looks more like a turkey. For in truth, the turkey is in comparison a much more respectable bird, and withal a true original Native of America. Eagles have been found in all countries, but the turkey was peculiar to ours; the first of the species seen in Europe, being brought to France by the Jesuits from Canada, and served up at the wedding table of Charles the Ninth. He is, besides (though a little vain and silly, it is true, but not the worse emblem for that) a bird of courage, and would not hesitate to attack a grenadier of the British guards, who should presume to invade his farmyard with a red coat on."

White-headed Eagle.

Mentored by William Bartram, Alexander Wilson (1766–1813) is considered the father of American ornithology. Wilson's nine-volume book, *American Ornithology* (1808–1814) included a spectacular image of a bald eagle, based on Peale's specimen, lording over Niagara Falls. (Wilson's work, later expanded by Napoleon's nephew Charles Lucien Bonaparte, also influenced the young John James Audubon.)

THE GREAT SEAL

An important instrument of American symbolism, the Great Seal is the official "emblem" of the United States government. It is not only the official graphic representation of the nation, but the Great Seal is an actual metal stamp kept by the secretary of state, who uses it to emboss paper or wax seals, rendering documents or treaties "official." Like the Stars and Stripes, the Great Seal's design gradually evolved, but unlike the Stars and Stripes, the Great Seal's design process was thoroughly documented.

On July 2, 1776, the same day the Declaration of Independence was approved, Congress appointed a committee of three—Thomas Jefferson, Benjamin Franklin, and John Adams—to devise a great seal. Each had his own ideas about biblical or mythological figures appropriate to represent the nascent nation: Adams proffered Hercules, Franklin proposed Moses, and Jefferson suggested a biblical pillar of flame. Finding no compromise, the committee engaged Pierre Eugène

du Simitière to assist in the effort, who scuttled all of their suggestions and instead devised a seal that expressed America's multiethnic composition. Around a cluster of shields representing European nations that first settled the New World, was the motto *E pluribus unum*—"Out of many, one," sometimes translated as "Out of diversity, one," the first time the phrase was used to represent the United States. Simitière also included well-known Masonic symbols, a thirteen-stepped pyramid and the all-seeing eye. Congress, however, rejected the design.

A new committee formed in 1780, including James Lovell, John Morin Scott, and William Churchill Houston. These men sought the help of Francis Hopkinson (see page 29), who produced a design centered on a shield of thirteen diagonal stripes and a constellation of six-pointed stars. In the midst of full-scale war, Hopkinson suggested *Bello vel paci*—"For war or for peace"—as its motto. But this design, too, eventually fell by the wayside.

> Francis Hopkinson's original design drawing for the Great Seal incorporated a diagonally striped shield, a constellation of thirteen six-pointed stars, and figures representing war and peace.

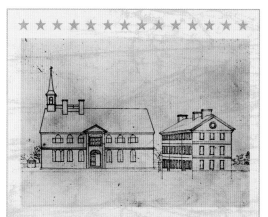

Pierre Eugène du Simitière

The earliest drawing of the Academy of Philadelphia depicts the lecture hall on the left, where the Orrery of Rittenhouse (see page 40) was kept, and the dormitory on the right. The drawing was made by Pierre Eugène du Simitière (1737–84). Born in Geneva, Switzerland, Simitière learned to draw in the West Indies before arriving in New York to pursue a career as a portraitist. (He was also given the honor of receiving Washington in his small Arch Street studio in 1779). Simitière, who John Adams described as a "curious little man," professed a talent for heraldry and would eventually design a special coin to commemorate Washington's liberation of Boston (incorporating, for the first time, Liberty in the form of a goddess), the State of New Jersey Seal, and aspects of the Great Seal. But Simitière's real passion—and downfall—was collecting, an obsession that soon filled his small house with shells, minerals, fossils, taxidermied animals, insects, butterflies, Indian costumes, drawings, paintings, newspaper clippings, broadsides, books, and coins and money—the last constituting the first substantial numismatic collection in America.

After relocating to Philadelphia, Simitière struggled to balance his will to buy with his lack of will to earn. Hoping the solution lay in the collection itself, he opened the American Museum in his little house, today regarded as among the first in America. Here, for an admission price of a half dollar, Simitière led people through his "Natural and Artificial Curiosities."

The American Museum had a short and unhappy life, as Simitière's ticket income was meager, and he refused to sell anything in his precious collection; historians believe he literally starved to death in 1784. His collections were publicly auctioned, but fortunately many important documents and drawings were acquired and preserved by the Library Company of Philadelphia.

The first Great Seal was brass, cut in Philadelphia in 1782, and was used officially for the first time by Charles Thomson on a document authorizing George Washington to negotiate with the British for humane treatment of prisoners of war. A special treaty seal was created in 1825, followed by a revised Great Seal in 1841. Tiffany & Company created the next Great Seal in 1885. When it began wearing out in 1902, it was replaced by a steel version of essentially the same design engraved by Bailey, Banks, and Biddle in 1904. In 1986, this die was retired and replaced with a new die made from a master produced by the Bureau of Engraving and Printing. This die is displayed in the Department of State.

The final versions of the Great Seal's front and reverse were drawn by James Trenchard and published in the October 1786 issue of *Columbia Magazine.*

William Barton was the first to incorporate an eagle with outstretched wings in the design of the Great Seal as a symbol of the United States. The pyramid (with thirteen levels) and all-seeing eye were commonly used Freemason symbols.

On May 4, 1782, yet another committee was called—Arthur Middleton, John Rutledge (eventually replaced by Arthur Lee), and Elias Boudinot. William Barton, the third artist to make a pass at the design, incorporated a 13-Star Flag, an eagle, the pyramid, a shield of stripes and eight-pointed stars, a Liberty column, Lady Liberty, a tricorn-hatted patriot, a dove, a suit of armor, a sword, a halo, and the motto *Virtus Invicta*. But this omnibus effort failed once again to win acceptance.

Finally, Charles Thomson, secretary of the Continental Congress, diplomatically and artfully assembled aspects of each committee's designs: a striped shield, a bald eagle clutching olive branches and thirteen arrows, thirteen stars, the motto *E pluribus unum*, and a reverse side including a pyramid and all-seeing eye.

"The colors of the pales (the vertical stripes) are those used in the flag of the United States of America," Thomson wrote. "White signifies purity and innocence, Red, hardiness & valour, and Blue, the color of the Chief (the broad band above the stripes) signifies vigilance, perseverance & justice." Finally, this design for the Great Seal was adopted on June 20, 1782, in time for the signing of the Treaty of Paris and the emergence of a sovereign nation.

A HOME FOR THE FEDERAL GOVERNMENT

Major Peter (Pierre) L'Enfant was a French-born American who served in the Revolutionary War in General Washington's staff. (L'Enfant, who arrived in America as Pierre, preferred "Peter" as an expression of his citizenship.) In 1783, he designed a medal, insignia, and diploma for the Society of Cincinnati. The diploma included a flag with stars arranged in an elegant ellipse, demonstrating his fine arts education and familiarity with the European Baroque style. L'Enfant helped design New York City's 1788 Grand Federal Procession, which included the creation of a banquet table seating six thousand people. Shaped like a great fan, ten 440-foot tables converged on a pavilion, festooned with striped flags.

Although possessed of genius, L'Enfant was incapable of tempering his personality to the demands of collaboration. Having lost the commission to shape the Federal City, L'Enfant managed to find more work, only to end in disappointment. His plans with Alexander Hamilton for Paterson, New Jersey, ended in recrimination; a lavish Philadelphia mansion for Robert Morris went over budget, propelling the client deeper into bankruptcy; and a job to fortify eastern cities led nowhere. Penniless, L'Enfant spent his last days in a boarding house, where he died in 1825. He was buried without tribute. But in 1910, his remains were exhumed and laid in state in the U.S. Capitol, on the same catafalque used for Abraham Lincoln. L'Enfant was buried on a knoll at Arlington National Cemetery, overlooking the city that arose from his vision.

Before the federal government permanently settled at the Potomac and Anacostia rivers, it had moved eleven times. On July 9, 1790, the "Act for Establishing the Temporary and Permanent Seat of the Government of the United States," known as the Residence Act, was only narrowly passed by Congress in New York City. Indeed, George Washington remarked that it was the most difficult issue to resolve in his political life, given that the choice of a site turned into an epic tug-of-war between northern and southern interests. A site below the Mason-Dixon Line was selected only when southern legislators agreed to permit the Federal government to absorb substantial debts incurred by northern states during the Revolutionary War. Pennsylvanians, however, fiercely adamant that the government be returned to its Philadelphia birthplace, accepted the deal only with the caveat that their city serve as the interim capitol for ten years, betting that Congressional partisanship, deadlock, and indecision—all well-known, by that time, as federal traits—would permanently cement the capital in Philadelphia. In other words, once settled in Philadelphia, in Philadelphia the government would stay. But the Pennsylvanians made a bad bet.

With strong interest by the architecturally passionate Thomas Jefferson and southern President George Washington, selection of the southern site was well underway by 1791, when Peter L'Enfant and Andrew Ellicott were dispatched to survey a 100-square mile piece of land near Georgetown, Maryland, encompassing the region were the Potomac and Anacostia rivers came together. They may have been assisted for a time by Benjamin Banneker, a free African American

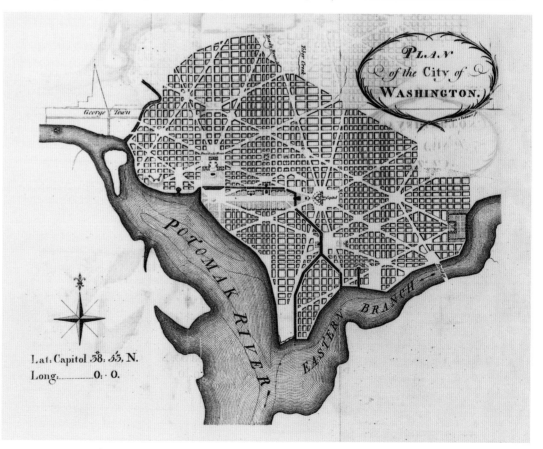

{ **Although it would be** modified by many architects and planners, L'Enfant's vision laid the groundwork for the present city of Washington, D.C.

who learned mathematics and astronomy from the Quakers. With the site's topography and natural features measured and drawn, L'Enfant planned a federal city that was, at that time, the most ambitious, optimistic, and sophisticated city ever proposed in America. An inspired work of city planning and symbolism, L'Enfant's city was meant to convey the grandiosity of the political revolution. L'Enfant, however, was notoriously difficult when it came to collaboration, and he lost the commission to Ellicott, who resumed the work, albeit keeping much of L'Enfant's original scheme.

Balance of power was stitched into urban fabric: thirteen grand avenues, named for each of the colonies (Vermont and Kentucky avenues were later added, as were other state names as the city and nation grew), created sweeping view corridors, linking sites where legislative, judicial, and executive branches of government would eventually be built. Pennsylvania Avenue was given special prominence, linking Capitol Hill and the what would eventually by known as the White House at its famous 1600 address. Since 1800,

when the government officially relocated to the Federal City, the District of Columbia has been the permanent national capital. However, on September 6, 2002, Congress convened in New York City, the first and only time in two hundred twelve years, in remembrance of 9/11.

When New York City was selected by Congress on September 13, 1788, to be the Capitol, L'Enfant was commissioned to convert the City Hall into the new Federal Hall. He incorporated an eagle in the pediment, hovering over thirteen stars in the frieze. Washington took the Presidential oath of office on the balcony.

Francis Hopkinson's portrait was painted by Thomas Sully in 1834.

Francis Hopkinson

Uniquely talented, Francis Hopkinson was not only a signer of the Declaration of Independence, an attorney, judge, and member of the Constitutional Convention, he was also a poet, writer, harpsichordist, organist, and composer, whose passion for all things patriotic resulted in volumes of hymns, poems, and allegories. (Credited as the composer of the first American opera, he passed on his love of music to his son, Joseph, a respected lawyer himself who, in 1798, wrote the lyrics in for "Hail, Columbia!")

Hopkinson's array of interests emulated his mentor Benjamin Franklin's wide field of vision. He was in the first class of students to enroll in Franklin's College of Philadelphia (ultimately to become the University of Pennsylvania) and indeed earned its first diploma. Charles Thomson, later secretary to the Continental Congress, taught Latin, and it was here that Hopkinson also came under the wing of David Rittenhouse, commencing a lifelong friendship with the astronomer (see page 40). And at the outbreak of Revolution, Hopkinson became a fierce and devoted patriot.

Hopkinson also fancied himself a visual artist, who, as documents indicate, played a central role in the evolution of the Stars and Stripes. Of special significance, Hopkinson served as chairman of the Navy Committee from 1776 to 1778, leading a group of men who would have been particularly interested in the development of the flag, since early

American flags were predominantly used at sea. After he designed a seal for the Board of Admiralty in 1780, which included a chevron of thirteen vertical red and white stripes, an anchor, and a ship, he submitted an invoice to Congress requesting compensation for his "Labours of Fancy." One of the labors he listed was designing the "Flag of the United States of America" as well as patterns for official seals and Continental currency. Hopkinson initially asked for "a quarter cask of the public wine" (about 14 gallons), surely more as a token of recognition than as payment. Congress denied payment, however (as it did to many people seeking money from the shallow government coffers), replying that Hopkinson "had not been the only one to work on the project." Hopkinson increased his request to $45. After months of correspondence, Congress continued to decline any payment, and he eventually abandoned his pursuit.

Not withstanding any explicit credit for contributing to the first Stars and Stripes, Hopkinson continued to demonstrate his great pride in the Revolution by organizing festivities. In 1788 he chaired and directed the crowning event of American patriotism in his life—the Grand Federal Procession. Held in several cities throughout the new nation, the procession was a richly symbolic and choreographed parade celebrating the ratification of the Constitution. Hopkinson died on May 9, 1791.

THE FIRST FLAG RESOLUTION

The Continental Congress, meeting in the State House in Philadelphia, adopted the Stars and Stripes as the national flag of the United States on June 14, 1777. The First Flag Resolution's thirty-one words were straightforward and without fanfare: "Resolved That the Flag of the 13 united states be 13 stripes alternate red and white, that the Union be 13 stars, white in a blue field representing a new constellation." The resolution was recorded in the official Congressional Journal, included among all of the business, both urgent and ordinary, that management of the Revolutionary War required, particularly at an anxious time when intelligence was warning of an impending British assault on Philadelphia. A loan for five thousand dollars was approved for Rhode Island; Captain John Paul Jones was assigned command of the small vessel, the *Ranger*; six dollars was reimbursed to John Arnell, a soldier, for a blanket lost in the engagement at Trenton; because the British were blockading ports, two thousand bushels of salt were to be sent to the "distressed" inhabitants of New York City.

No stirring rhetoric accompanied the Flag Resolution. No authors were noted. No debate was recorded. Ten weeks went by before it was first reported in the press. Just as the Declaration of Independence, the Constitution, and all the other documents that gave shape to the government painstakingly found their final form, the Stars and Stripes was equally inexact, evolving from elements in the Continental Colours, the Sons of Liberty flags, and other early American symbols.

THE DESIGN

The Flag Resolution was also silent about how the 13-Star Flag should be designed. Not only did the 1777 resolution offer nothing about star shapes, arrangements, or proportions, subsequent flag legislations in 1794 and 1818 were equally vague. As a result, flag makers improvised on star patterns, numbers of points, shapes, and proportions. Even "alternating red and white stripes" was subject to interpretation of arrangement.

The omission of a particular design, while frustrating any attempt by historians to discover an "original flag design" or the person who "designed" the first Stars and Stripes, instead sheds light on the realities of 18th-century textiles production.

Prior to the Industrial Revolution, "design" meant, more or less, artistry or "fancy" work. Mass production and the capacity to duplicate in quantity a design based on a template was in its infancy at best, particularly in the colonies. Textile production and flag making was largely done by hand, one flag at a time, by individuals spread throughout the colonies. Some flags were entirely sewn from parts; others were painted on silk sheets. Unlike the Great Seal and early currency or coinage, which had to be as uniform as possible to foil misrepresentation or counterfeiting, flags required far less uniformity to the 18th-century mind. Simply to be recognized as an American flag, particularly at sea, was adequate. Flags varied significantly given the inconsistencies of dyes, paints, and textiles.

Quite clearly, a specific "design" meant little to those who were involved in the creation of the Stars and Stripes and who authored the Flag Resolution. What mattered more, however, particularly to the people who were at the center of a revolution of *ideas,* communicated through *symbols,* was the *meaning* behind the Stars and the Stripes.

Born John Paul in Scotland in 1747, the naval hero came to the Americas in 1773, when he added Jones to his name. His life intersected with flag history several times. On December 3, 1775, Jones raised, for the first time, the Continental Colours on the ship *Alfred,* on which he served as a young officer. On June 14, 1777, the day the 13-Star Flag was created, Jones was appointed Commander of the *Ranger,* on which, on February 14, 1778, its flag was saluted by the French fleet. On September 23, 1779, Jones' exploits aboard the *Bonhomme Richard* helped instill a sense of national pride in the flag. Jones died in Paris in 1792, amid the French Revolution, whose chaos resulted in an undistinguished burial. When his grave was discovered in 1905, President Theodore Roosevelt ordered five ships of the U.S. Navy to escort the remains across the Atlantic, where they were interred at the United States Naval Academy in Annapolis.

FLAGS AND THE HIGH SEAS

Americans officially began to organize their own navy in October 1775, when George Washington and the Continental Congress authorized the purchase of its first ships to protect coastal cities and patrol trade routes. During the Revolutionary War, military and privateer vessels used many different flags, including the Continental Colours, the Stars and Stripes, and ensigns with rattlesnakes and pine trees—the latter testifying to the strategic importance of New England's timber supply for masts. Not only did these flags identify a vessel's nationality, facilitating admittance to ports

Resolved That the Flag of the united states [consist] of 13 stripes alternate red and white, that the Union be 13 stars white in a blue field representing a new constellation.—

The original Flag Resolution as it appeared in Thomson's handwritten journals reveals that a phrase was edited. The phrases "consists of" and "be represented by" were eliminated.

or harbors but they also served as visual symbols for communications between vessels both friendly and hostile. Accordingly, naval exploits were among the first to create the legend of the Stars and Stripes in the popular mind, especially the exploits of John Paul Jones.

Captain John Paul Jones won his greatest naval accomplishment while in command of the *Bonhomme Richard* for the U.S. Navy. Jones set sail from France in search of the enemy off the shore of Britain. On September 23, 1779, his lookouts caught sight of an English flotilla, led by the *Serapis*, a newly built, fifty-gun warship commanded by Captain Richard Pearson. The *Serapis* got off the first volley, exploding gunpowder kegs on the deck of the *Bonhomme Richard*, instantly killing many of the heavy gunners.

For three hours, the ships pummeled each other with cannon, grenades, and rifle fire. Dozens of corpses and body parts bloodied the decks. With his ship taking on water, Jones decided that his best chance was to tie the *Bonhomme Richard* to the *Serapis* and board her with his remaining fighters. As the *Bonhomme Richard* passed the *Serapis*, she caught the anchor line, and the two frigates were bound together in a tangle of lines and hooks. Running side by side, and at close range, each ship fired furiously on the other, from below and above.

Over half of Pearson's crew was dead or fatally wounded. Fifty-six American sailors were dead. Both ships were on fire, and the *Bonhomme Richard* was sinking. When the Stars and Stripes was shot off the

mast, both sides guessed it might be a sign of surrender, to which Jones, according to legend, raged, "I have not yet begun to fight!"

Joining his gunners at a 12-pounder cannon, they aimed at the midsection of the *Serapis* and fired a cannonball that detonated the gunpowder store in the enemy's hull. The immense explosion blew out the base of the main mast, sending the whole mast assembly into the North Sea, dragging its lines and sails. In all there were nearly three hundred dead crewmen. Pearson ordered his remaining men to strike the red British Meteor Ensign in defeat.

Since the *Bonhomme Richard* was too damaged to sail (it sank the next day), John Paul Jones and his men boarded the *Serapis*, imprisoning Pearson and his crew. They ran up the Stars and Stripes and set sail for safe port in Holland.

{ **A French depiction** of the battle between the *Bonhomme Richard* and *Serapis* shows the fractured mast.

{ **The Revenue-Marine** was created on August 2, 1790, under Secretary of the Treasury Alexander Hamilton, to enforce law and order on the high seas. Its official flag, featuring an eagle, an arc of thirteen stars, and sixteen vertical stripes (recognizing the number of states at the time), was created in 1799. In 1862, the service was renamed the Marine Cutter Service, and on January 28, 1915, it became the United States Coast Guard. The cotton Marine Cutter flag above dates from the 1860s.

{ **Both red-and-white** and blue-and-white striped flags, like the one above, are shown in depictions of the battle of the *Serapis*.

13

STAR FLAG

state | THE 13 COLONIES
president | GEORGE WASHINGTON
material | WOOL BUNTING AND COTTON
date made | C.1790
admissions dates | 1787–1790
flag date | JUNE 14, 1777
dimensions | 30" x 44"
period in use | 18 YEARS

Proclamation Act
of 1763

Territory
Northwest of the
River Ohio

COLONIES & PROVINCES TO STATES & COMMONWEALTHS

The 13-Star Flag first flew over a loosely organized, feuding, and tentative Confederation that had the Atlantic Ocean as its eastern edge and a vague western border that dissolved into a vast, mostly uncharted wilderness. Early colonial borders had been mandated by King George III whose Proclamation Act of 1763 decreed a limit to westward colonial expansion into dangerous territory and land claimed by their greatest rival, France. Roughly tracing the crest of the Appalachians and the headwaters of Atlantic-spilling rivers, the boundary was meant to prevent conflicts between colonists and natives. Colonists, nonetheless, regularly disregarded the decree by settling lands on its western side. The Peace Treaty of 1783, which formally ended the Revolutionary War, invalidated the Proclamation Line, suddenly expanding American intentions—and land claims—to the eastern banks of the Mississippi River. Some states simply extended their borders indefinitely into this great unknown, often overlapping other claims. Connecticut, for instance, assumed dominion over all land between its 41° and 42° latitudinal borders, extending all the way through present-day Ohio, Indiana, and Illinois. Land that would one day become Vermont was claimed by New York, Massachusetts, Connecticut, and New Hampshire. Some colonies went even further, insisting that holdings stretched "sea-to-sea."

The Northwest Ordinance of 1787, enacted by the Confederation Congress, rescinded most colonial claims to the interior by federalizing the northern half of the frontier, as the Territory Northwest of the River Ohio. Not only would this ordinance set the stage for the physical expansion of the nation and westward migrations, it also prohibited slavery west of the Ohio River, affirmed freedom of religion, and mandated *habeas corpus* in what were remote and lawless lands.

Not until the Constitution was ratified in 1789 (Delaware was the first state to do so in 1787) would the Territory Southwest of the River Ohio organize the remainder of the land east of the Mississippi. It would take years for the states to gradually relinquish claims in these lands and set their borders among each other.

The Northwest Ordinance also created policies to guide the transformation of a territory into a state, ultimately affecting the design of the flag. Once the territorial boundaries were set, Congress would appoint a governor for a three-year term, a secretary, and three judges to administer law and order. Upon the settlement of five thousand free males of voting age, a territorial legislature (or general assembly) could be organized, with one non-voting delegate allowed to attend Congress to represent the territory. When the territory's population reached sixty thousand, the territorial legislature could then submit a state constitution to Congress. If Congress deemed the Constitution worthy and in keeping with the nation's ideals, then the territory could be admitted as a state. Its electorate could then choose their own governor, representatives, and other officials.

The 13-Star Flag in Art and War

★ ★ ★ ★ ★ ★ ★ ★ ★ ★ ★ ★ ★ ★ ★ ★ ★

Although the 13-Star Flag was formalized in 1777, four years before the end of the Revolutionary War, very little evidence suggests use of the flag was common during the war, particularly on land. Iconic works of art paint a different picture and saturated the popular imagination. But most of these great works of art were painted long after the events took place.

One of the best known images of the Stars and Stripes is the iconic 1850 painting of *Washington Crossing the Delaware* by Emmanuel Gottlieb Leutze (1816–1868). Painted in Germany nearly seventy-five years after the actual Christmas Eve crossing in 1776, Leutze depicted Washington with a medallion arrangement flag (held by future president James Monroe), although no evidence exists that Washington carried a Stars and Stripes at any time during the Revolutionary War.

If Washington did carry an ensign, it was likely a simple blue field with stars—without stripes—as depicted in Charles Wilson Peale's original *George Washington at the Battle of Princeton*, painted in 1779. John Trumbull, another warrior and patriot (his epitaph reads "To his country he gave sword and his pencil"), also incorporated an array of flags in his stirring depictions of Revolutionary events. *The Surrender of General Burgoyne at Saratoga*, which includes a flag with stars arranged in a square, was completed in 1821, four decades after that event.

Completely hand sewn, this 13-Star Flag is a remarkable early version of what would become known as the "Great Luminary Pattern," where the individual stars are arranged to form a single star. With only thirteen states, each segment of the star is limited to a single line, and three stars make the core. Notice how each of the stars points in a different direction, a way that flag makers graphically enlivened their flags. Each of the stripes is made from individual strips of wool bunting, the white stripes slightly narrower than the red. Cotton was often used for the stars, since wool bunting would easily unravel if cut at such tight angles. The cotton hoist strip and metal grommets were added after 1850.

TEN 13-STAR PATTERNS

Since the Flag Resolution did not stipulate any official star arrangement, all kinds of patterns proliferated on flags, banners, ensigns, and pennants. Flags might have stars with five-, six-, seven-, or eight-pointed stars, and individual stars might point in any direction, often in a variety of directions on the same flag.

A circular arrangement of stars was a favorite of painters, currency and coin designers, and some flag makers, since the ring suggested unity and perpetuity. Called "medallion" patterns, these flags sometimes featured a (sometimes larger) central star or corner stars.

Straight rows of stars, too, were simple to lay out and have been used in many configurations, including even or staggered rows. (Rows might have one, two, three, four, or five stars.) Stars were also arranged vertically, in columns. Sometimes the stars were arranged in a square border. Still others included an arc of thirteen stars. One famous version of this type of flag, once thought to have been flown during the Revolutionary War, included a large "76" to commemorate the year of independence (page 51).

There is speculation that 12-Star Flags were once made, since Georgia, heavily Tory, was hesitant about endorsing independence. But examples are so far non-existent.

LINEAR PATTERN FAN
PAPER | C.1876 | 44" x 61"

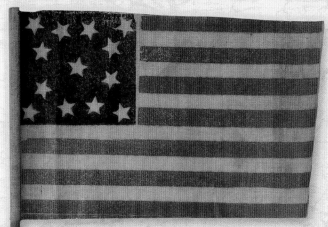

MEDALLION PATTERN VARIANT
WOOL | C.1876 | 30" x 60"

QUINCUNX PATTERN
COTTON | C.1870 | 44" x 61"

CIRCULAR PATTERN YACHT ENSIGN
WOOL | C.1850 | 57" x 93"

5-3-5 LINEAR PATTERN

WOOL | C.1860–1870 | 36″ x 60″

ELLIPTICAL PATTERN

CALICO COTTON | C.1880 | 44″ x 61″

MEDALLION PATTERN VARIANT

COTTON | C.1876 | 44″ x 61″

4-5-4 LINEAR PATTERN

COTTON | C.1860–1870 | 44″ x 61″

4-5-4 ARC LINEAR PATTERN

COTTON | C.1860–1870 | 44″ x 61″

ARC PATTERN BANNER

WOOL | C.1870 | 29″ x 64″

THE STRIPES

Simple graphic stripes have been used since antiquity on flags, coats of arms, and other forms of symbolic heraldry. In colonial America, stripes (horizontal, vertical, and diagonal) appeared on actual flags and in an abundance of drawings, engravings, and other illustrations depicting flags. The flag of the East India Company and the Continental Colours consisted of a striped field, together with a Union Jack. The Philadelphia Light Troop used a flag that included a canton of stripes. Rattlesnake and pine tree flags sometimes incorporated striped fields. And John Paul Jones displayed a striped red, white, and blue ensign that came to be known as the *Serapis* flag.

A uniquely American flag with stripes appeared for the first time, accounts suggest, in Boston, where it was displayed by the Sons of Liberty in the mid-1760s.

Why were stripes a potent symbol of colonial resistance? Stripes have, throughout history, often been associated with negative, sinister, and even devilish connotations. Throughout Europe, prostitutes were often required to wear striped stockings. And later, prisoners were made to wear striped clothing. The barbershop pole was red-and-white striped to symbolize arteries and bandages, since barbers treated maladies by bloodletting. (Blue stripes were later added to the poles to symbolize veins.) Even the modern football, hockey, or basketball referee, figures of authority who administer penalties wear stripes!

But by far, the most common use of the word "stripes" in colonial America was in reference to corporal punishment. To be sentenced to stripes was to be whipped with a leather cord across the bare back, with such force, one European writer described, "that the Blood flies at every stroke," leaving welts and scars. Such was the skill and strength of those exacting the punishment that the stripes could be laid out in even rows, "on the whole Breadth of a Man's Back, by the side of each other, with Great Dexterity, from the top of the Man's shoulders, down to the Waste-band of his Breeches." A practice given moral sanction in the Bible, striping was a common punishment in Puritan society, a fearsome instrument for enforcing slavery and bondage, and on the high seas, a means to maintain shipboard order, inflicted on negligent or disobedient crewmen. Men and women were tied to pillories, masts, and trees to be whipped, linking the stripes in later symbolism and political propaganda to the Liberty Pole.

To anyone in the colonies, stripes meant painful, debilitating injury, exacted on thieves, extortionists, counterfeiters, blasphemers, critics, treasonous subjects, disloyal soldiers and sailors, and prostitutes. Especially grievous crimes, if not deserving of a death sentence, sometimes merited a combination of stripes and a branded letter burned on the forehead, a ghoulish abbreviation advertising one's crime. Flagellations were carried out publicly to maximize deterrence and humiliation; "These public examples it is hoped, will prevail on all who hear of them to fear and not to do so wickedly."

When the notorious Stamp Act of 1765 was announced in the *Boston Evening Post*, the proclamation spelled out explicit warnings that counterfeiters shall be "set upon the Gallows with a Rope about his neck, for the Space of an Hour, and then shall be publickly [sic] whipped not exceeding twenty Stripes, and shall then be committed to the House of Correction . . . and be kept to hard Labour for the Space of three Years."

Nobody living in colonial America could have missed the meaning of striped flags raised against the godly crosses of the Union Jack. While flags with thirteen red and white stripes obviously represented united

In this British political cartoon of 1783, George Washington (in a dress) "stripes" Mother Britannia with a thirteen-strapped whip, (a variation on the more common cat 'o-nine tails whip), while men representing France, Spain, and the Netherlands cheer him on.

colonies, the stripes were more importantly a symbol of provocation and defiance, just as the Rattlesnake flag was a symbol of danger and warning, and the Great Seal's eagle, vigilance. In fact, the Sons of Liberty, those who were the first to provoke and violently resist British subjugation, adopted a red-and-white striped banner to communicate their defiance explicitly.

Revolutionary rhetoric filled the newspapers, pamphlets, and meeting hall and tavern speeches by such agitators as Paul Revere and John Hancock. The rhetoric, aimed at stirring up support for opposition

As early as November 12, 1785, a private merchant produced coins with stripes, emulating buttons from Revolutionary War military uniforms.

to the British and a boycott of their goods, always included images of blood, tyranny, and slavery. Colonists constantly warned of "enslavement" by the Crown. That British rulers and overlords sought to harvest America's natural resources, while forbidding or suppressing the development of any substantial colonial manufacturing capacity, was perceived by colonists as an affliction that would condemn the industrious American to perpetual servitude. "We dread nothing but slavery," John Hancock cried in his fiery speech in 1774 to commemorate the Boston Massacre. (Such statements, it must be pointed out, were usually made without any consideration given to the American enslavement of Africans.) Striped

flags sent a clear warning to colonists of the spectre of abusive British rule, of the infliction of stripes on the collective American backside, and to the British that the Revolutionaries were ready to wear their stripes proudly.

Certainly the British regarded such flags with disdain, judging them morally equivalent to symbols of piracy. However, on at least one occasion the American stripes garnered more respect on the high seas than did the British Union Jack. As an observant sailor noted in 1790, "A Capt. Kendricks, commanding an American ship, had been trading a considerable time on the coast, and the Spaniards treated him with the greatest civility, so that Spain has the temerity to dare the maritime power of Britain, and yet truckles to the American stripes."

A printed cotton handkerchief, attributed to John Hewson, was made for Martha Washington in 1775 and incorporates flags with rattlesnakes, stripes, trees, and Union Jacks.

The Significance of 13 *According to an English Satirist*

★ ★

"Thirteen is a number peculiarly belonging to the rebels. A party of naval prisoners lately returned from Jersey say that the rations among the rebels are thirteen dried clams per day; that the titular Lord Stirling takes thirteen glasses of grog every morning, has thirteen enormous rum bunches on his nose, and that (when duly impregnated) he always makes thirteen attempts before he can walk; that Mr. Washington has thirteen toes to his feet (the extra ones having grown since the Declaration of Independence), and the same number of teeth in each jaw; that the Sachem Schuyler has a topknot of thirteen stiff hairs, which erect themselves on the crown of his head when he grows mad; that the old Putnam had thirteen pounds of his posterior bit off in an encounter with a Connecticut bear ('twas then he

lost the balance of his mind); that it takes thirteen Congress paper dollars to equal one penny stirling; that Polly Wayne was just thirteen hours in subduing Stony Point, and as many seconds in leaving it; that a well-organized rebel household has thirteen children, all of whom expect to be generals and members of the high and mighty Congress of the 'thirteen united States' when they attain thirteen years; that Mrs. Washington has a mottled tomcat (which she calls in a complimentary way Hamilton) with thirteen yellow rings around his tail, and that his flaunting it suggested to the Congress the adoption of the same number of stripes for the rebel flag. From the Journal of Captain Smythe, Royal Army, January 1780."

—From *History of the Flag of the United States* by George Henry Preble

THE SONS OF LIBERTY FLAG

A striped flag floats over a group of colonists listening to a reading of the Declaration of Independence. This illustration was included in a 1783 history of England.

The British Stamp Act of 1765 required that all paper used in the colonies be officially stamped, so that any newspaper, publication, license or deed, or contract would require payment of a tax. Opposition immediately erupted, and one group in particular, known variously as the "Loyall Nine," "Liberty Boys," or, most popularly, "The Sons of Liberty," were the first to provoke actively against this transgression in particular and monarchical authority in general.

The Sons of Liberty was the first group to adopt a red and white striped flag as a symbol of colonial defiance. They were particularly inspired by the English politician John Wilkes, who in 1763 published an attack on King George in Volume 45 of his *North Briton* newspaper. Wilkes was sent to the Tower of London, and one of the men who printed the paper, John Williams, was sentenced to the pillory. Some speculate that the nine stripes seen on some Sons of Liberty flags represented 4 + 5 for "45."

The Sons of Liberty held rallies, speeches, and demonstrations around Liberty Poles and hoisted striped flags into Liberty Trees. Not only did they hang and burn effigies of royal officials and tax collectors, but they incited mob attacks on tax officials' homes and offices. For those loyalists unlucky enough to fall into the hands of such a gang, being tarred and feathered was an especially brutal outcome. One victim, it is said, later presented a patch of his detached skin, destroyed by the burning tar, to King George, pleading for a pension.

When William Pitt intervened on behalf of the colonists and managed to convince his fellow Lords to repeal the Stamp Act, colonists celebrated in the streets, thinking that a path had been cleared to liberty, colonial representation in Parliament, and fuller autonomy. But more taxes and tariffs inevitably followed, including one on tea, which famously resulted in the Boston Tea Party and the eventual escalation of Boston's street resistance into full-blown armed conflict.

The Bostonian Society preserves what some believe is the earliest existant striped flag, contributed in 1893 by John Fernald, who obtained it from the granddaughter of a Samuel Adams (not the patriot). The Boston Society also preserves one of the original lanterns hung from a Liberty Tree on March 8, 1766.

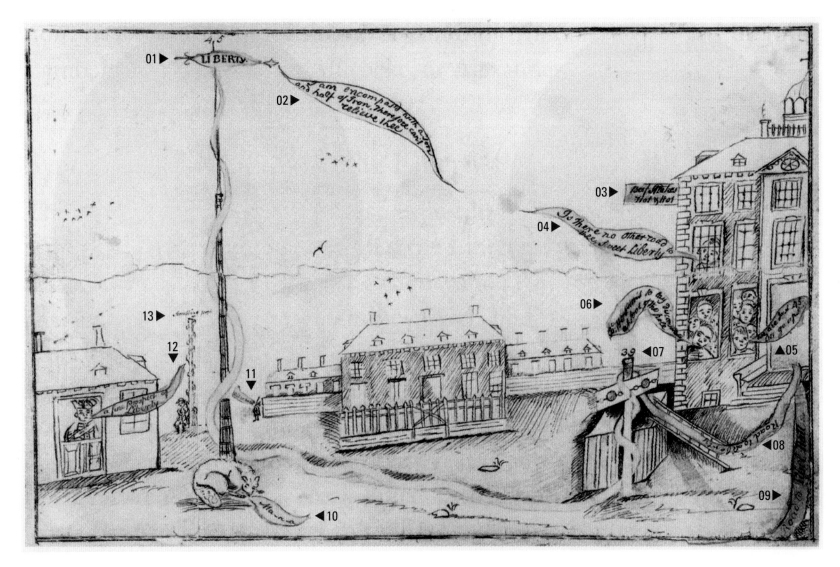

And one extraordinary *bon mot*, from the 1779 South Carolina *American Journal and General Advertiser,* summed up the message: "In the beginning of the war, an American cruizer [sic] having captured a British ship, the Master coming on board the cruizer, and not having heard of any Reprisals made by the Americans at sea, seemed in no little Suprize, and asked the Commander whether he really meant, and had authority, to make Prize of him; upon being assured that it was truly so, he cast his eyes upon the Colours, and inquired further, what Motto the Flag had, and what was particularly intended by the STRIPES. Oh, Sir, replied the American Commander, the meaning of our Colours is to be found among the Maxims of the wisest Prince that ever reigned—STRIPES *for the back of fools.*"

The Road to Liberty, a political cartoon attributed to Pierre Eugène du Simitière, incorporates the Liberty Pole, pillory, John Wilkes, and the struggle for liberty. The "Road to Liberty" leads into "Libel Hall," where patriots are locked. From there, the road leads through the pillory and stocks, surmounted by the number 39, which, from biblical times, was the maximum number of times a criminal could be striped. The road then continues up the Liberty Pole surmounted with the number 45, a reference to the John Wilkes publication. Iron bands were sometimes added to Liberty Poles to prevent Tories from cutting them down.

01 45—Liberty
02 "I am encompas'd with a ton and half of iron, therefore can't relieve thee."
03 Beef Stakes Hot & Hot
04 Is there no other road to thee sweet Liberty?
05 We are just 45. All go [up.]
06 He seems to lay [inconsolable] at foot of the pole.
07 39
08 Road to Liberty
09 Road to Libel Hall
10 Ma-a-a
11 All is well.
12 A fine prospect of liberty.
13 Scribbling Post

THE STARS

None of the histories of the Stars and Stripes written since the 19th century (see page 125) have attempted to explain the most obvious origin of stars as a symbol for the new nation: the radical and revolutionary great experiment, "a new constellation." Plainly, the phrase was chosen for a reason, being that it was, in fact, the only metaphorical phrase in the First Flag Resolution. But what did it mean?

DAVID RITTENHOUSE

Constellation was indisputably an astronomical term, familiar to anyone living in the 18th century. And there was only one person in Philadelphia in 1777 whose name and intellectual contributions were virtually synonymous with astronomy—David Rittenhouse.

David Rittenhouse was born on April 8, 1732, in a small hamlet outside of Philadelphia, the great-grandson of the man who in 1690 built the first paper mill in America. By the time he was seventeen, he had made his first clock. In 1751 Rittenhouse and his brother began a clock-making business in Norritown, Pennsylvania,

{ **An engraving** of David Rittenhouse, based on Charles Wilson Peale's 1796 posthumous portrait. Peale's portraits of Washington, Franklin, and Jefferson are among the most iconic national images.

which soon produced some of the finest tall case clocks, surveying instruments, and compasses in the colonies. In the evening David studied Newton's *Principia* and taught himself mathematics and astronomy. His grasp of lenses, mechanics, arithmetic, calculus (known as fluxions), and even surveying, came so effortlessly that Rittenhouse was later dispatched to the Pennsylvania-Maryland boundary, where his surveys became the basis of Mason and Dixon's "line."

Rittenhouse's talents caught the attention of the Reverend Thomas Barton, a distinguished minister and man of letters in Philadelphia, who became an intellectual mentor. Their families even merged when Barton married Rittenhouse's sister, Esther. One of their sons, Benjamin, became a noted naturalist. His brother William, who assisted in the development of the Great Seal, was deeply influenced by Rittenhouse and eventually wrote a voluminous biography of his uncle.

Soon Rittenhouse and his family moved into the city, where his circle of important figures widened. He was given charge of the clocks on the State House, later known as Independence Hall, and he was elected a member of the American Philosophical Society in 1768.

That same year Rittenhouse announced that the impending "transit of Venus," when the mysterious planet would pass in front of the sun, would provide a rare opportunity for astronomical observation. Eager to connect the American Philosophical Society with the prestige of such an auspicious event, William Smith, Benjamin Franklin, and Thomas Barton persuaded the Pennsylvania legislature to grant £100 for the purchase of the necessary telescopes. Since the transit would require observations from several different locations, Rittenhouse built the main observatory at Norritown. He also built a wooden observatory in the square in front of Independence Hall, no doubt attracting the attention and curiosity of everyone meeting there.

When time for the transit arrived, members of the American Philosophical Society volunteered to assist at the telescopes and record calculations, and chief among the collaborators was Francis Hopkinson (see page 29). Rittenhouse, so overcome with emotion as the tiny speck appeared on the outside edge of the solar disc, literally fainted with excitement. Revived in a moment, he made observations that, when published, received a mark of distinction that aspired to the greatness of London's Royal Society.

Bigger and brighter accomplishments soon followed. Rittenhouse's mastery of clock making perfectly complemented 18th-century ideas about astronomy, and in particular, the motions of celestial bodies. Earlier, William Penn had contributed a print of an English orrery to Franklin's Free Library. An orrery, named for the Earl of Orrery who commissioned such a machine in England, was an astronomical model that approximated the movements of planets around the sun. Rittenhouse, who was already incorporating astronomical features in his clocks, began to design on paper his own orrery that would, in every sense of the word, eclipse any yet made.

Nobody in Philadelphia was disappointed with the result. When the machine was completed in 1770, it was the marvel of the city, the most sophisticated scientific instrument ever made in Philadelphia, let alone the continent. Remember, a quarter-century would pass before Eli Whitney would invent the cotton gin, a simple hand-cranked mechanism that was considered the height of technology in 1794. The orrery, by comparison, was infinitely more complex and dazzling.

Everyone who mattered went to see it. Even the stoic John Adams recounted, after seeing the orrery, on his way to the first Continental Congress, that "the most beautiful machine . . . exhibits almost every motion in the astronomical world." Writing from Monticello, Jefferson later recalled that "the amazing mechanical representation of the solar system you have conceived and executed, has never been surpassed . . ." Given that knowledge of the stars and heavens was central to navigation, seasonal and weather predictions (and hence agriculture), even health and well being—as astronomy and astrology had not yet been cleanly separated as science and superstition—the orrery was celebrated as both a practical and scientific achievement, one that demonstrated the potential of America to rival the scientific accomplishments of Europe.

But a drama unfolded in 1770, when Rittenhouse was given an honorary degree by the College of New Jersey (renamed Princeton University), whose president, John Witherspoon, seized the opportunity to purchase the machine. When the transaction—more a kidnapping to Philadelphians—was revealed in the press, Smith and Barton were dumbfounded, unable to accept that the orrery would be taken from a "city" to a "village."

Passions were calmed when a compromise was struck. Rittenhouse would delay the transfer of the orrery to

New Jersey until a second one was ready. Once again, all the members and trustees of the Society and Academy were transfixed by the instrument unveiled in 1772. The second orrery was even larger and more complex than the first. Dozens of gears allowed Rittenhouse to pinpoint the position of celestial bodies (even taking into account elliptical orbits) thousands of years into the past or future. The State of Pennsylvania awarded Rittenhouse £300, an "unprecedented sum," according to one historian, as a tribute to his genius. (By comparison, when Franklin purchased the largest building in Philadelphia for the Academy, he paid just over £700.) The orrery, encased in a fine mahogany cabinet, was placed at the Academy of Philadelphia (where the Continental Congress sometimes met), only two blocks from Independence Hall. Thomas Jefferson, proud of his friend's achievement, urged Rittenhouse to sever the reference to the English "orrery" and instead call the machine the *Planetarium Americanum*.

REVOLUTION OF CELESTIAL BODIES

Rittenhouse was now a famous man and was invited to deliver a lecture at the American Philosophical Society on February 24, 1775. Beginning with the history of astronomy, "the most sublime of the human Sciences," Rittenhouse worked his way through Copernicus and Newton to Enlightenment themes so central to the American Revolution. He spoke passionately about the relationship between the inner workings of nature, the struggle for liberty, and self-government.

The orrery of Rittenhouse, built in 1770, was a complex array of gears and dials that tracked the elliptical movements of the planets, moons, and stars, with an accuracy unrivaled in the 18th century. On the three-dimensional panel, the planets, carved from ivory, both rotated on their axes and revolved around the gilded sun. The front panel with its silvered dials was painted with golden, starry constellations, with an outer ring that located the zodiacal constellations. The drift of constellations was even figured into the motions, as the outer ring rotated 1° in 72 year intervals! (Note the painted stars had varying numbers of points, and some were depicted as comets streaking through the firmament.) The orrery was kept at the Academy of Philadelphia, just two blocks from Independence Hall.

Nature, he explained, indeed the entire cosmos, was the handiwork of a Divine Creator. Clocklike in precision and harmony, the mysteries of the universe (which, he predicted, would one day be found to contain a plurality of inhabited worlds) could be observed and understood by reasonable men dedicated to learning. Government among men ought to emulate the beauty, integrity, and balance of nature. Reason and accomplishment, regardless of one's origins, religious beliefs, or class, must be the soul of the republic. Hereditary privilege had no place in this radical world view.

Rittenhouse's widely attended lecture on February 24, 1775, was considered important enough for the American Philosophical Society to commission a printing by John Dunlap to be distributed to delegates arriving at the Continental Congress on January 1, 1776.

Rittenhouse's anti-slavery statement predated even his close friend Thomas Paine's abolitionist publication, and the establishment, on April 14, of the Society for the Relief of Free Negroes Unlawfully Held in Bondage. Thomas Jefferson would soon draft the Declaration of Independence, which also included anti-slavery statements, edited out, however, by other delegates.

Buoyed by the prestige of Rittenhouse's orrery, the Society petitioned the Pennsylvania Legislature to sponsor the construction of a permanent observatory. (After the war, Francis Hopkinson would even lobby the legislature to create a permanent position for Rittenhouse: State Astronomer.) Colonists intimately understood how knowledge of the heavens provided important economic and military advantages, as demonstrated by John Harrison's discovery of longitude in 1761.

However, the commitment to independence and total war sidelined the observatory project, as everyone's attention—and precious resources—were directed to the cause. Rittenhouse devoted himself wholeheartedly to the war effort. In October 1776, he was appointed engineer to the Committee of Safety, responsible for protecting Philadelphia from attack; and within a year he was made a member and president of the committee. Given his experience in working metal, he oversaw the production of armaments.

Politically, Rittenhouse became a prominent force in the Pennsylvania Legislature. In January 1776, he was unanimously elected Treasurer of the Commonwealth, with the unenviable task of collecting taxes from an incredulous, scattered, and financially strained populace to help fund the war, while dealing with, at the same time, an essentially bankrupt treasury. Rittenhouse wrote most of the 1776 Pennsylvania Constitution, which echoed his own words and thoughts in the 1775 lecture. He was elected to Benjamin Franklin's seat in the Pennsylvania Legislature, freeing Franklin to devote his time to the Continental Congress. All of these responsibilities closely tied Rittenhouse to the Continental Congress, since the funding and defense of Pennsylvania was by de facto the defense of the struggling "federal" government.

But at the start of the summer of 1777, "crisis" best described the state of Philadelphia. With dwindling supplies, money, munitions, and men, the Americans had scant resources to defend the city from the British.

In the midst of these uncertain times, on June 14, 1777, the First Flag Resolution appeared in the record: "Resolved That the Flag of the 13 united states be 13 stripes alternate red and white, that the Union be 13 stars, white in a blue field representing a new constellation."

The Nova Constellation (or *Constellatio Nova*) coin was first minted in silver in 1783 in Philadelphia. A copper version (seen here) was produced in 1785 in Manchester, England. A clear reference to the First Flag Resolution, the coin features thirteen six-pointed stars surrounding the all-seeing eye. Notice the similarity between the style of stars on the Orrery and the coin. These coins were commissioned by Robert Morris, who served as Superintendent of Finance in 1783. Both Francis Hopkinson and David Rittenhouse were consulted about the design and casting of the *Nova Constellatio* coin. President Washington appointed Rittenhouse the first director of the United States Mint in 1793.

Revolutionary War era "almanacks" provided detailed information about stars and constellations, even relating monthly occurrences to health. Many almanacks throughout the American colonies recognized Rittenhouse on the cover. "Our customers are requested to observe," announced John Dunlap's *Father Abraham's 1778 Almanack*, "that the ingenious David Rittenhouse, A.M. of this city has favoured us with the astronomical calculations of our Almanack for this year, therefore they may be most firmly relied on."

"Few admired Rittenhouse more unrestrainedly than Francis Hopkinson," wrote his biographer, Brooke Hindle, "and none sought as eagerly to place the man on a pedestal where he would be celebrated and free for creative scientific work." Not only did Hopkinson oversee the earlier astronomical observations from his telescope station in Independence Square but he also worked intimately with Rittenhouse on government matters.

A "new constellation" could not have been chosen independently of astronomical meaning. Indeed, what other metaphor could more powerfully convey the magnitude and importance of the new nation than the splendor of the cosmos? The new constellation linked the nation to science and divinity, and this linked the nation to greatness. "New constellation" brilliantly evoked the radically novel government being forged. But it also implied a commonly held belief that liberty was "endowed" by divinity, what Thomas Paine called "so celestial an article as FREEDOM," and that the "great experiment" could succeed only through God's favor—*Annuit Coeptis*. And finally, a constellation was an image created by the *union* of individual points of light—*e pluribus unum*.

After the War, Rittenhouse continued to devote his energy to the nascent government and to science; he even became the first director of the U.S. Mint. (Thomas Paine began a newspaper in Boston called the *Federal Orrery*.) In 1786 he built a fine Georgian house at Forth and Arch streets in Philadelphia, next to an octagonal observatory (the first one in America) he had constructed earlier on the site. Here Rittenhouse, Hopkinson, du Simitière, Franklin, and others maintained a Wednesday evening gathering, a kind of scientific, philosophical, artistic, musical, and political salon, that Jefferson, serving as minister in France, lamented "he would rather sit in . . . than spend a whole week in Paris." When his fellow scientist and friend, Benjamin Franklin, died in 1790, Rittenhouse served as a pallbearer. Franklin not only left Rittenhouse his cherished telescope, for use on his observatory, but Rittenhouse stepped into his shoes when he was elected the next president of the American Philosophical Society. Rittenhouse was also elected to the Royal Society in London, the most prestigious honor a scientist could attain in those days.

Rittenhouse died on June 26, 1796, and was buried next to his city observatory. His orreries still reside at Princeton University and the University of Pennsylvania, testament to the fact that the Revolutionaries, who created the "new constellation," were literally stargazers.

Given that the resolution appeared among business known to emanate from the Continental Navy Board, historians believe that the flag resolution, too, was a product of its work. The fact that flags were predominantly used on ships supports this idea. This Navy Board had three members: John Nixon, John Wharton, and Francis Hopkinson.

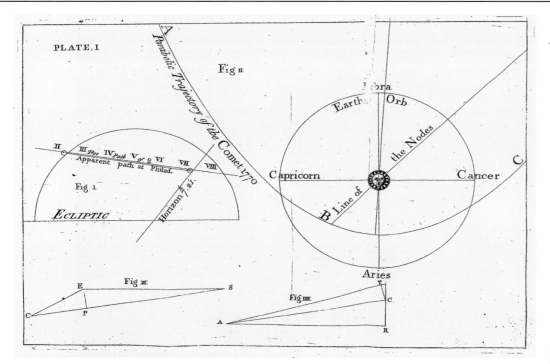

PLATE. I

The path of the Lexell Comet, as drawn by David Rittenhouse, based on his 1770 observations. His report and diagrams were published in the *Transactions of the American Philosophical Society*.

A SONG for the 5th of MARCH.
To the Tune of Once the Gods of the Greeks, &c.

I.

WHEN the *Foes* of the Land, our Deſtruction
      had plan'd
They ſent *ragged* TROOPS for our *Maſters*;
But from former Defeat they muſt now underſtand,
   Their *Wolves* ſhall not prowle in our PASTURES.

II.

Old *Hiſtory* ſhows, and AMERICA knows,
   That *Tyrants* make Carnage their Food;
But that we will oppoſe all ſuch inſolent Foes;
   Experience hath wrote it in Blood.

III.

No *Traitor* to come, as we dare to preſume,
   Will ſolicit an Army for BOSTON;
New-England's brave HEROES denounce their ſad
   That *Britain* will mourn ſhe has loſt one. (Doom

IV.

By the *Banner of Freedom* determin'd we'll ſtand,
   Waving high o'er our *Countrymens* Graves;
From the deep Vault of Death they give forth the
   " Revenge us, or live to be Slaves." (Command

V.

Awaken'd; we learn, 'tis a common Concern,
   All AMERICA ſwarms to the Field;
Not a Coward that waſtes one mean Tho't on his Life
   Not a Wretch that has Life, and would yield.

VI.

Bleſt FREEDOM's the Prize, thither tend all their
   Stern Valour each Viſage inflames;   (Eyes
The Lands they have won, and ſtill Claim as their
   And no *Tyrant* ſhall raviſh their Claims. (own

VII.

A Ray of bright Glory now Beams from afar,
   Bleſt dawn of *AN EMPIRE* to riſe;
The AMERICAN Enſign now ſparkles a Star,
   Which ſhall ſhortly flame wide thro' the Skies.

VIII.

Strong knit is the Band, which unites the bleſt Land,
   No *Dæmon* the Union can ſever;
Here's a Glaſs to fair *Freedom*, come give us your
May the ORATOR flouriſh for ever.   (Hand;

SINISTER AND AUSPICIOUS EVENTS

"A Song for the 5th of March," written to commemorate the Boston Massacre, is often cited as the first time the word "star" was used in reference to an American flag, or ensign. Flag historian George Henry Preble thought it was first published in the March 10, 1774, edition of the *Massachusetts Spy*, but it was actually published earlier in the February 28 edition of the *Boston Post Boy*. What Preble also failed to realize was that the line, "The American Ensign now sparkles a Star," was literally a metaphor—ensign referred not to a flag, but to the sky over Boston, and "A Ray of bright Glory now Beams from afar . . . Which shall shortly flame wide thro' the Skies," was a direct reference to the 1770 comet.

Paul Revere copied Henry Pellham's drawing in this famous engraving he printed and sold in March 1770. It shows the bloody massacre perpetrated in King Street, Boston, on March 5, 1770, by a party of the 29th Regiment. Among the men killed that night was Crispus Attucks, a free black man whom Revere portrayed as white, demonstrating the racial divisions present in Colonial society.

The comet was first discovered in Europe by Charles Messier of France (although it is named after Anders Johan Lexell, a Russian astronomer and mathematician who computed the comet's orbit). As it approached Earth, it became so bright that it was visible with the naked eye, even during the day. (The Lexell Comet, in fact, came closer to Earth than any other, approximately within three million kilometers.) David Rittenhouse, unaware of the work of his European counterparts, noticed the comet on June 25, 1770, and charted its velocity and path. Astronomers publicly predicted that the comet would appear again on its return cycle, which explains the line, "What shall shortly flame wide thro' the Skies," but they did not understand that Jupiter's gravity would prevent a return pass by the Earth.

Both the comet and the massacre were widely reported in colonial newspapers for years to come. Comets had, for millennia, been regarded as omens, both good and bad, depending on the culture and circumstances. This comet's appearance was linked in people's minds to the prospects of a better future.

"A Song for the 5th of March" demonstrated the relationship people noted between astronomical and political events. Notice too the recurrent images of "tyrant" and "blood" and "slaves," reflecting the subjugation that colonists felt under British rule.

STARS OF EVERY SHAPE AND STYLE

{ **Someone considered** this 41-Star canton special enough to keep even though it lost its stripes. The three different star sizes are beautifully arranged to form one large illuminary. The center star likely recognized the forty-first state, Montana. Two pentagram-shaped arrangements of the medium-sized stars are rotated, while the remaining small stars are overlapping triangles.

  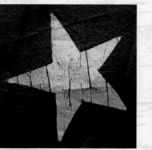 

Stars painted in metallic gold or pressed onto silk with thin sheets of gilding (left) were used for special flags. A thin border (right) might be painted to give the star greater emphasis.

Double-appliqué stars were cut and sewn to each side of the blue canton. Hand-sewn stitches typically traced the star's perimeter, while machine-sewn stitches traversed for rapid production and extra strength.

Paper stars (left) were pasted onto the base flag fabric. Quick and simple felt stars (right) were used on a movie prop flag.

"Peek a boo" or single appliqué stars were made by cutting a star-shaped hole in the canton fabric and letting the star "shine through" to the flag's reverse side.

Embroidered stars on modern flags can be sewn in seconds by sophisticated machines.

Shiny sequin stars stitched onto irridescent silk flags added sparkle.

Painted, printed, or clamp-dyed stars could (left to right) have a border to grant significance; be resist dyed for sharp simplicity; be printed but repaired later with white thread; or be painted with a hint of a highlight to create an illusion of depth.

THE LEGEND OF BETSY ROSS

No other person has dominated speculation about the origin of the Stars and Stripes than Elizabeth (née Griscom) Ross Ashburn Claypoole, better known as Betsy Ross. Despite lack of evidence—many historians maintain there is no evidence whatsoever—people still believe that she was the "author," "designer," "maker" (or even all three!) of the very first Stars and Stripes.

Elizabeth Griscom was born into a Quaker family in Philadelphia on January 1, 1752. When she was twenty-one, she eloped with John Ross (a nephew of George Ross, a signer of the Declaration of Independence) to New Jersey. Both had apprenticed to a Philadelphia "upholder" or upholsterer, one of the trades involving textiles and "needlework." Since the groom was Episcopalian, the marriage alienated the bride from the Quaker community.

John Ross, however, was killed in 1776, three years into their marriage, by an accidental gunpowder detonation. A year later, Betsy married Joseph Ashburn. They had two daughters, Zilah and Elizabeth. Ashburn himself died in 1782, while a prisoner of war in England. A year after his death, Betsy married John Claypoole, a man who had been imprisoned with Ashburn, and who had in fact brought news of his death back to her in Philadelphia.

Betsy and John had four daughters who survived into adulthood—Clarissa, Susanna, Rachel, and Jane—and a fifth, Harriet, who did not survive infancy. The couple joined a newly formed Quaker sect, known as "Fighting Quakers" or "Free Quakers," who abandoned the traditional pacifist stance, instead supporting armed resistance to the Crown.

Throughout widowhood, remarriage, and child rearing, Betsy provided not only for her immediate family, including her ailing husband (he, too, was wounded in battle), but for her widowed daughter Clarissa's six children as well, with her upholstery and needlework services, conducted from a small domicile on Arch Street. According to John Balderstan, a descendant, the clan was in part supported financially by their Quaker Meeting House.

THE STORY

Nearly a century after the First Flag Resolution, one of Betsy Ross's grandsons, William Jackson Canby (son of Jane Claypoole), first publicly proposed, in a speech delivered to the Historical Society of Pennsylvania, that his grandmother made the first American flag with her own hands upon request from George Washington. Canby presented a series of signed affidavits, taken in 1870–71, from a daughter, granddaughter, and niece of Ross, attesting to stories that had been told to them while they themselves were children. (To this day, these affidavits are the only physical evidence, albeit hearsay, that gives the Ross story any credibility.)

According to the legend, George Washington, Robert Morris, and George Ross visited Betsy's upholstery shop and prepared in her parlor a drawing of what they thought the 13-Star Flag should look like. Washington proposed a six-pointed star, easily made by overlapping triangles of fabric. Betsy suggested instead a five-pointed star. She even demonstrated how a such a star could be easily snipped from cleverly folded white fabric. The men departed; Betsy gathered materials and sewed the prototype flag.

In 1872, an associate of Canby's, Charles J. Lukens, gave a speech at the Musical Fund Hall in Philadelphia to "heighten the pageantry of the Centennial," which was being planned as an elaborate World's Fair in Philadelphia. However, a monumental display documenting the history of the Stars and Stripes in the main building of the exposition omitted any reference at all to Betsy Ross.

Schuyler Hamilton's book, *The History of the National Flag*, published in Philadelphia in 1853, and considered to be the first book singly dedicated to the Stars and Stripes, made no mention of Betsy Ross. (Nor did Hamilton, for that matter, mention Betsy Ross when he delivered a lecture in 1877, seven years after Canby's lecture, at the New York Historical Society. Canby's assertions were first widely published in the most substantial history of the flag by that time, George Henry Preble's *Our Flag* (see page 125). In 1898, Addie Guthrie Weaver followed with another book that promoted the story. Finally, in 1909, William's brother George Canby and nephew Lloyd Balderston expanded the legend in their own book, *The Evolution of the American Flag*.

While it is known that Betsy Ross did make flags after the Revolutionary War, no documentary evidence proves or even supports the Betsy Ross tale.

239 ARCH STREET

A Georgian abode, originally numbered 89 Arch Street, is thought to have sheltered John and Betsy Ross as tenants between 1773 and 1786. It is now called the "Betsy Ross Flag House."

The saga of the house began in 1893, when an amateur painter, Charles Weisgerber, entered a city competition to render a historical Philadelphia event. Weisgerber solicited William Canby's help, and his entry, a 9 x 12 foot painting called *Birth of Our Nation's Flag*, won first prize. Even though the scene was pure invention (not a single confirmed portrait of Betsy Ross has survived), the painting reinforced in the popular mind the tale of Betsy Ross.

Silk "gift flags" were sewn by Betsy Ross's ninety-two-year-old granddaughter, Rachel Albright, cousin of William J. Canby, in 1902. The embroidered stars are arranged in a circular ring, often called a "Betsy Ross" pattern, widely believed by Americans to be the nation's first flag. But this pattern was only one of several arrangements used on 13-Star Flags. None of them was ever designated as the "official" arrangement.

On December 19, 1898, The American Flag House and Betsy Ross Memorial Association was formed by Weisgerber and a New York City attorney, Colonel John Quincy Adams, named for the former president but related to a different Adams family who counted Samuel Adams a forebear. On June 14, 1898 (a day that would later be designated Flag Day), Charles and Olga Mund sold 239 Arch Street for twenty-five thousand dollars to the John Quincy Adams Company (distinct from the Association) co-owned by Adams and Weisgerber. Weisgerber and his family moved into the house.

That same year, the John Quincy Adams Company printed certificates, featuring a chromolithograph of Weisgerber's painting, that were then offered to subscribers in the Betsy Ross Association. By June 15, 1899, ten thousand dollars worth of the subscriptions had been sold, even despite at least one account of hucksters selling counterfeit copies in New York City saloons. On June 30, 1900, the *New York Times* ran a news item including an interview with Col. Adams, who was upset by allegations of financial impropriety and of little evidence that 239 Arch Street was even indeed inhabited at any time by Betsy Ross. In the article, Adams admitted that of each 10¢ subscription (upwards of one million had been sold by that time), the Company received 7.5¢, with 2.5¢ going to the Betsy Ross Association. The article also quoted Adams' assertion that not only did Betsy Ross sew the first flag, but his ancestor Samuel Adams was the first to press

for a national flag. He also embellished the original story that on the way to their meeting with Betsy Ross, Washington, Morris, and Ross dropped in on John Hancock, who, being bedridden with a cold, declined to accompany them, but did happen to have at his bedside red, white, and blue bunting which he contributed to the effort!

On February 18, 1902, city deeds record that Weisgerber and Adams conveyed the house to the Betsy Ross Association "in consideration of $19,000 under and subject to a mortgage of $6,000," thereby recouping their original $25,000 purchase. In 1905, the Association attempted to convince the U.S. Congress to purchase the property as a national historic landmark, an effort that was torpedoed by a Philadelphia historian who disputed its authenticity. In 1907, the Association tried to interest the City of Philadelphia in the property, but they too declined. Weisgerber and his family vacated the house and moved to Washington, D.C., where he devised a similar scheme to solicit money for the preservation of the Francis Scott Key mansion.

For the next three decades, the structure sank further into dilapidation, given the Association's lack of financial resources. After the collapse of Weisgerber's parallel effort in Washington, he returned to the house and attracted public attention when he flew an American flag at night, despite complaints from citizens. Finally in 1937, the Betsy Ross Association donated the house to the City of Philadelphia—on condition that the city forgive thirty years of unpaid property taxes. A. Atwater Kent, an industrialist who manufactured automobile ignitions and radios, funded its restoration. Architect R. Brognard Okie returned the structure to its original 18th-century condition. Ross's grave site was eventually moved to the courtyard from the Free Quaker Burying Ground. Since then, the Betsy Ross House has given sanctuary to the legend of Betsy Ross, violated only once when anti-war protestors took over the house in 1971.

★ ★ ★ ★ ★ ★ ★ ★ ★ ★ ★ ★ ★ ★

William J. Canby listed his occupation in an 1870 census as "conveyancer." Such professionals dealt with property deeds and titles, often written in elaborate hand script or calligraphy. His office was at 154 South Fourth Street, around the corner from Independence Hall, and two blocks from the "Betsy Ross House" on Arch Street. (His brother George, who would later complete his book, was a plumber and gas fitter, who operated from a shop on Arch Street.) In 1876, while working for the Washington Gas Light Company (the utility that first installed gas lanterns on the U.S. Capitol grounds), Canby sent a letter to the Librarian of Congress Ainsworth Rand Spofford, offering to "restore" the Declaration of Independence, after seeing the severely damaged parchment at the Centennial Exposition in Philadelphia. Canby's offer to "retrace" the Declaration parchment with ink "known to be for all practical purposes, imperishable" was declined. Canby refused to contribute to the "subscription" to preserve the so-called Betsy Ross House.

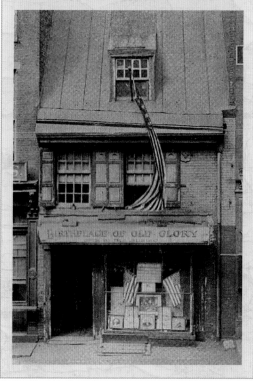

14

STAR FLAG

state | VERMONT
president | GEORGE WASHINGTON
material | WOOL BUNTING
date made | C.1791
admissions date | MARCH 4, 1791
flag date | UNOFFICIAL
dimensions | 54" x 84"
period in use | N/A

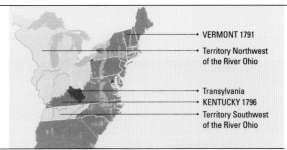

VERMONT 1791
Territory Northwest of the River Ohio
Transylvania
KENTUCKY 1796
Territory Southwest of the River Ohio

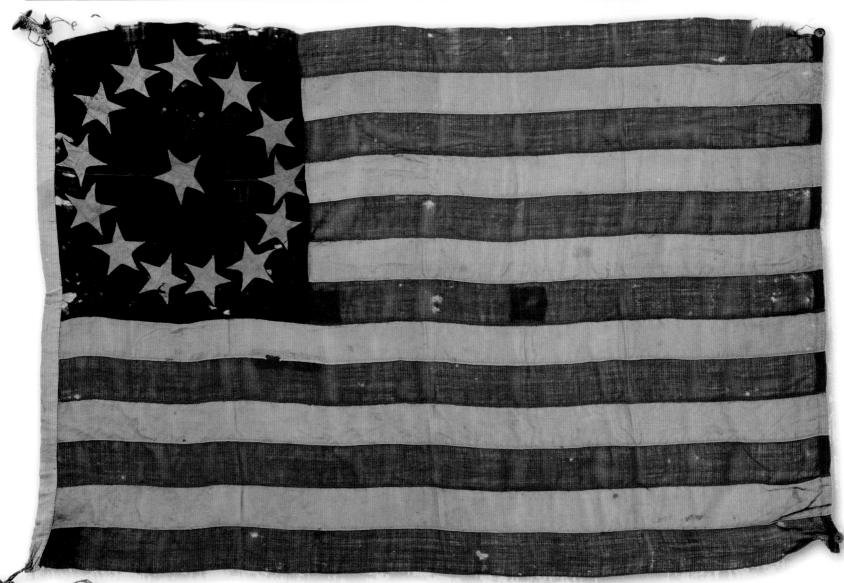

Period 14-Star Flags are exceptionally rare, since they were never official and Vermont was admitted in the 18th century—a period from which few flags survive. The wooden toggles, tied to the flag's hoist strip by a line, were attached to the halyard for hoisting and securing the flag on the pole or mast. Double-stitched hems were often made on a flag's fly end, reinforcing the ends of the stripe seams. Solid lead washers added weight to stabilize the flag when hung vertically.

VERMONT & KENTUCKY

Established as a French territory, and later acquired by the British, Vermont was claimed by Massachusetts, New York, New Hampshire, and Connecticut. The different claimants made land grants to settlers—sometimes for the same property—leading to border altercations, most famously when Ethan Allen led his "Green Mountain Boys" in armed raids to repel New York's settlement. In January 1777, Vermont declared itself an independent republic with its own president, Thomas Chittenden, and passed its own constitution on July 4th. It was the first constitution to outlaw slavery in the Americas.

Vermont's loyalty to the Revolutionary cause was demonstrated in August 1777 when British General John Burgoyne, positioned across the border in New York, sent Lt. Colonel Friedrich Baum to capture storehouses of supplies in Bennington, since his army's provisions were diminishing. Together with New Hampshire reinforcements, led by General John Stark ("There are your enemies, the redcoats and the Tories. They are ours, or this night Molly Stark sleeps a widow!"), Vermont troops commanded by Seth Warner attacked and decisively defeated Baum's forces, killing him and capturing close to one thousand of the enemy.

The resupply mission a failure, Burgoyne was left even weaker, setting the stage for his defeat at Saratoga two months later in October. By the 1790s Vermont was pressing for statehood. Fearing that Vermont's admission would embolden western territories to also claim statehood, James Madison opposed the application, as Virginia claimed all of Kentucky. Thomas Jefferson, however, who once visited the state on a botany expedition, supported Vermonters, and on March 4, 1791, it became the 14th state.

KENTUCKY

Kentucky's road to statehood was more arduous. Starting in August 1774, a North Carolina judge, Richard Henderson, began laying claim to a twenty-million acre expanse, which he envisioned first as Louisa Colony, but later renamed Transylvania. Daniel Boone blazed a trail through the forested mountains—under constant threat from Shawnee and Cherokee attack—starting in

The Stalla Quarta Decima, "Fourteenth Star" coin was minted in 1785 by the Republic of Vermont, its design based on the thirteen-star "Nova Constellatio coppers."

Tennessee, winding up through Virginia, west through the Cumberland Gap and into Kentucky, ending at a place he called Boonesborough, site of a timber fortification. Rejected entry into the Continental Congress, Transylvania was reabsorbed as a Virginia county in 1777. But Kentucky settlers began organizing for separation from Virginia, arguing that they were not represented in its legislature, and ill-protected by such a distant government. In 1784 James Wilkinson arrived on the scene, pushing for Kentucky independence and even secretly colluding with the Spanish in New Orleans for Kentucky to join Spain and control trade on the Mississippi River.

(The plan failed, and Wilkinson's destiny would later intertwine with Aaron Burr in another nefarious plot.) Only after ten contentious and bitter conventions, and four federal enabling acts, did Kentucky became the 15th state on June 1, 1792.

FLAGS THAT MADE HISTORY

THE "76" FLAG

This flag was originally thought to have been flown at the Battle of Bennington on August 16, 1777. Scholars now dispute this claim, since the flag is made of cotton and sewn with cotton thread, a technology only developed in the 1800s. Nonetheless, it is one of the oldest known cotton flags, made as early as 1812. Graphically distinctive, the 13-Star Flag features a distinctive "76" celebrating the year of Independence, and eleven seven-pointed stars arranged in a beautiful arc. Two additional stars inhabit the canton's upper corners. One theory suggests that the flag was made by Nathaniel Fillmore, a veteran of the Battle of Bennington, for his son, Colonel Septa Fillmore.

When 2,200 New York troops were threatened by 14,000 British soldiers at Plattsburg on Lake Champlain, Vermont, Governor Martin Chittenden raised an alarm to their neighbors. Septa Fillmore led 2,500 Vermonters, who, together with the New Yorkers, repelled the British from Lake Champlain, a turning point in the War of 1812.

In 1887, a souvenir hunter tore the top stripe and one star from the flag, during a Grand Army of the Republic parade in Minneapolis. In 1996, the flag, whose red and blue dyes had severely faded, was stabilized at the Museum of American Textile History.

current fly length

original fly length

{ The Star-Spangled Banner lost several feet of its fly end, in addition to other fragments, including a piece of its canton and one of its stars. Historians speculate the red chevron was added to commemorate "Armistead."

15
STAR FLAG

state | KENTUCKY
president | GEORGE WASHINGTON
material | WOOL BUNTING
date made | 1813
admissions date | JUNE 1, 1792
flag date | MAY 1, 1795
dimensions | 30' x 34'
period in use | 25 YEARS

KENTUCKY
1792

The Second Flag Act

★ ★ ★ ★ ★ ★ ★ ★ ★ ★ ★ ★ ★ ★ ★

On December 23, 1793, Senator Stephen R. Bradley, a member of Vermont's first Congressional delegation, introduced a bill to officially alter "the Flag of the United States." Arising on the heels of passionate debates about the balance of power between the Federal government and individual states, the discussion about the merits of preserving or changing the 13-Star Flag was itself a reflection of just how the United States should define itself as a nation.

After three readings in the Senate, the bill easily passed, but when it arrived in the House, it aroused a far more spirited debate. Representative Benjamin Goodhue of Massachusetts complained that adding two stars and stripes for Vermont and Kentucky would set a bad precedent. "The flag ought to be permanent," he argued, predicting—correctly— that flag changes could go on for a century. Representative Samuel Lyman, also of Massachusetts, argued that new states would take offense if excluded on the national banner. Nathaniel Niles, even though a representative from Vermont, agreed with the detractors, but felt passage would clear the way for debate of more pressing issues. Israel Smith, another Vermonter, concurred, pointing out that changing the flag would cost him over five hundred dollars and each owner of a naval vessel sixty dollars. A last-minute motion "to fix the flag forever" failed, and the original bill passed the House of Representatives by a vote of fifty to forty-two.

President George Washington signed the Flag Act on January 13, 1794. America was now represented by a 15-star, 15-stripe banner, the first and only time the flag officially had more than thirteen stripes.

Like the First Flag Resolution, the language was direct and to the point. Once again lawmakers avoided any proscription about the actual design. The bill's brevity and the disposition of the Congress during deliberation (many legislators complained that the debate was trivial) emphasized how the Stars and Stripes was still a symbol in search of passionate devotion. The 15-star, 15-stripe flag, it turns out, although created in a spirit of relative indifference, would be the flag that most powerfully and permanently captured the imagination and pride of the American people.

THE STAR-SPANGLED BANNER

According to Marilyn Zoidis, Senior Curator of the Star-Spangled Banner Project (1999–2006), the Star-Spangled Banner, a garrison flag made by Mary Pickersgill, measured 30 x 42 feet. Extraordinary for the time was not the size of the flag, but the $405.90 the government paid Pickersgill. Hand-sewn in about seven weeks during the summer of 1813, Pickersgill used British hand-loomed wool bunting for the stripes and American cotton for the stars. Indigo was used for the blue; cochineal for the red (see pages 95–97). This order, which included a smaller 17 x 25 foot storm flag, required all able hands in the household to help. This included Mary's daughter Caroline, three nieces, and an African American indentured servant, Grace Wisher. The girls—aged ten to nineteen years old—worked late into the night with Pickersgill to complete the order. Quickly the house on Albemarle Street was filled with red, white, and blue bunting, and the emerging flag soon overwhelmed the cramped space. Pickersgill moved the operation across the street to the local brewery and assembled the flag into fifteen red and white stripes and added fifteen cotton stars to the blue canton, then the official design of the American flag. In August 1813, the Star-Spangled Banner was delivered to the fort as George Armistead prepared for war.

THE PRESERVATION OF THE STAR-SPANGLED BANNER

Textiles are among the most difficult museum objects to preserve and display safely. Photons, airborne particles, insects, bacteria, mold, humidity, vibrations, gravity, and temperature fluctuations all constitute potential threats to the aged textile fibers and dyes. The Star-Spangled Banner, because of its age, condition, and size presents special preservation challenges.

For decades the flag was folded and unfolded for display and storage, transported in a canvas sail bag, exposed to weather and fluctuating light, with pieces trimmed away as tokens for particular people. In 1914, a linen backing was sewn directly to the flag with a interlocking network of 1.7 million stitches. Because the flag was hung by its hoist for decades, the weight of the flag and its backing was stretched by gravity, further weakening the fibers. Dirt, dust, and other pollutants sullied the fibers and colors.

In 1996, the National Museum of American History gathered experts to assess the condition of the flag and develop a preservation plan. A special laboratory was constructed, sealed behind glass viewing walls so that visitors to the museum could watch the conservation process. State of the art filtration systems dehumidified the air, removing, for instance chlorine from the airborne moisture.

Because the flag is so large and needed to rest flat during the conservation process, engineers designed an enormous stage with a platform that could suspend conservationists safely above the flag. Sliding panels under the stage allowed access to the flag from below.

Conservators removed the linen backing, snipping every single stitch that had joined the flag to its linen backing, releasing the tension on the flag's woolen fibers. Inch by inch, the conservators then dabbed the wool bunting (and cotton stars) with swabs moistened with a solution of water and acetone to lift dirt and particles from the fibers. (Acetone allowed the water to evaporate quickly so the fibers would not be damaged.) Because gravity is one of the Star-Spangled Banner's worst enemies, the flag can never be hung vertically as it once has. Instead, the Star-Spangled Banner will be displayed in the center of the National Museum of American History, on a table with a gentle 10° incline stage, protected in a glass-enclosed space with a precisely controlled atmosphere. A state-of-the-art gaseous fire suppression system will guard the flag from fire. This work has rescued the Star-Spangled Banner from further deterioration and has ensured its preservation for at least five hundred years.

The earliest known photograph of the Star-Spangled Banner was taken by George Henry Preble in the Boston Navy Yard in 1873.

THE WAR OF 1812

By 1812 the status of the original thirteen states was by and large settled, and the process for the admittance of new states was affirmed by Vermont and Kentucky. The Louisiana Purchase expanded, on a breathtaking scale, the nation's horizon. Deftly defusing national anxiety about the character of presidential power, George Washington, a leader unlike so many of his historic predecessors, served two terms and then quietly—and eagerly—retired to Mount Vernon, a willful relinquishment of power that doubtlessly mystified his European counterparts. Four more presidents followed, and although elected from both sides of a bitterly divided political arena, the systematic and peaceful transfers of presidential power proved a hallmark of American democracy. The Constitution, it seemed, had taken root.

As the idea of nationhood was growing stronger, the trade disputes between Britain and the United States would boil over into war, once again testing the metal of American independence and sovereignty. While architectural heritage would be one of the War of 1812's casualties, two icons that would forever cement the nation's symbolic identity would emerge from the war: the Garrison Flag of Fort McHenry would become the Star-Spangled Banner, and the song of the same name, written by Francis Scott Key, would eventually become the National Anthem.

FIRE AND RAIN

Heat pervaded Washington, D.C. in late August 1814, when news of British advances on the city reached President Madison. With hardly an equipped army in place to defend the capital, the Americans knew they could do little to save Washington from the oncoming assault. The federal city had to rely on a hastily mustered patchwork of Maryland militias, volunteer tradesmen, and farmers to repel the British invasion. Even the president and his cabinet took up sidearms to protect themselves. Their defenses, as expected, proved entirely inadequate.

As British soldiers closed in on the city, people frantically gathered children and belongings, joining a stream of refugees fleeing over the Potomac's few bridges. To escape capture, President Madison hastened his own retreat. Once across the river, he ordered the main bridge destroyed, preventing a British pursuit into Maryland, but stranding those citizens left in the city.

Dolley Payne Todd Madison, who had served as "First Lady" to the widower President Jefferson, and now her own husband, remained at the President's House, watching for the advancing British troops through a spy glass. When they appeared, she and her staff scrambled to save what they could—important papers, silver, and Gilbert Stuart's full-length portrait of George Washington. Because the frame was too large to carry, Madison ordered the canvas cut and rolled, instructing even that it be burned

THE TAKING OF THE CITY OF WASHINGTON IN AMERICA

THE CITY OF WASHINGTON THE CAPITAL OF THE UNITED STATES OF AMERICA WAS TAKEN BY THE BRITISH FORCES UNDER MAJOR GEN'L ROSS

An 1814 English depiction of the burning of Washington boasted that $30 million worth of property was destroyed in the city.

In Gilbert Stuart's portrait of George Washington, the chair is decorated with stars and stripes, an eagle is on the table, and a rainbow appears in the sky.

if there was a chance of it falling into British hands. Dolley Madison then fled the city in search of her husband. At the State Department, a resourceful public servant, Stephen Pleasonton, concealed the Declaration of Independence in a linen pouch and spirited it away to safety in Virginia.

Easily overcoming the feeble defenses, the British entered Washington. To deepen the insult of so effortlessly subduing the capital, British commanders and officers spent the night in the President's House, drinking its store of wine, carousing, and vandalizing its interiors. From the opposite bank of the Potomac the next day, American soldiers and displaced citizens watched helplessly as torches and incendiary bombs were set upon the President's House, the Capitol, the War and Treasury buildings, the arsenal, and other public structures and bridges. Flames were so intense that the glow could be seen from Baltimore, forty miles distant.

The next day, freakish American weather added to the sense of defeat. An afternoon thunderstorm, though it doused the flames and kept the rest of Washington from burning, spawned what may have been a tornado that touched down on the Mall and ripped through the center of Washington. Buildings were upended, entire trees wrenched from the ground, and men killed. Astonished British soldiers witnessed cannons being sent airborne. By sunset, Washington was a scene of blackened, wet calamity.

FORT McHENRY FLAG

Now that Washington was laid to waste, Major-General Robert Ross and Admiral Alexander Cochrane set sail for Baltimore, eager to double the insult. Baltimore had become, by the start of the War of 1812, the most important seafaring city in America, whose populace thrived from a prodigious global trade. Its fifty thousand citizens made it the third largest American city after New York and Philadelphia. Stately red brick houses, warehouses, and prosperous mills were packed around its safe Chesapeake harbor. The British considered the city a particularly deserving target. Deemed a "nest of pirates," its shipping companies and capitalist merchants had aided England's mortal enemy, Napoleon Bonaparte, attacked royal ships, and confounded British trade and supply efforts.

Major George Armistead commanded Baltimore's defenses, headquartered at Fort McHenry with one thousand troops. If ships tried to pass alongside the fort, through the narrow of the Patapsco River and into Baltimore harbor, its guns would have a clear broadside shot through enemy hulls. The fort's 24-pound cannonballs would devastate any naval invasion.

On the morning of August 12, however, the thirty-ship British armada came into view of Fort McHenry. From miles out, the British could see, over the earthworks and ramparts that had been laid in the days of the Revolution, the enormous 15-star, 15-stripe American flag. Its fly was over 40 feet long, each of the stars 2 feet across. The blue union rested on a red

Born in 1776, Mary Young was the daughter of Rebecca Young, a Philadelphia flag maker. Following the death of her father, and later an uncle who cared for them, Rebecca taught her daughter to sew and make flags. In 1795, Mary and John Pickersgill were married, but he died in London in 1805, leaving the widow to care for a daughter and her own widowed mother. Together the three women moved to Baltimore, where they started a flag-making business, providing "colours" to the city's maritime tradesmen.

Dolley Madison sat for Matthew Brady in 1848, one year before her death. She is the first First Lady of whom we have a photographic image. Martha Washington and Abigail Adams both died before the first photographic print was made in 1826.

The Star-Spangled banner.

O! say, can ye see by the dawn's early light
What so proudly we hail'd by the twilight's last gleaming?
Whose bright stars & broad stripes, through the clouds of the fight,
O'er the ramparts we watch'd were so gallantly streaming?
And the rocket's red glare, the bombs bursting in air,
Gave proof through the night that our flag was still there.
O! say does that star-spangled banner yet wave
O'er the land of the free & the home of the brave?

On that shore, dimly seen through the mists of the deep,
Where the foe's haughty host in dread silence reposes,
What is that which the breeze, o'er the towering steep,
As it fitfully blows, half-conceals, half-discloses?
Now it catches the gleam of the morning's first beam,
In full glory reflected, now shines on the stream.
'Tis the star-spangled banner—O! long may it wave
O'er the land of the free & the home of the brave.

And where is that host that so vauntingly swore
That the havoc of war & the battle's confusion
A home & a country should leave us no more?
Their blood has wash'd out their foul footstep's pollution.
No refuge could save the hireling & slave,
From the terror of flight or the gloom of the grave.
And the star-spangled banner in triumph doth wave
O'er the land of the free & the home of the brave.

O! thus be it ever when freemen shall stand
Between their lov'd homes & the war's desolation.
Blest with vict'ry & peace, may the heav'n rescued land
Praise the power that hath made & preserv'd us a nation.
Then conquer we must—when our cause it is just,
And this be our motto—In God is our trust—
And the star-spangled banner in triumph shall wave
O'er the land of the free and the home of the brave.

Washington
Oct 21 — 40.   F Key

stripe, of the customary white. Gusty Chesapeake winds lifted the immense drape into the sky. Armistead had ordered the flag made the year before, in anticipation of such a British attack. Mary Pickersgill, a Baltimore seamstress and flagmaker, was commissioned for the project. What Armistead wanted was a garrison flag so enormous that the British would have no chance of missing it above the fortress. Americans were not about to cower under a small flag.

General Ross started with a ground attack on the morning of September 13, sending three thousand British troops ashore. They were repelled by well-prepared Americans numbering ten thousand. Admiral Cochrane then opened with naval fire the next day, directing his cannons on Fort McHenry. Americans had scuttled ships in the water to block a close approach, but a new British rocket, engineered by William Congreve, was designed to deliver fiery destruction while keeping its launchers out of the defending cannon's range. With long wooden tails, the missiles sailed nearly two miles and exploded above their targets, sending downward jagged shards of incendiary metal—an invention of another British weaponnier, Henry Shrapnel. "This was to me a most distressing circumstance," Armistead later recounted to the secretary of war, James Monroe, "as it left us exposed to a constant and tremendous shower of shells, without the most remote possibility of our doing him the slightest injury."

Twilight fell. The bombardment intensified. Baltimore's residents, knowing the fate of Washington, either fled the city or anxiously waited into the night to see if the fort would hold.

From their ships, British officers could see little. Their bomb's flashes were swallowed by thick smoke; red tracers from the Congreve missiles arced through the dark sky. For hours, nobody could spot the American flag or a signal of surrender.

The cacophony, it was written, was staggering. Simultaneous explosions shattered windows throughout the city. One menacing 180-pound iron bomb crashed through the roof of the fort's magazine, where all of the barrels of gunpowder and ammunition were stored. But the bomb did not detonate. Had it exploded, the immense chain reaction would have reduced the fort to rubble, and likely killed most of it defenders. In the middle of the night the British tried another ground attack with 1,200 men and ladders, intent on breaching the fort's walls. They too were repelled by gunfire. Dozens were injured by the thunderstorm of metal. Four Americans were killed. By dawn, twenty-five hours of constant shelling had passed.

As the sun rose over the horizon, Francis Scott Key, a Georgetown lawyer and amateur poet, who had come to negotiate the release of an imprisoned friend, Dr. William Beanes, was himself detained temporarily by the British. Aboard the small vessel the *President*, anxious to know if Baltimore would suffer the fate of Washington, Key was comforted by the site of the American flag (visible through the clearing smoke and fog), waving over the defended fort, and the retreat of the British.

Over the next two days, Key wrote the poem, "The Defence of Fort McHenry," that would deepen America's devotion to the Stars and Stripes, and make a legend of the Fort McHenry Flag. The poem would eventually become better known as the song, "The Star-Spangled Banner."

THE SONG, "THE STAR-SPANGLED BANNER"

Over the next century, "The Star-Spangled Banner" grew in popularity, especially when sung at public gatherings. The national anthem was first performed at a major sporting event on September 5, 1918, during the World Series. Officials had considered canceling the Series with U.S. troops risking their lives in battle, but reconsidered because soldiers' morale was boosted with news of the Series. During the "Seventh Inning Stretch" of the first game, fielded in Comiskey Park in Chicago, a band spontaneously struck up the anthem. Spectators rose to their feet, removed their hats, and joined in the singing. The Boston Red Sox, led by Babe Ruth, beat the Chicago Cubs, four games to two.

The first time the national anthem was sung before the first pitch of a baseball game was during the same Series, but in Boston on September 9, 1918. It was not until 1942, however, that the National Anthem began to be played before every athletic event. Not until March 3, 1931, did "The Star-Spangled Banner" officially become the national anthem.

Not only were innumerable sheet music editions of Francis Scott Key's song published since 1814, but many other songs about the Star-Spangled Banner were composed, including this 1836 tune with words by the "Savannah Georgian signed 'Orlando'" and music by George F. Cole.

Francis Scott Key moved into a brick house in Georgetown in about 1805, where he and his wife Mary raised their eleven children, and where, in a small shed addition, he practiced law with his uncle, Philip Barton Key. The family remained in the house until 1833, when construction of the C&O Canal along the property diminished its residential tranquility. Key continued his law practice in the original house, serving as a District Attorney for Washington D.C. (appointed by President Andrew Jackson), a position that led him to argue cases before the Supreme Court. Key was also instrumental in starting the American Colonization Society, which led to the nation of Liberia. He died in 1843.

In 1907 an association formed to preserve what was left of the Key Mansion. Having little success with fundraising, the association solicited Charles Weisgerber (see page 48) for help, hoping to duplicate his successful "preservation" of the Betsy Ross House. In 1908 he painted a scene of Key gazing at Fort McHenry for its membership certificates. But the association eventually dissolved. In 1912, the house owners removed its roof and facade. On March 6, 1913, Weisgerber purchased what remained of a pile of the "old original lumber," documenting the acquisition with a notarized affidavit. In time for the 1914 Star-Spangled Banner Centennial, he had yet another batch of certificates printed for sale. The episode was emblematic of 19th-century preservation attitudes, as the last remaining pieces of the house were hawked to raise money for the structure's preservation!

16
STAR FLAG

state | TENNESSEE
president | GEORGE WASHINGTON
material | COTTON
date made | C.1830
admissions date | JUNE 1, 1796
flag date | UNOFFICIAL
dimensions | 42" x 91"
period in use | N/A

Territory Northwest
of the River Ohio

Franklin

TENNESSEE 1796

TENNESSEE

Early explorers who ventured west beyond the ridge of the Appalachians, to a land considered a dangerous frontier inhabited by hostile natives, returned with stories of spectacular river valleys that held promise of great agricultural enterprise. Organized out of the Territory Southwest of the River Ohio, which was ceded by North Carolina to the federal government, the boundaries of Tennessee, the sixteenth state, were delineated by extending North Carolina's north and south borders westward, from the ridge of the Great Smoky Mountains to the Mississippi River.

Orignally known as Frankland, three counties of present-day eastern Tennessee formed a "state" from 1784 to 1788 (five more counties eventually joined), independent of North Carolina, which laid claim to the land at the time. John Sevier was elected governor, and a state legislature was convened with the capital at Greenville. But the government failed to gain a two-thirds majority in Congress to achieve statehood, even though they adopted the name Franklin to muster (unsuccessfully) diplomatic support of the famous Philadelphian.

The unofficial 16-Star Flag, endearingly humble, roughly laid out and constructed from thin cotton sheeting, commemorated Tennessee's admission to the Union. The imbalanced star arrangement suggests how this flag was likely originally made, starting as a 13-Star Flag, but then acquiring the outer stars as Vermont, Kentucky, and Tennessee were admitted to the Union; the maker added three additional stars in the corners, resulting in a slightly off-balance arrangement. The flag is also unusual since it has only nine stripes, and even more unusual since the canton rests on a red stripe.

Davy Crockett's exploits, many doubtlessly exaggerated, helped mythologize the image of the intrepid pioneer and frontiersman—learned in the ways of the wilderness, self-reliant, and tough. Born in Greene County, Tennessee, Crockett eventually settled in Franklin County, where he was elected to Congress during the presidency of Andrew Jackson, a fellow Tennessean. After breaking with Jackson politically (he was opposed to Jackson's Indian Removal Act), Crockett lost reelection to Adam Huntsman, who had lost a leg in battle with the Creeks.

"Since you have chosen to elect a man with a timber toe to succeed me," Crockett famously said, "you may all go to hell, and I will go to Texas."

In Texas, Crockett joined Commander William Travis's forces and although hopelessly outnumbered by over 1,500 of Sana Anna's troops at the siege of the Alamo, refused to surrender. Crockett died in battle on March 6, 1836. There were no Texan survivors.

17

STAR FLAG

state | OHIO
president | THOMAS JEFFERSON
material | WOOL BUNTING
date made | C.1803
admissions date | MARCH 1, 1803
flag date | UNOFFICIAL
dimensions | 45" x 86"
period in use | N/A

• Illinois Territory
• Michigan Territory
• OHIO 1803
• Indiana Territory

• Mississippi Territory

Demonstrating the contrasting designs and character of antique flags, a far more formal and purposefully laid out specimen recognized Ohio statehood with an over-scaled central star, a device commonly used by flag makers to honor a new state. The stars were then carefully sewed to the canton so the points radiated out from the centerpoint of the arrangement.

OHIO

When it passed the Enabling Act of April 30, 1802, Congress authorized settlers in Ohio to organize a territorial government, and ultimately to become a state, the first to be carved out of the Territory Northwest of the River Ohio.

Ohio's first non-native settlement was Marietta, which grew out of a fortification built by Rufus Putnam, a Revolutionary War officer, surveyor, and founder of the Ohio Company. The town was named in honor of Marie Antoinette, a gesture of appreciation for French patronage of the American Revolution.

Marie Antoinette, ironically, would lose her head as a result of the American-inspired French Revolution.

As a part of its general claim to all lands between the 41st and 42nd parallel (sometimes extending even to the Pacific!), Connecticut held fast to the "Western Reserve," a 500,000-acre area on Lake Erie's southern shore. Within the Reserve was the Fire Lands, set aside for Yankees whose homes were torched by the British. Many of the towns were named for Connecticut towns, and its capital was named for the leader of a Connecticut surveying company, Moses Cleaveland.

Upon writing a state constitution in 1803, Congress welcomed Ohio into the Union. (The surrounding territory was then divided to create the Indiana Territory to the west, with the future Michigan split east to west.) But only in 1953 did an Ohio historian discover that Congress had never formally accepted Ohio statehood. To correct the oversight, President Dwight Eisenhower signed a retroactive act on August 7, 1953, especially delivered to Washington, D.C. from Ohio, on horseback, that declared March 1, 1803, the official date of the state's admission.

THE LOUISIANA PURCHASE

The Louisiana Purchase propelled America beyond the Mississippi River to the Continental Divide, enveloping over half a billion acres, doubling the nation's territory, and setting the stage for the surge to the Pacific. Not only did it terminate French presence and influence in the wilderness south of Quebec but it also brought the United States into closer conflict with Spain's empire and inched America into yet another confrontation with Britain in the Pacific Northwest. And there were conflicts at home, too. Jefferson worried about the impact of the Purchase on Federalism, and New England states once again expressed concern over the spectre of western power.

Jefferson's agents in France, including the future President James Monroe, were focused on purchasing only the city of New Orleans, but were stupefied when Napoleon offered the entire Louisiana territory for fifteen million dollars. Unable to pass up such a bargain, Jefferson authorized (without the consent of Congress) the Louisiana Purchase to be signed. President Jefferson announced the purchase on Independence Day, 1803. The vast extent of the land was impossible for Americans to imagine, and very little was known about the character of the place—some even speculated that live, ferocius mammoths inhabited the lands beyond the Mississippi.

Meriwether Lewis and William Clark's journey of the Corps of Discovery, which lasted two years, captured the imagination of Americans with the scale, beauty, and awesome resources contained within the continent's interior. They went as explorers (mostly conducting the voyage on rivers), starting in St.

Louis, Missouri. In preparation for the trip, Lewis and Clark went first to Philadelphia where William Bartram, Thomas Barton, David Rittenhouse, and Andrew Ellicot gave crash courses on botany, zoology, astronomy, and stellar navigation.

The first state to come out of the Purchase was Louisiana, which joined the Union on April 13, 1812. Less than three years later, Colonel Andrew Jackson's reputation was cemented, and his road to the presidency ignited, when he defeated Admiral Cochrane's attack on New Orleans. The state became the center of a cotton economy, linked to the shores of Galveston, Houston, and Natchez. The water of the Mississippi carried untold tons of cotton bales. Following Louisiana statehood, the remaining land of the purchase was renamed Missouri Territory.

{ A Currier & Ives print of 1842 depicts a medallion pattern flag flying over the January 8, 1815, Battle of New Orleans, where cotton bales were used for barricades.

{ A profusion of flags fly at a patriotic concert at the 1904 Lousiana Purchase Exposition held in St. Louis, organized by all of the states encompassed by the original treaty: Louisiana, Arkansas, Oklahoma, Texas, Colorado, Missouri, Kansas, Nebraska, South Dakota, North Dakota, Montana, Minnesota, New Mexico, Wyoming, Montana, and Iowa.

18

STAR FLAG

state | LOUISIANA
president | JAMES MADISON
material | WOOL BUNTING
date made | C.1812
admissions date | APRIL 30, 1812
flag date | UNOFFICIAL
dimensions | 66" x 93"
period in use | N/A

Missouri Territory

Illinois Territory

Michigan Territory

Indiana Territory

Mississippi Territory

LOUISIANA 1812

Spanish Florida

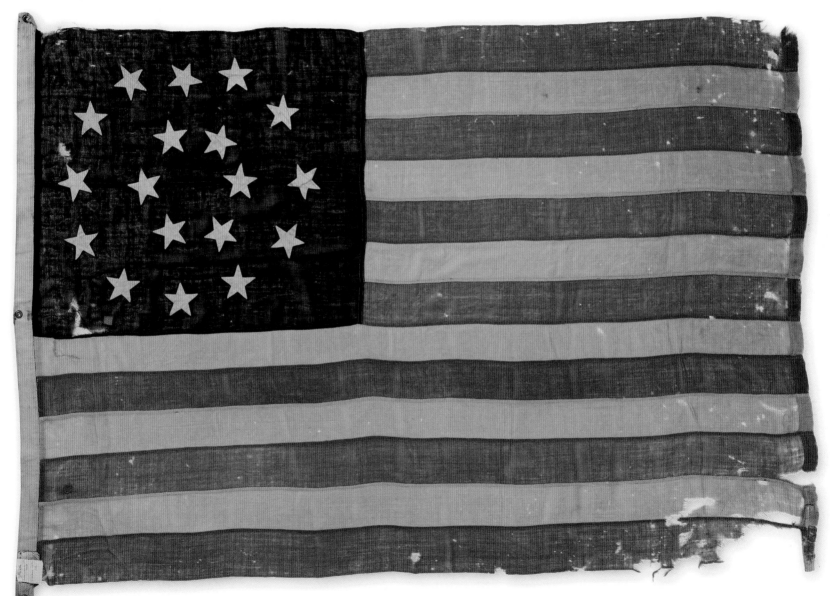

This regal 18-Star wool bunting flag features a double medallion arrangement of cotton stars. The outer ring of thirteen stars embraces a smaller ring of five stars representing new states.

19

STAR FLAG

state | INDIANA
president | JAMES MADISON
material | LINEN
date made | C.1870
admissions date | DECEMBER 11, 1816
flag date | UNOFFICIAL
dimensions | 5" x 8"
period in use | N/A

Illinois Territory
Michigan Territory
Missouri Territory
INDIANA 1816

Spanish Florida

INDIANA

President John Adams signed a bill, shepherded through Congress by future president William Henry Harrison, on May 7, 1800, which split the Territory Northwest of the River Ohio into two. The western part became the newly designated Indiana Territory, with Saint Vincennes as its capital. In 1805, a line was extended east and west from the southernmost bank of Lake Michigan to split Indiana Territory itself,

the northern part now called Michigan Territory. Four years later, in 1809, the territory was redrawn yet again, creating Illinois Territory to the west.

The Indiana Territory legislature petitioned for statehood in 1811, but the outbreak of the War of 1812 derailed the measure, delaying statehood until 1816. Indiana's Constitution forbade slavery, and with Mississippi statehood close at hand, the practice

of admitting one "free" state and one "slave" state to preserve Congressional equilibrium began.

Indiana's population more than doubled from 1820 to 1830 because of emigraton from Kentucky and Ohio. Indiana is also distinguished as the first state to require government funding of public schools: "Knowledge and learning generally diffused, through a community, being essential to the preservation of a free Government."

The Third Flag Act

★ ★

The Third Flag Act of 1818 reaffirmed the symbolic genesis of the 13-Star Flag, but created the process that would guide all subsequent flag changes and eventually lead to the 50-Star Flag. With independence from foreign interference reaffirmed by the defeat of Britain once again, and with pioneers venturing ever westward, Congress focused its attention on how the Stars and Stripes should reflect these realities.

On December 9, 1816 (when there were nineteen states), Representative Peter Hercules Wendover of New York City introduced a resolution to form a committee to consider changes to the 15-Star, 15-Stripe Flag. It was not until 1817, however, after yet another state, Mississippi, was admitted, that House members began debating. Unlike the previous flag legislations, the Third Flag Act inspired considerable debate, particularly in the House of Representatives, demonstrating how the flag's symbolism had strengthened since 1777, and how much the War of 1812 had intensified the Stars and Stripes as a symbol of national importance.

All kinds of ideas about changing the flag were tabled. One proposal suggested eliminating the current twenty stars, and replacing with only seven—to indicate the newest states—and letting the thirteen original states be represented by the stripes. Another was to balance twenty stars with twenty stripes. Yet another even proposed that the flag could feature a random number of stripes. Most agreed that adding a new stripe for each state, presumably by making each skinnier and skinnier, would "decrease their magnitude." All of these ideas were rejected.

Much of the debate about the flag was, at heart, a debate about the very nature of Republican democracy—its capacity to honor precedent but adapt to new realities, to evoke the past but embrace the future.

Finally a solution was accepted on April 14, 1818, when the idea to revert to the original thirteen stripes but add one new star for every new state satisfied those who yearned to honor the founders and those who sought recognition for new Americans. (This resolution also clarified, for the first time, that the

{ **While the Third Flag Act** was being debated, Congress met in the "Old Brick Capitol." Following the British destruction of the Capitol in 1814, many congressmen vocally demanded the government be relocated to Philadelphia. Local businessmen, fearing such a devastating economic loss, swung into action. In the following weeks, they paid for and built a brick meeting hall, where Congress could comfortably meet until the new structure on Capitol Hill was completed. The Old Brick Capitol was torn down in 1932 to clear the site for construction of the U.S. Supreme Court.

stripes be horizontal.) Each new flag would become official on the Fourth of July following the previous year's admissions, strengthening the tradition of commemorating the events surrounding the Declaration of Independence.

But like the previous flag legislations, no specifics guided the actual design of the flag. Wendover preferred that star arrangements be left up to individuals. President James Monroe, after signing the bill into law, suggested stars be arranged in four rows of five stars, but flag makers throughout the land preferred to use their own artistic license.

In fact, the flag raised over the wooden Capitol dome to celebrate the legislation was a Great Luminary pattern, with a 14-foot fly. The flag was made by Captain Samuel G. Reid, a naval hero of the War of 1812. "I have just time to inform you," Wendover wrote to Reid, "that the new flag for the Congress Hall arrived here per mail this day, and was hoisted up to replace the old one at two o'clock, and has given much satisfaction to all who have seen it. . . I am pleased with its form and proportions, and have no doubt it will satisfy the public mind."

MISSISSIPPI

Americans first settled Mississippi in 1798, at Natchez, the oldest settlement on the Mississippi River, the first capital of the Mississippi Territory. Beginning in the 19th century, Natchez was the center of the cotton trade in the South, supplying and brokering vast amounts of raw material to foreign textile markets and the burgeoning native textile industry in New England. For a time, it was the wealthiest city in America, indicating the fundamental importance of textiles to the nation's economy and trade.

The original Mississippi Territory created in 1798 was a strip of land extending about one hundred miles north to south and from the Mississippi River to the Chattahoochee on the Georgia border. The territory was increased in 1804 and 1812 to reach from Tennessee to the Gulf. On December 10, 1817, Congress admitted Mississippi to the Union as the twentieth state. However, Mississippi became the second state to secede from the Union on January 9, 1861, and over eighty thousand of its residents served in the Confederate Army. After the Confederacy was defeated, the Union readmitted Mississippi in 1870 as a state.

One of the most exuberant houses of Natchez was Longwood, the home of Haller Nutt, a wealthy cotton baron, physician, and scientist. Nutt, a loyalist during the Civil War, died destitute after Confederates destroyed his crops and stock holds. The octagonal house he began before the war and left incomplete was designed by Samuel Sloan of Philadelphia.

20
STAR FLAG

state | MISSISSIPPI
president | JAMES MONROE
material | WOOL BUNTING
date made | C.1818
admissions date | DECEMBER 10, 1817
flag date | JULY 4, 1818
dimensions | 36" x 60"
period in use | 1 YEAR

Illinois Territory
Michigan Territory
Missouri Territory

MISSISSIPPI 1817

Spanish Florida

This 20-Star Flag dates from 1818 and was
the third official flag of the United States. President
James Monroe favored such a simple arrangement
of stars in rows. However, each row of stars points
in the opposite direction, subtly energizing the flag.
Because Illinois statehood followed Mississippi's
entry into the Union in less than a year, authentic
20-Star Flags are difficult to find.

21
STAR FLAG

state | ILLINOIS
president | JAMES MONROE
material | WOOL BUNTING
date made | C.1819
admissions date | DECEMBER 3, 1818
flag date | JULY 4, 1819
dimensions | 57" x 93"
period in use | 1 YEAR

ILLINOIS

When the original Northwest Ordinance created the Territory Northwest of the River Ohio, officials anticipated that three states would eventually coalesce, each with its own extensive Great Lakes coastline. But six states would eventually emerge, with Illinois being the third.

Daniel Pope Cook (for whom Cook County was eventually named), came to Illinois Territory from Kentucky and soon purchased a newspaper that he named the *Western Intelligencer*. In the paper, Cook championed the idea of statehood (some suggest he was eager to beat neighboring Missouri into the Union), and soon the Territorial Legislature approved the idea. On December 3, 1818, Illinois became the twenty-first state. Illinois Territory was created with its northern border just skimming a ten-mile stretch of Lake Michigan's southern end. Statehood pushed the border an extra forty-one miles north, to include Chicago and a longer shoreline.

In 1857, the Black Hawk War led to the removal of native presence in the state; a young Abraham Lincoln served in the Illinois milita during the battle.

The **21-Star Flag** has an unusual arrangement of stars in vertical, rather than the more customary horizontal, rows. Curiously, the flag only sports twelve stripes, starting with a white one at the top. It was not unusual for a flag maker to only put nine or eleven stripes on a flag, perhaps indicating a shortage of materials. Only when flag manufacturing became an industry did flags consistently include thirteen stripes.

22
STAR FLAG

state | ALABAMA
president | JAMES MONROE
material | WOOL BUNTING
date made | C.1850
admissions date | DECEMBER 14, 1819
flag date | UNOFFICIAL
dimensions | 70" x 138"
period in use | N/A

Michigan Territory
Arkansaw Territory
ILLINOIS 1819
ALABAMA 1819

The 22-Star Flag has stars arranged in orderly horizontal rows; each star points upward in what would become a standard design feature of 20th-century flags. This flag displays handstitched stars applied to the front (obverse) of the flag with peek holes in the canton to the reverse side. The treadle-sewn stripes suggest that this flag was made for the fiftieth anniversary celebration of Alabama statehood, since stitching machines were not invented until the 1850s. Since Alabama entered the Union on December 14, 1819, ninety days before Maine, the 22-Star Flag was never "official."

ALABAMA

Deep in the American south, the War of 1812 had an enormous impact on the eventual shape of the southeast, where the interests of the United States, Britain, Spain, and native Americans collided. At the center of the collision was Andrew Jackson. Following Jackson's heroic defense of New Orleans, be liberated Mobile, which gave Alabama Territory a port and coastline along the Gulf of Mexico, regarded as prerequisites to statehood. Jackson also prosecuted a concurrent but overlapping war with Alabama's Creek nation. His victory resulted in the cession of twenty-one million Creek acres in Georgia and Alabama.

Later, as president, Andrew Jackson signed the Indian Removal Act which effectively pushed all natives west across the Mississippi River. On December 14, 1819, Alabama became the twenty-second state.

★ ★ ★ ★ ★ ★ ★ ★ ★ ★ ★ ★ ★ ★ ★

Andrew Jackson at the Hickory Grounds in Alabama (the last capital of the Creek Nation), where his Tennessee forces, under a 15-Star Flag, engaged the British. (Jackson was known as Old Hickory not because of this battle, but because of his toughness, which people likened to hardwood.) Jackson was the first pioneer to become president, and the last president who served in the Revolutionary War. Another distinction fell upon Jackson on January 30, 1835, when he became the first president to survive an assassination attempt. While attending a funeral service at the U.S. Capitol, Richard Lawrence, a "supposed maniac" who believed he was Richard III, deprived of fortune and throne by the U.S. government, stepped out from behind a column with a pair of pistols aimed at the president's back. The city's famous humidity, however, caused both pistols to misfire, allowing bystanders to subdue Lawrence. President Jackson, newspapers reported, joined in beating the assailant with his cane. After hearing trial evidence, the jury acquited on grounds of insanity. The prosecutor, Francis Scott Key, had Lawrence committed to an asylum.

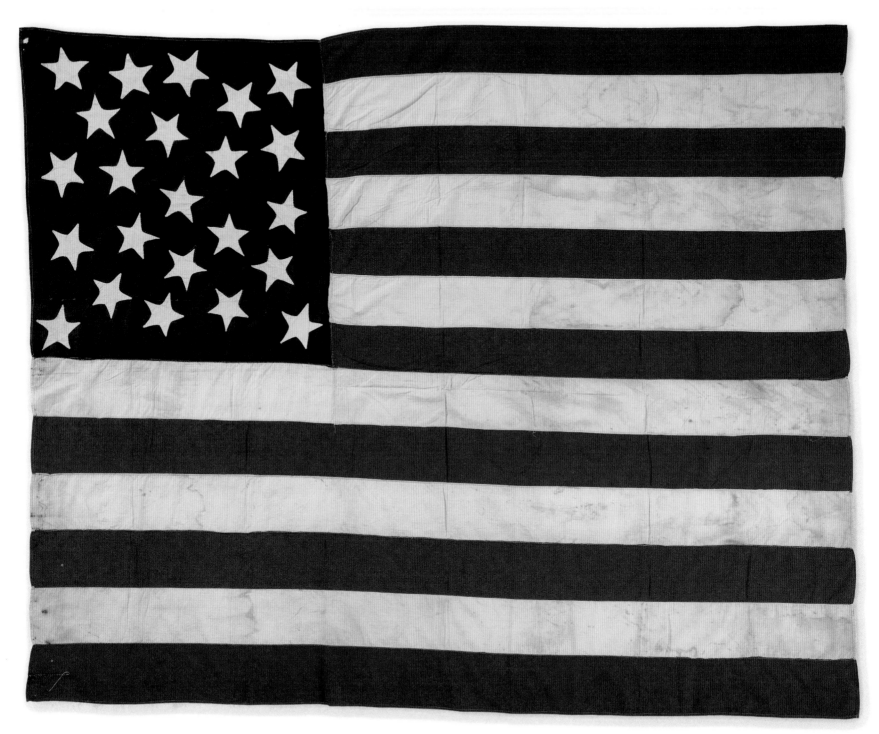

Because Missouri was not officially admitted until August 10, after the Fourth of July when new flags became official, the 23-Star Flag was used for only one year. The stars are arranged in a double medallion with a center star and four corner stars. Each star is positioned so that a single point leads on the inner side of the rings to the center. Although this flag's central star is placed with one point oriented upward, it was by no means the rule.

23
STAR FLAG

state | MAINE
president | JAMES MONROE
material | WOOL BUNTING
date made | C.1820
admissions date | MARCH 15, 1820
flag date | JULY 4, 1820
dimensions | 62" x 79"
period in use | 2 YEARS

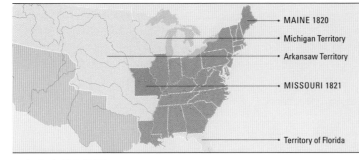

- MAINE 1820
- Michigan Territory
- Arkansaw Territory
- MISSOURI 1821
- Territory of Florida

Maine's international border with Canada was a source of enduring tension that actually sparked the bloodless Aroostok War between settlers and loggers claiming overlapping forests. After General Winfield Scott was sent as a demonstration of force in 1839, an armed clash was avoided. In 1842 Secretary of State Daniel Webster signed a treaty with Canada that settled the border.

MAINE

Maine was a part of Massachusetts when separatists began agitating for statehood in the 18th century, but it was not until 1819 that a vote to formally pursue statehood gained voters' approval. Settlers in Maine objected to what they perceived as lackluster representation by the state government in distant Boston.

Maine's petition for statehood, however, provoked a debate destined to be remembered as a turning point in the nation's history. Strongly abolitionist, Maine's statehood petition collided with Missouri Territory's own statehood effort in the U.S. Congress, splitting the pro- and anti-slavery factions, who were already deeply divided over textile tariffs. A district of Massachusetts, Maine was, along with its mother state, one of the first to prohibit slavery, while the expansion of the cotton economy into Missouri's river valleys was followed by slavery itself.

MISSOURI

After the Louisiana Purchase, the land that would become the state of Louisiana was designated as the Orleans Territory. The remaining part was designated the Louisiana Territory in 1805 but was renamed the Missouri Territory in 1812. (In 1807 President Thomas Jefferson appointed Meriwether Lewis governor of the Louisiana Territory, but in 1809 Lewis, despondent, committed suicide. William Clark served as governor of the Missouri Territory in 1813.) Starting in 1796, alternately slave and free states were admitted to the Union: Tennessee, Ohio, Louisiana, Indiana, Mississippi, Illinois, Alabama, Maine, and Missouri. The Missouri Compromise allowed Missouri to enter the Union as a slave state and Maine as a free state, thus keeping the balance of slave and free states in Congress. Although Missouri was admitted a slave state, the rest of the original Louisiana Purchase north of the 36°30' parallel was declared "forever" off-limits to slavery. The compromise, like a wedge driven deeper into wood, widened the fissure that already traveled across America.

"I had a long time ceased to read newspapers or pay attention to public affairs," Thomas Jefferson wrote from Monticello, "confident they were in good hands and content to be a passenger in our bark to the shore from which I am not distant. But this momentous question, like a fire bell in the night, awakened and filled one with terror. I considered it at once as the knell of the Union."

Harriet Beecher Stowe wrote *Uncle Tom's Cabin* in Brunswick, Maine. Published in 1852, the book profoundly strengthened the abolitionist cause. Ten years later, Abraham Lincoln welcomed her to the White House, calling her the "little lady who started a big war."

24

STAR FLAG

state | MISSOURI
president | JAMES MONROE
material | WOOL BUNTING
date made | C.1822
admissions date | AUGUST 10, 1821
flag date | JULY 4, 1822
dimensions | 36" x 56"
period in use | 14 YEARS

MISSOURI

The 24-Star Flag, born of the Missouri Compromise, represented the status quo of America on the eve of its Demicentennial, its fiftieth birthday. Just as the Revolutionaries aroused Americans to arms with warnings of British enslavement, now America's own opposition to and embrace of slavery would test the fabric of the Republic. The flag's exaggerated fly length is emphasized by the four long rows of stars. What is particularly unusual about this flag is that the flag maker chose to apply the stars to the back (reverse) side of the flag and allowed them to "peek" through to the front (obverse) side. Typically, if stars are applied only to one side, they are applied to the obverse, or front, side and peek through to the back.

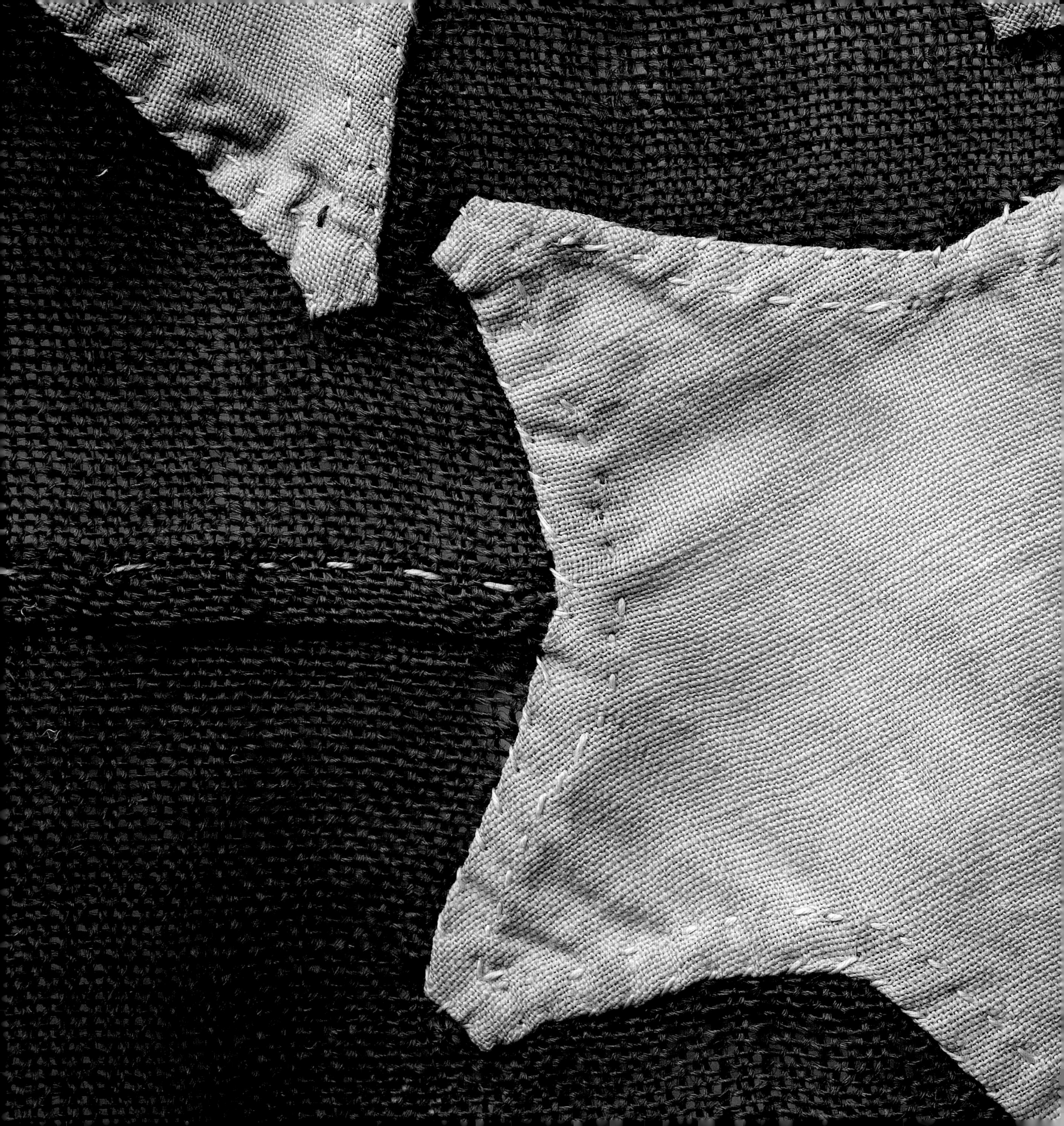

PART TWO: *1826–1875*

THE 25-STAR FLAG TO THE 37-STAR FLAG

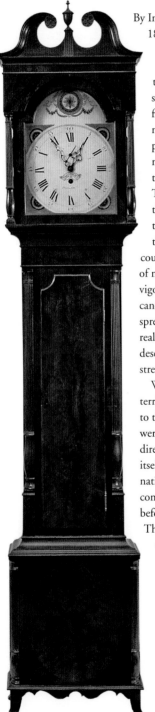

By Independence Day, 1826, the United States had grown to include well over ten million people, spread across twenty-five states. Over the next fifty years, the population would nearly quintuple to fifty million. Territories extended the national domain to the Pacific through the wilds of Oregon country. America's sense of nationhood had vigorously taken root, its canopy now beginning to spread over much vaster realms of forest, prairie, desert, mountain, and stream and river.

With vast new territories opening up to the west, Americans were setting forth in all directions. Commerce itself was reaching the nation's interior with the completion, only the year before, of the Erie Canal. That same year, work on the Santa Fe Trail was authorized.

Eli Whitney, who with his simple cotton gin set in motion a vast expansion of the national economy (but who never profited from his invention), had died in 1825. Already, the symbiotic relationship between textile mills in Lowell, Massachusetts, and the cotton plantations in the South, shattered any myths about American ingenuity and industriousness. The dark core of this success was, of course, slavery, now deeply entrenched in the fiber of the South, where in 1826 twice as many slaves were held in bondage than in 1776.

The federal government had now been in Washington, D.C. for a quarter of a century, had seen five presidents, was in its 19th Congress, and Chief Justice John Marshall (the longest serving of any who would ever occupy that chair on the Supreme Court) brilliantly established and demonstrated, for thirty-five years, the importance of the judiciary. The principle of the balance of power would endure with great stability, but American politics were anything but demure and civil or predictable. The party created by some of the nation's founders, the Federalists, was already laid to rest; and quite literally, a new generation of Americans had taken up the reins, when John Adams's son, John Quincy, won the presidency.

His health failing, Thomas Jefferson was spending his final years contentedly away from politics at his beloved home and farm on the hilltop overlooking the University of Virginia, another of his creations. Surrounded by his books and plants, instruments and artifacts, Jefferson restored his friendship with John Adams, damaged in the bitter election of 1800, through dozens of letters. His fellow revolutionary's replies, full of observations and recollections, completed the cross-stitch, repairing the seam that had joined them together in 1776. Anticipating the milestone July 4th of 1826,

towns, villages, cities, and capitals began preparing months ahead for the festivities. Parades, military demonstrations, feasts, toasts, lectures, concerts, sermons, rallies, and picnics would both solemnly and jubilantly mark the day. "The worthy patriots of Ulster County," historian Robert P. Hay wrote, planned to use two thousand pounds of gunpowder to create an explosion that they hoped would echo throughout New England. The mayor of Washington, D.C. would make his city's demonstrations especially poignant; even though his greatest wish, to have Thomas Jefferson present in the capital city that day, was undermined by the apologetic Jefferson's illness.

Amidst all the jubilations of July 4th, the day took on an even deeper importance for Americans when disheartening news—emanating from two different places, Braintree, Massachusetts, and Monticello, Virginia—converged in the nation's collective consciousness.

Thomas Jefferson, seriously weakened, semi-conscious in his bed, periodically woke to ask, "Is it yet the Fourth?" When the sun rose, and America reached its fiftieth birthday, Jefferson died.

Meanwhile, John Adams, then in his ninety-first year, but vigorous and fully engaged in the tending of his own farm, suddenly fell ill after a walk. By six o'clock in the evening, he too died, his last words believed to have been, "Jefferson lives."

That two of the Founding Fathers, the last two still living, one a Northerner, one a Southerner, would expire on the fiftieth anniversary of the birth of the Declaration of Independence, was beyond the comprehension of people everywhere. Disbelief led naturally and quickly to the conviction that only divine affirmation of the political ideas of republicanism, equality, and liberty could have sponsored such an act of symbolic simultaneity. This incredible occurrence deepened and honed reflections on what America's 1826 anniversary meant, with interpretations and exultations flowing from newspaper columns, lecterns, and pulpits. Special editions of Jefferson and Adams memorabilia were published, memorial parades held in even the smallest of towns, and flags were lowered to half-mast everywhere when news eventually arrived in places as distant as the Sandwich Islands. Yale mathematicians

Following Jefferson's death, his family was forced to auction most of Monticello's contents to pay off his debt. Dr. Robley Dunglison, a professor of medicine at the University of Virginia, who cared for Jefferson in his last days, attended the auction where he hoped to purchase this 1812 clock. Unaware that Jefferson's daughter Martha asked a relative, Nicholas Trist, to bid on the clock for her, so that she might give it to the doctor in appreciation of his care, Dunglison placed his own bids. Trist outbid Dunglison by five dollars. Martha then gave the clock to Dunglison, whose descendants contributed the clock to the Pennsylvania Historical Society in 1894. The clock was eventually returned to Monticello, where it remains.

earnestly calculated the odds, which they assured the public stretched into the unfathomable millions, of such an event taking place again, reaffirming in Americans' minds that the fantastic improbability was indeed proof of the Revolutionary motto, *Annuit Coeptis*.

Neither of these great men, fellow-citizens, could have died, at any time, without leaving an immense void in our American society. They have been so intimately, and for so long a time, blended with the history of the country, and especially so united, in our thoughts and recollections, with the events of the Revolution, that the death of either would have touched the chords of public sympathy. We should have felt that one great link, connecting us with former times, was broken; that we had lost something more, as it were, of the presence of the Revolution itself, and of the act of independence, and were driven on, by another great remove from the days of our country's early distinction, to meet posterity and to mix with the future. Like the mariner, whom the currents of the ocean and the winds carry along, till he sees the stars which have directed his course and lighted his pathless way descend, one by one, beneath the rising horizon, we should have felt that the stream of time had borne us onward till another great luminary, whose light had cheered us and whose guidance we had followed, had sunk away from our sight.

—Daniel Webster Eulogizing
Thomas Jefferson and John Adams

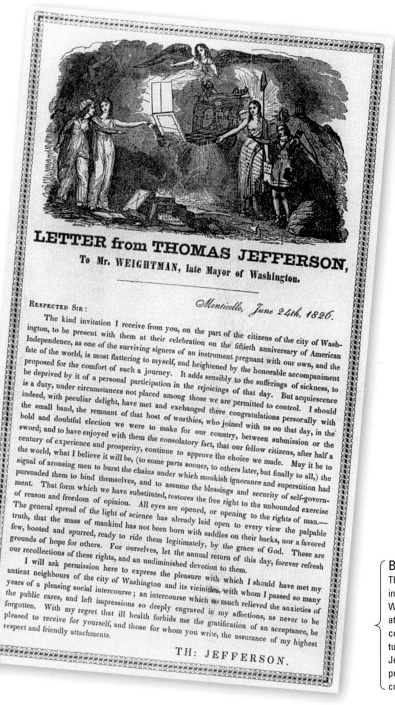

Because of failing health, Thomas Jefferson declined an invitation from Mayor Roger C. Weightman of Washington, D.C. to attend the fiftieth anniversary celebrations of Independence. It turned out to be the last letter Jefferson wrote. The text was printed that same year on a commemorative silk scarf.

This peculiar 25-Star Flag symbolizes the volatilities and divisions that would challenge the nation between 1826 and 1876. Its square canton, made of cotton robbed by sunlight of its blue, rests on a red stripe, sometimes called a "war stripe." Twenty-four five-pointed stars gather around a larger six-pointed star, suggesting a flag for Arkansas, the twenty-fifth state. However, machine stitching along the stripes suggests the flag is Civil War vintage, and possibly one that was made to reaffirm the loyalty of states remaining in the Union.

ARKANSAS

25
STAR FLAG

state | ARKANSAS
president | ANDREW JACKSON
material | COTTON
date made | C.1836
admissions date | JUNE 15, 1836
flag date | JULY 4, 1836
dimensions | 81" x 141"
period in use | 1 YEAR

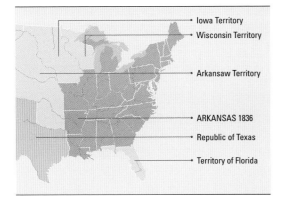

Iowa Territory
Wisconsin Territory

Arkansaw Territory

ARKANSAS 1836
Republic of Texas
Territory of Florida

Arkansas Territory came to be in 1819, encompassing land between Louisiana and Missouri, but extending west along the Red River and then north along 100° longitude, and back again to the northern line of Tennessee. Even though Iowa, Missouri, Arkansas, and Louisiana were, in theory, to share equivalent lengths of Mississippi River banks as their eastern borders, Missourians managed to secure the "lower boot," considered by their southern neighbors as an intrusion. Once again, political and geographic interplay linked events in Arkansas and Michigan, as indicated on page 80.

★ ★

Jim Bowie was a slave trader, knife fighter, sugar producer, and land speculator whose exploits in Louisiana and Arkansas included fraudulent land schemes that required the U.S. Supreme Court to invalidate some of his deeds. Born in Kentucky, Bowie and his brother, Rezin, headed to Texas after the War of 1812. (Rezin gave him the legendary Bowie Knife, a huge blade that was 10½ inches long and 2 inches wide.) Bowie accepted Mexican citizenship and planned to build cotton and wool mills across the Rio Grande. However, swept up in the Texas Revolution in which he led men against the Mexicans, Bowie ended up within the precincts of the Alamo. He was thirty-nine years old, and already near death from tuberculosis, when he was executed by Santa Anna's troops, who shot him in the head.

This 25-Star Flag testifies to the increasing availability of quality cotton textiles in the United States. While the wool flags were still predominantly made of British bunting, the explosive growth of cotton production in the United States provided quality fabric for such flags as the one above.

The Smithsonian Institution

★ ★

When James Smithson, an eccentric and wealthy British aristocrat and collector, died in 1829, his will instructed that his entire estate be used for an "Establishment for the increase & diffusion of Knowledge among men." James Smithson, it turns out, did not want his "Institution" to be built in his native country, but in the United States (a place that he had never been to), for reasons that historians have never been able to fully explain.

Predictably, Smithson's vague words stirred up fierce debate among Washington's politicians, who for ten years argued about how exactly Smithson's instructions should be interpreted. Congressman John Quincy Adams, the most ardent champion of the bequest's lofty intellectual premise, zealously urged that Smithson's gift be used for an appropriate place of higher learning. Senator John Calhoun, however, interpreted the bequest as yet another encroachment of state's rights and a dangerous expansion of Federal power—not to mention that any acceptance of English gold was "beneath the dignity" of a nation that had only twenty years before watched English soldiers burn its Capitol.

Meanwhile, the money itself—one hundred thousand dollars in gold bullion—arrived to the U.S. Treasury in 1838, and as swiftly as it was deposited, was withdrawn and invested in bonds for the new states of Arkansas and Michigan. Within a year, the money had evaporated. Infuriated, Adams demanded the government redeem the bequest with interest, and hoping to avoid scandal, Congress agreed to do so in 1841.

But another five years would lapse before President James K. Polk signed an act establishing the Smithsonian Institution on August 10, 1846. And another ten years would pass before architect James Renwick's "Castle" was built on the Mall, to be joined over the next century by over a dozen additional museums, zoos, laboratories, libraries, and research centers (most arranged in a series of architectural monuments outlining the Mall), including the National Museum of American History, established in 1946. Today, the most famous American Flag, the Star-Spangled Banner, symbol of American independence from Britain, is preserved by an institution created by an English fortune and built in the center of a city burned and ransacked by English soldiers.

Alexander Graham Bell, a Smithsonian regent, personally oversaw the exhumation of Smithson's remains near Genoa, Italy, and their transfer to the United States where, in 1904, President Theodore Roosevelt ordered a formal military procession to the Castle for the flag-draped casket.

MICHIGAN

26
STAR FLAG

state | MICHIGAN
president | ANDREW JACKSON
material | WOOL
date made | C.1837
admissions date | JANUARY 26, 1837
flag date | JULY 4, 1837
dimensions | 67″ x 107″
period in use | 8 YEARS

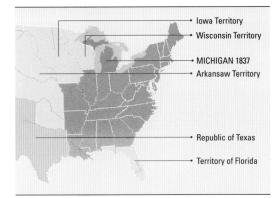

Iowa Territory
Wisconsin Territory
MICHIGAN 1837
Arkansaw Territory
Republic of Texas
Territory of Florida

Continuing the sectional tempo of state admission, Michigan, the next state to emerge from the slave-free Territory Northwest of the River Ohio, counterbalanced the slave state of Arkansas. Because Detroit had been captured by the British when the Great Lakes were theaters of naval battles during the War of 1812, Michigan's boundaries were only restored to American sovereignty after the Treaty of Ghent in 1814.

Significant migrations to the interior filled Michigan with enough settlers to begin statehood appeals in 1836. But Ohio congressmen quashed Michigan's application because of a dispute over a thin wedge of land known as the "Toledo Strip," located along the Michigan-Ohio border. When state militias encamped on opposite sides of the Maumee River, prepared to settle the issue with guns, cooler heads in Congress prevailed, convincing Michigan to relinquish its claim to Toledo in exchange for the federal grant of the Upper Peninsula.

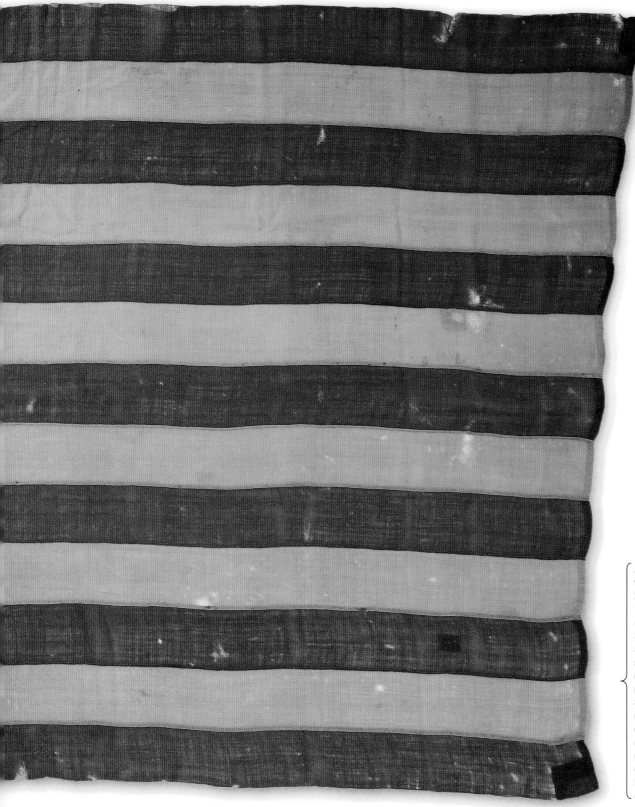

Authentic pre-Civil War flags comprise less than one percent of flags that have survived into the 21st century. Among collectors, the "Great Star" or "Great Luminary" flags are the most coveted of 19th-century geometric patterns. Believing that a Great Star pattern would be one most easily recognized across great distances at sea, Captain Samuel Reid suggested to President James Monroe that such a design should be the official star pattern; Reid was making an important point, since most Stars and Stripes were made for maritime use. In fact, it was not until 1837, the year that the 26-Star Flag became official, that the infantry was authorized to carry the national flag. Entirely hand-sewn, with whip-stitched grommets, the single-appliqué linen stars seen here oxidized to gold over time. The "puffy" stars have blunt points that nestle into each other, helping to dramatize the shape of the conglomerate star.

27

STAR FLAG

state | FLORIDA
president | JAMES K. POLK
material | COTTON
date made | C.1845
admissions date | MARCH 3, 1845
flag date | JULY 4, 1845
dimensions | 60" x 60"
period in use | 1 YEAR

Arkansaw Territory •
• Wisconsin Territory
• Iowa Territory

Republic of Texas •
• West Florida
• FLORIDA 1845

FLORIDA

From the day Juan Ponce de León landed in Florida in 1513, nearly three centuries passed before this final section of Atlantic seaboard was brought into the American fold. In 1810, a successful rebellion in West Florida created the Free and Independent Republic of West Florida, a little nation that existed for a mere twelve weeks, until President James Madison expanded the border of the Louisiana Territory eastward, absorbing the Republic. What remained of Spanish claims was now sequestered on the Florida peninsula. There, agitated by the heat and humidity and complicated by mosquito-infested swampy terrain, Creek and Seminole tribes, the Spanish, white settlers, escaped slaves from bordering states, and British interests collided. Three particularly bloody "Seminole" wars, between 1817–18, 1835–42, and 1855–58, in addition to the War of 1812, were fought before Florida was "subdued" and the fate of its natives sealed.

John Quincy Adams, serving as President James Monroe's secretary of state, negotiated the 1819 Adams-Onís Treaty. In exchange for the Spanish cession of Florida, the treaty reaffirmed (for the time being) Spanish sovereignty in the southwest. But more importantly, a boundary, known as the Adams-Onís Line, which traveled over Texas and then along the 42nd parallel, clearly delineated the transcontinental boundary between the United States and Spain. For the first time, a path could be traced over the American dominion from the Atlantic to the Pacific.

A delegate went to Congress in 1821, and the Territory of Florida united East Florida with West Florida the following year. President Andrew Jackson, who had ruthlessly prosecuted the First Seminole War, was determined to settle the Florida question and launched the Second Seminole War, an expensive quagmire that would trudge through three more presidents, and establish the reputation of a fourth, General Zachary Taylor, before finally ending in 1842, clearing the way for Florida statehood the day before President John Tyler left office.

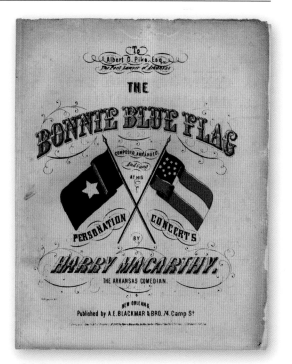

Nearly square in shape, the 27-Star Flag is among the rarest in the collection. Because Texas statehood soon followed, very few authentic flags from Florida's brief period as the nation's newest state have survived. Lengths of cotton were stitched together to make each stripe. But the flag maker, who apparently only had 25-inch widths of blue cloth, had to add a strip to the canton's lower section to accommodate the width of its seven neighboring stripes, making a square-shaped flag with a square canton. The sharply pointed stars were arranged in a staggered 5-4, 5-4, 5-4 pattern, each randomly rotated, so that the viewer's eye gets frozen nowhere.

A flag with a single star, known as the "Bonnie Blue," represented the short-lived Free and Independent Republic of West Florida. The Bonnie Blue Flag, carried into Texas by settlers from Western Florida, may have inspired the Texas Lone Star Flag. During the Civil War, the Bonnie Blue Flag was resurrected as an important symbol of solidarity, Southern unity, and resistance, often accompanying other Confederate flags.

TEXAS

Having been under control of Spain, France, Mexico, the Confederacy, and its own Republic, Texas has flown a myriad of flags during its mythic history, including many versions of the Lone Star Flag.

When Sam Houston and his troops avenged the Alamo by defeating the Mexican army at San Jacinto on April 21, 1836, and capturing the great nemesis Antonio Lopéz de Santa Anna cowering in tall grass, Texas won its independence and announced national sovereignty. President James K. Polk, driven by expansionist ambitions (unlike his opponent Henry Clay), won the 1844 election with a campaign promise to bring Texas into the Union. When, in 1845 Polk and Congress made Texas the twenty-eighth state, Mexico moved to retake its territory, particularly the land between the Rio Grande and Nueces rivers, an area of great dispute. When U.S. Cavalry troops moved into the area, it provoked a Mexican attack, killing eleven Americans. Considering this a hostile invasion, Polk was able to rally Congress into passing a Declaration of War.

★ ★ ★ ★ ★ ★ ★ ★ ★ ★ ★ ★ ★ ★ ★

Sam Houston, born in Virginia and raised in Tennessee (partly by Cherokee Indians), caught the attention of Andrew Jackson, under whom he valiantly served, becoming seriously wounded in battle with the Creeks. Having honed his political connections as a lawyer and Freemason, Houston was sent to Congress in 1823 to represent Tennesseans and later elected governor of Tennessee. Shattered by a failed marriage, Houston resigned his governorship and left Tennessee. His wanderings led him to Washington, D.C., where an altercation with a congressman brought him to trial in the House of Representatives, defended by the author of "The Star-Spangled Banner" and lawyer, Francis Scott Key.

Houston eventually came to Texas in 1832, the place that he would shape most profoundly, serving as president of Texas twice, a U.S. senator, and governor of Texas. (He is the only American to serve as governor of two different states.) Refusing to support secession, Houston was discharged from office.

FLAGS THAT MADE HISTORY

THE ALAMO FLAG

On October 13, 1835, in New Orleans, men gathered in the café in the glass-roofed Banks Arcade, built by merchant Thomas Banks, who supported Texas independence. There they mustered two volunteer regiments of one hundred twenty men, whose drab uniforms gave them the name "New Orleans Greys."

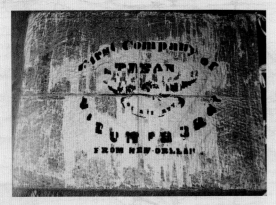

Before the end of the month, they were in Texas, where appreciative women presented them with a blue silk flag, emblazoned with an eagle. The New Orleans Greys distinguished themselves as one of the bravest volunteer units and fought at all of the major Texas battles, including the Alamo, where General Santa Anna captured their flag.

Some believe the New Orleans Greys flag to be the only flag flown at the Alamo that survived. However, the flag has an uncertain destiny. Texas Attorney General John A. Keeling claims to have discovered the flag in 1933 while visiting Mexico's National History Museum in the Chapultepec Castle in Mexico City. Over the next several decades, both the Texas legislature and the U.S. Congress sought to convince Mexican authorities to return the flag, but never succeeded. Museum officials even claimed that the flag had been burned or lost, but as recently as 2005, reports surfaced that the flag was indeed still in the collection.

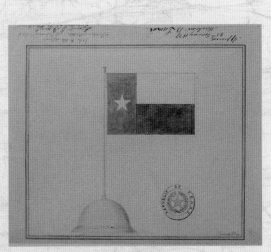

The Lone Star of Texas Flag was officially adopted as the national flag of the Republic of Texas on January 25, 1839. Peter Krag's original design is preserved at the Texas State Library. Illustrations preceding this one sometimes reversed the red and white stripes.

28

STAR FLAG

state | TEXAS
president | JAMES K. POLK
material | COTTON
date made | C.1846
admissions date | DECEMBER 29, 1845
flag date | JULY 4, 1846
dimensions | 52" x 107"
period in use | 1 YEAR

Arkansaw Territory
Wisconsin Territory
Iowa Territory

TEXAS 1845

This most unusual 28-Star Flag, made entirely with cotton, stretches its stripes wide. A "Great Luminary" pattern, with two points oriented upward, bursts to the edges of its little canton.

Similarly elongated and peculiar, this second 28-Star Flag opted for a rectangular canton, with disciplined rows of painted stars, given emphasis by slight shadows. The flag has only eleven stripes, alternating red, white, and blue. Small metal rings along the hoist strip were likely used to display the flag vertically.

FROM FIBER TO FLAG

U nderstanding the origin and manufacture of textiles is an important part of appreciating historic American flags. Generally, textiles can be grouped into three general categories. Textiles made from animal sources such as wool or silk have protein as their structure. Plant-based fibers, composed of cellulose, include cotton and flax. Synthetic fibers are made from a number of different chemical components and industrial processes; among the hundreds of synthetics are rayon, nylon, and polyester.

Textile production has a complex history: an interplay of agriculture, husbandry, craft, mechanization, invention, trade and tariff politics, and economics. Textile production is as ancient as human culture, and is based on handwork, simple tools, and fibers and dyestuffs gathered from natural sources. With the development of international trade, the role of textiles became central to the economies of regions, cities, nations, and empires. Textile production was so lucrative that it became one of the principal engines of the Industrial Revolution. The machine designs, manufacturing processes, and dyestuff preparations were closely guarded state secrets, given the competitive advantages and profits each might promise.

Historic Stars and Stripes were principally made of silk, wool, cotton, and a smaller percentage of linen. While each type of textile had certain advantages or disadvantages in terms of durability, weight, appearance, or colorfastness, the choice of textile may have simply depended on local availability. Flags could also have components made of different textiles. It was not uncommon, for instance, for the field to be made of wool and the stars cotton.

CONVERSION INTO YARN

Before cotton, silk, linen, or yarn can be made into fabric, the raw fibers need to be converted to yarn or thread. The length of fiber is known as the staple. The longer the staple, the smoother the twisted yarn, since fewer ends have a chance to protrude from the surface. Cotton fibers are the shortest, depending on the variety of plant, producing staple lengths anywhere from half an inch to three inches in length. Short wool fibers (up to 3 inches) are used for woolen yarns, while longer wool fibers (between 3 and 8 inches) are used for worsteds. Fabric made with linen fibers, which can be as long as 20 inches, produce less lint. Silk produces by far the longest natural fibers; a single cocoon can produce a filament up to 4 thousand feet in length—a phenomenon that gives silk its smooth surface. (Synthetic fibers can be produced in continuous filaments of unlimited length.) While each type of textile requires specific methods, some general terms follow.

OPENING AND BLENDING

Wool or cotton bales, packed densely, are opened by machines to decompress the masses and separate the fibers. Another set of mechanical actions removes impurities and flattens the fibers into laps.

CARDING

The next stage, known as carding, when fibers are untangled and worked to be straight and parallel, was once achieved by hand with flat wooden tools covered in grids of wire needles. Massive machines now accomplish the task with rolling cylinders covered with wire needles. The machines extrude the carded fibers as loose, rope-shaped strands known as *card sliver*.

A man feeds wool into a carding machine at the American Wool Company in Boston in 1912. The huge series of rollers straightens the fibers for the spinning process.

DOUBLING

An additional stage, called *doubling*, combines slivers into denser conglomerates that produce a stronger yarn.

COMBING

In cotton production, a secondary carding stage, known as *combing*, straightens the fibers even more and separates out short or loose fibers (known as *noils*), resulting in *comb sliver*.

DRAWING OUT, SLUBBING, AND ROVING

Comb slivers next enter the drawing out and slubbing machines that progressively lengthen the fibers by pulling the staples and making an introductory twist, winding the roving on bobbins. The roving frame machines lengthen and twist the fibers even finer.

SPINNING

Finally, the spinning process combines the fibers into yarn with the desired amount of twist; more twist produces stronger and smoother yarns. Warp yarns, because they need to maintain tension during the weaving process, require a greater amount of twist during spinning than their counterpart weft yarns. To make very strong warp yarn, another stage twists plys together, producing two-ply or three-ply yarn, for instance. In contrast, weft yarns do not receive as much twist during spinning as do warp yarns.

WEAVING FIBERS INTO FABRIC

Like spinning, weaving began as a craft performed with hands and rudimentary tools and instruments. Over centuries, weaving methods became more and more elaborate and mechanized, vastly increasing the speed and volume with which fabric could be woven. Consequently, commercially made fabric replaced, by and large, homemade textiles. The textile industry was among the first to absorb women—and children, until labor laws were enacted—into the industrial workplace. The loom is at the center of the weaving process, the framework that holds and coordinates two sets of yarn (the *warp* and the *weft*) as they are intermingled to form fabric. Warp yarns are held in tension, equally spaced by the warp beam and the cloth beam. The *shuttle*, which holds a bobbin, or spool, of weft yarn, is passed over or under warp yarns, in any number of patterns, to create the desired weave. Each cross through the width of the loom is known as a *pick*. The action of lifting warp threads to create the space through which the weft could pass, known as *shedding*, was performed by hand on early looms, and later automatically by mechanized looms. After each pass of the shuttle, the weft yarns are tamped together with variable force, to achieve the desired tightness. As the fabric is created, it is gathered and rolled onto the beam while more warp yarn is released. During colonial times, most people preferred a plain weave. However, in the early 1820s, the Jacquard loom attachment came to America, resulting in more complex patterns.

{ Men, women, and children amidst a field of cotton in Mississippi.

ANIMAL (PROTEIN) FIBERS

WOOL

Wool was the common textile material (particularly in an inexpensive lightweight weave known as *bunting*) used to make American flags. Several factors made it an ideal fabric for flags, especially when used aboard ocean-going vessels. While wool fibers are highly absorptive of water, the lightness of a bunting weave allowed flags to dry more quickly than denser weaves. The light weave, through which air could travel, allowed breezes and gusts of wind to lift the flag. Wool is also more elastic than cotton, and it has a natural resistance to mildew, unlike cotton or linen. And wool fibers accepted most dyes, showing off bold colors that could be identified across considerable distances.

Until the Civil War and the subsequent establishment of an American woolen textile industry, bunting was produced in Great Britain, particularly in Essex. According to one British textile historian, bunting "was made almost entirely by female labour," commonly woven in broad 19- to 22-inch widths or a narrower 11-inch width. Its production fluctuated with demand by British naval or military campaigns, as times of war required more bunting for more flags, sometimes disrupting its availability in the colonial marketplaces. As early as 1780, American colonial shop owners advertised the availability of British bunting "for ships colours" in such newspapers as the *Pennsylvania Packet.* Conversely, flag makers, such as Rebecca Young in 1781, included appeals in some advertisements for "any person having BUNTING for sale."

After a wool pile was sheared from the sheep, it was cleaned. Particles such as seeds or leaves were removed by hand, while oils and soil were removed by careful washing. The wool fibers were then separated from the hair-like kemp fibers and then sorted for quality, based on the fibers' fineness—the finer the better.

Carding was done by hand or later with increasingly sophisticated machines that used thousands of combing needles to straighten and align the wool fibers.

Spinning converted the fibers into yarn, which was then woven into the fabric. Woolens were made of a loosely spun yarn that gave the finished fabric a fuzzy appearance. *Worsted* was made of long-staple fibers that were carded and more tightly spun, giving the fabric a smoother quality. Virgin wool was made from entirely new fibers, while *shoddy* was made, either wholly or partially, from recycled rags and fibers of lesser quality. *Fulling* was a finishing process whereby fabric was shrunk, thickened, or given textures through the application of steam, friction, or pressure. Dyeing, which could occur at several different stages, gave wool its color.

Fiercely protective of its textile technology and lucrative weaving industry, British law forbade colonists from importing raw wool and especially prohibited the export of textile technology or migration of skilled textile workers from Britain. That colonists were forced to pay a premium for finished fabric was yet another grievance that fueled the Revolution.

Ironically, any wool flags made during the Revolutionary War would have been made of British bunting, likely made in Sudbury, England, a town northeast of London.

Most wool fabric for flags was woven in a loose plain weave, the warp and weft yarns alternating over and above each other. The openness of the weave allowed gusts of wind to float the flags spiritedly.

During World War I, First Lady Edith Wilson, eager to demonstrate the importance of self-sufficiency and contribution, oversaw the care of a flock of sheep that grazed on the White House lawn. Wool from the sheep was contributed to the Red Cross for the war effort. Wool production was also important for soldiers' uniforms.

But it was not until the 1850s that an American wool industry began to take shape, after English designs for looms were either memorized and recreated abroad or smuggled directly into the Americas. And it was not until after the Civil War that American-made bunting was widely used for Stars and Stripes, even acquiring the support of law when Benjamin Butler, a member of Congress and an investor in Massachusetts wool mills, promoted legislation to require all American flags be made of domestically produced bunting.

SILK

Silk is a protein fiber produced by certain caterpillars for their cocoons, most notably *Bombyx mori*, known as the silkworm. Sericulture is the science of cultivating silkworms and their food source, the mulberry leaf. First developed in ancient China, the methods of silk production disseminated via the Silk Road to India, Persia, and eventually Europe. Italians, particularly around Lake Como, became master sericulturists.

Lyons, France, became a great center of silk weaving after Joseph-Marie Jacquard invented his automated loom, the first to weave fabrics mechanically with

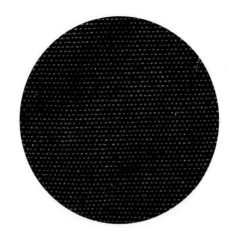

This 13-Star banner with a gold fringe dates from the 1870s and was likely made of American silk.

Silk flags or banners could be woven in a far tighter, less porous weave than everyday silk, allowing its smooth surface to be painted.

Silk mills, such as this one in Paterson, employed thousands of men, women, and children. Labor disputes were common and in 1913, when owners wanted to assign one worker to operate four looms instead of two, a strike ensued. Nearly a month into the walkout, mill owners, in an attempt to assert that striking was unpatriotic and shame workers back to their looms, held "Flag Day" on March 17. Giant American flags were unfurled over factories. Workers responded by wearing cards that declared, "We wove the flag. We dyed the flag. We won't scab under the flag." The workers did not return for another four months.

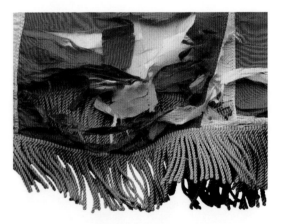

Conservation of silk flags presents certain challenges. Aging and exposure to light and water can weaken the fine fibers. When silk was treated with metallic chemicals to increase its bulk, the chemical reactions could make fibers more brittle. This silk flag, made in the 1860s, is so delicate that the slightest touch can damage its fibers.

patterns. The loom's action was directed by cards punched with holes—a precursor, historians theorize, to the modern computer.

American colonists attempted to cultivate silkworms and provide raw material to English weavers, but never succeeded because of technical inexperience and unsuitable ecology. Silk fabric had to be imported until 1839, when silk production began on a large scale in the Old Gun Mill in Paterson, New Jersey. By the 1880s, silk production had become so extensive that Paterson was nicknamed "Silk City" and the "Lyons of America." (The demand for silk supported a competitive industry in Pennsylvania as well.) Raw silk fibers still were not produced anywhere in the Americas but were imported from China, Japan, and Italy. Silk cocoons from Italy, particularly from Piedmont, were regarded as premium; Chinese cocoons were the poorest. The fibers were then spun, dyed (enhanced by the soft water of the Passaic River), and woven into broadcloths and ribbons. The invention of rayon curtailed silk production by 1930.

Silk was particularly suited for flags, but because of its expense, it was typically reserved for ceremonial flags, displayed on special occasions. Unlike wool, it would have been unsuitable for an everyday flag, particularly aboard vessels where it would be exposed to weather. Triangular in cross-section, silk fibers refract light, giving silk its hallmark luster and shine. Silk displays dyes vividly and evenly.

The majority of flags definitively documented to be from the Revolutionary War period that survive today are silk. During the Civil War, cavalry guidons (small flags used as unit markers) were also sometimes made of silk, since it fluttered in the wind and shimmered in the sun.

PLANT (CELLULOSE) FIBERS

A cotton fabric made with red and white yarns resulted in a lighter shade for the stripes.

The red and white stripes of this 33-Star Flag, dating from 1859, were made by weaving the red and white yarns into a striped twill fabric. The blue canton was printed on a plain white cotton weave, leaving the white fabric for stars.

COTTON

Cotton was a crop and industry central to the development of American commerce, trade, and industrialization. Many storekeepers in colonial America offered all kinds of cotton fabric for sale. But domestic production of cotton textiles did not begin in America until 1790, when Samuel Slater managed to elude authorities, disguised as a farmer, to smuggle his knowledge of British spinning machines to Pawtucket, Rhode Island. Here he opened America's first mill for spinning cotton yarn. (Sewing thread, however, was not developed until much later.) Later, Francis Cabot Lowell, an American who also memorized the workings of textile machines while visiting Great Britain, established the Boston Manufacturing Company in 1813, the first company that could entirely process raw cotton fiber into finished cloth. Lowell died in 1817, but his partners greatly expanded the enterprise, creating an entire town in 1826 on the Merrimack River, whose surging water powered the machines. The town was named in honor of Lowell. Over the next decades, cotton mills producing a vast array of fabrics and products proliferated, both in the North and in the South following the Civil War.

Types of cotton weaves were numerous. Plain weaves (evenly alternating warp and weft) included calico and muslin. Common and cheap, both originated in India, and were widely used by the masses. Canvas or duck was a heavier, tighter plain weave that was popular in maritime applications—sails were made of duck—because of its toughness. Wax, glazings, or oil coatings could make canvas more water repellent.

Twill, an especially tight and durable fabric, was produced by weaving weft yarns over at least two warps, resulting in its characteristic diagonal striping. (The denim jean, designed to withstand the wear and tear of heavy labor, particularly mining, is a twill.) When twill was used for flags, the stripes could be woven directly into the fabric instead of dyed, painted, or sewn on.

A cotton bunting was invented and patented in the mid-19th century, often marketed as "moth proof."

Despite the predominance of cotton in American life, this fabric had several disadvantages when used for flags. Generally, cottons held dye less resplendently, and quickly faded when exposed to sunlight (see page 94). If cotton flags were exposed to inclement weather, they dried more slowly than woolen ones. Aesthetically, cotton did not drape as elegantly as wool, nor did it unfurl in swells of wind as readily or dramatically. Nevertheless, many American flags were made entirely of cotton, since wool shortages, especially in times of war, were common.

President George Washington personally signed the patent Eli Whitney submitted in 1794 for the cotton gin. His invention profoundly changed the American south, since it made mass cultivation of short-staple cotton hugely profitable.

LINEN

Flax was cultivated by ancient Egyptians in wet coastal and river lowlands, and linen, the fabric it produced, remained an important commodity through Roman, medieval, and modern times. Irish weavers became expert producers of fine linen, and the Dutch developed renown for their ability to bleach the fabric.

While linen was a fiber important to life in the 18th century, the rise of cotton production and industrialization in the next century significantly eclipsed the popularity of flaxen cloth. Linen cultivation and preparation was more labor intensive than cotton, requiring several stages to ferment, separate, card, and soften the stiff fibers to allow for spinning. The stiffness that made linen much more resistant to dyes than cotton, silk, or wool also made it a less desirable choice for flags, which were meant to drape and furl.

Using linen parts, however, to adorn wool flag fields was practiced—especially prior to 1815—before Francis Cabot Lowell's mills made cotton fabric cheaper than linen. Linen thread too, because of its strength, was important for the needlework on early American flags, since the technology for making reliably strong cotton thread did not occur until the 19th century.

Linum usitatissimum, the plant whose woody stem yields linen fibers, has been used for millennia—even by prehistoric people—for cloth, ropes, and nets. Ancient Egyptians produced linen cloth of great quality, samples of which survive to this day because of its use to enshroud mummies.

A hand-cut and hand-sewn linen star rests on a cotton canton (see page 46).

A STITCHING PRIMER

Because flags were much simpler to lay out and assemble than garments, the types of stitches used were fairly straightforward and common. Until the invention of the sewing machine, all flags had to be stitched by hand—or teams of hands! Identifying stitches can help identify the age of a flag. Hand-stitching, which varies in quality, can be identified by its irregularities, unlike most machine stitching, which precisely creates equally-spaced stitches. However, especially skillful hand-stitching can be so even and straight that it's mistaken as having been done by machine.

Hand-stitching alone does not guarantee that a flag was made before the invention of the sewing machine. Some flags were made with a combination of machine and hand stitches, while other flags may have been made with hand stitches in 1805, perhaps, but then repaired with a machine many decades later.

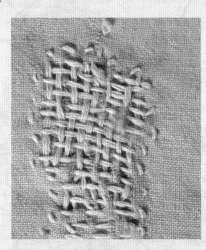

Darning or patches were used to repair holes or tears in flag bunting.

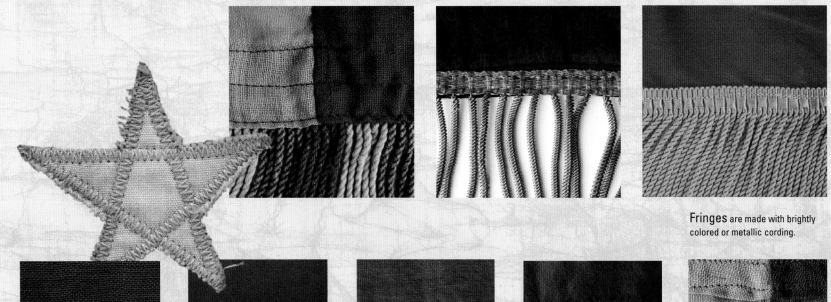

Fringes are made with brightly colored or metallic cording.

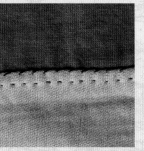

The Running Stitch is the simplest way to join pieces of fabric, with an in-and-out hand-stitch forming straight lines.

The Zig-Zag Stitch is both decorative and strong.

A Whip Stitch is a diagonal stitch used to join flat pieces together.

The Chain Stitch is an interlocking pattern made on a machine, consisting of a double loop of thread.

A hem reinforces the hoist end of a flag, where the end of the stripes are folded up onto themselves and stitched.

Hemp Rope Loop

FLAG HARDWARE AND ROPES

To hold a flag securely against strong wind, many kinds of grommets, ropes, weights, and rings were used. Stitched grommets were the simplest, used when metal was unavailable. Lead grommets and weights were among the earliest metal attachments to appear, followed by pewter, brass, and steel versions.

Stitched Grommet

Carved Wooden Toggle

Lead Weight

Civil War-Era Brass Grommet

Patent Grommet

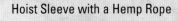

Hoist Sleeve with a Hemp Rope

Steel Rings

THE COLORS OF LIBERTY

{ Workers in Passaic, New Jersey, around 1909, tend silk yarns.

The natural colors of fibers range across whites, browns, beiges, and grays. Stars and Stripes were given their reds, whites, blues, golds, or silvers by dyeing, painting, or printing, or, in some cases, a combination of those methods. (Bleaching, the removal of color from textiles, was achieved through a number of methods, see page 96.) Dyeing is the permanent use of natural or chemical agents to color textiles. For especially elaborate or ceremonial flags, usually made of silk, flag makers often painted the designs onto the completed flag. Printing, whereby flags were stamped by hand or sent through printing machines, allowed for flags to be cheaply and speedily manufactured.

Bleaching and dyeing methods occurred at different stages of the textile-making process, depending on the desired result and type of fiber.

STOCK DYEING

Fibers in their raw state are immersed in a dye bath, a method that allows the most fundamentally colored textiles.

YARN (SKEIN) DYEING

Finished yarns are lowered into a dye bath.

PIECE DYEING

Whole sections of fabric are submerged in a dye solution.

RESIST DYEING

Physical tools or substances, such as wax, create patterns by preventing dye from reaching, and hence coloring, certain portions of a textile.

Color Variation and Fading

★ ★

{ A cotton 45-Star Flag from 1896 demonstrates blue's tendency to severely fade on cotton, and even vanish entirely, while the red remains essentially unchanged.

Method of production, dye concentration, even genetic strains and growing seasons, determined the shades of flag colors before standardization in the 20th century. The type of textile influenced the intensity of color as well. Silk showed off colors brilliantly. Wool fibers held dye more readily for vibrant or "true" color, more so than cotton or linen—hence the phrase "dyed in the wool."

Fastness is the propensity of a fabric to retain its color, described as "lightfastness" or "washfastness." Given the range of dye quality, different fabrics, and their age, antique American flags can have blues that range from near purple through greenish blues to gray, while reds can zone from deep maroon to orange and pink.

Wind, rain, and light act against fabric colors too, while dirt and dust can sully colors. Since red and blue are at opposite ends of the spectrum, they each have, respectively, low and high wavelengths. With the higher wavelength, or higher energy, blue typically fades more quickly than red. With age, whites in cotton or silk tend to yellow; in wool white generally turns gray or greenish-gray.

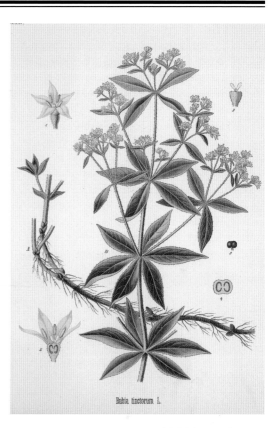

RED

Red, the color of "hardiness and valour" (according to Charles Thomson), of blood, of stripes, and of crosses on World War I nurses' uniforms, was created with a number of natural dyes. Madder (*Rubia tinctorum*) was the most usual botanical source for red. This leafy plant's roots contained the compound alizarin, which when combined with different mordants, produced a variety of reds, oranges, and yellows. British army redcoats were dyed with madder. "Turkey Red," an especially vibrant and colorfast madder hue discovered by Muslim weavers, was made by a complex and closely guarded secret process that produced a deeper and faster red used to color Turkish carpets, for instance.

Until the invention of synthetic dyes in the mid-19th century, colors had to be created with minerals, plants, animals, or other natural sources. Because all dyes fade to varying degrees when exposed to sunlight or water, merchants, explorers, and craftsmen constantly searched for more intense dyes, methods to make them more colorfast, and entirely new sources for different shades of colors. The age of exploration expanded the colorists' repertoire with the discovery of New World plants and the adoption of native American techniques.

One such source for red came from the tropical brazilwood tree, *Caesalpinia echinata*, first brought to Europeans' attention via trade with the Far East. The dyestuff entered the palette when Portuguese explorers discovered vast tracts of the trees growing in South America. Despite being a weaker and less reliable source for red, the forests were aggressively logged and exploited commercially. The dye was so desirable and important that it gave a nation its name: Brazil.

But the most lurid and vivid natural source of red discovered in the New World was obtained from carminic acid found in a dried female cochineal (*Dactylopius coccus*), an insect indigenous to Mesoamerica. Among the many regional names for the insect was *nocheztli*, "blood of the nopal cactus." Since cochineal only feed on cacti from the genus *Opuntia*, natives learned to cultivate such crops to attract the dye-bearing bugs. Up to seventy thousand individual insects were needed to produce one pound of dye. While assiduously keeping the source of this red a secret, the Spanish introduced the brilliant red to color-hungry Europe, where it became wildly popular. Cochineal, being particularly colorfast in wool fibers—the period's predominant textile for weaving—became second only to gold in export value.

Rubia tinctorum L.

{ A 19th-century botanical print of madder, *Rubia tinctorum*.

{ Red-coated British soldiers brutalizing colonists in New York, circa. 1778, from a French handcolored print.

WHITE

Raw cotton, linen, wool, and silk could range in color from white to yellow to brown to gray, so textiles sold as white fabric required a surprising amount of skill and labor to achieve a uniformly colorless appearance.

How bleaching was achieved depended on the type of fiber, since bleaching methods suitable for cotton could destroy silk, and whitening methods that worked for wool did not succeed with linen. Bleaching methods developed parallel to the Industrial Revolution's transformation of textile production, as scientific discoveries radically improved the lengthy and laborious methods of traditional bleaching.

Pliny described the ancient Roman method for whitening wool by rubbing the fibers with sulfuric earth. Eventually, people discovered that wool fibers were whitened when exposed to sulfuric gas produced by burning carboniferous materials, such as coal, in a closed chamber, a process known as *stoving*. Peroxide compounds, discovered in 1818, gradually replaced this process, since chemical whitening was faster and produced better results.

The age-old method of whitening cellulose textiles, such as linen or cotton, was by simple exposure to sun, often by spreading fabric out on open fields. But that alone seldom guaranteed uniformly white results, so intervening steps were discovered that worked in concert with light. "Bleachers" or "whitsers" specialized in this trade. The Dutch, in particular, regarded themselves as bleaching specialists and developed a significant industry fabric whitener for European textile firms. Submerging fabrics in lye (sodium hydroxide), buttermilk, and water also enhanced sun-bleaching.

In 1774, just as the events leading to the American Revolution were unfolding, the Swedish chemist Carl Wilhelm Scheele inadvertently discovered chlorine, and soon bleachers were experimenting with chlorine gas, despite its toxic fumes.

Charles Tennant, a Glasgow bleacher, discovered a stable bleaching power in 1799 and revolutionized the whitening industry, making the process fast, efficient, and safe. Not until World War I, however, was liquid chlorine bleach (sodium hypochlorite) formulated and manufactured for bleaching.

{ **A 1782 illustration** shows the workings of a bleach house, where fabric strips were washed in vats, boiled, immersed in troughs of water, wrung out, and glazed.

{ **Jacob van Ruisdael's** "View of Haarlem" C. 1670 captures scenes of fabric being stretched out on Dutch pastures to take advantage of sunlight for whitening.

A piece of indigo "cake," the final product of the cultivation, fermentation, and drying process.

BLUE

Throughout history, blue was one of the most sought-after, elusive, and costly colors to produce. Renaissance painters, for instance, had to rely on tremendously expensive ground lapis lazuli to produce brilliant hues for their skies. But for dyeing fabric, weavers had to use woad or indigo. Although the plants were common in Europe and Asia, respectively, the process of extracting indigotine from the leaves was elaborate and labor intensive.

Indigo (*Indigoferra tinctoria*) was first cultivated, historians believe, in India (from whence it got its name), and was introduced to the Mediterranean in antiquity. Woad (*Isatis tinctora*), a similar plant, was used as early as 1000 BC and was widely cultivated in Europe until the 18th century. Since woad cultivation was suited to temperate Europe, and tropical indigo was not, indigo imports were often banned in order to protect native woad industries. However, indigo had a much higher concentration of indogitine than woad and provided a superior and faster blue. Slave labor in the Carolinas made indigo even more affordable and abundant, and woad, as it were, fell out of fashion.

Another dye was discovered at the start of the 18th century, when a Berlin chemist mixed blood, potash, and cochineal. Unaware that his potash sample was impure, he stumbled on a new blue source, known as *Berliner Blau* or Prussian Blue. But it was not until the 1820s that scientists were able to refine the formula to make Prussian Blue a viable dye.

An 18th-century engraving depicts the laborious steps of indigo production often involving Indian and slave labor. Only experienced supervisors could successfully extract the blue dye.

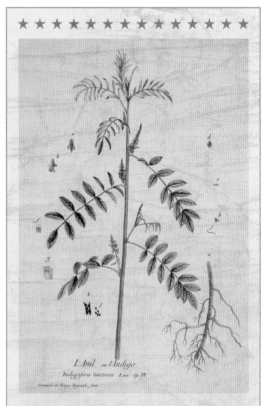

L.Anil ou l'Indigo
Indigofera tinctoria Linn. Sp. Pl.

Eliza Lucas Pinckney

In 1742, Eliza Lucas Pinckney (1722–1793), a resourceful South Carolinian, established the first indigo plantation in the Americas. The daughter of a British military officer, Pinckney was educated in England, where she developed a lifelong interest in botany.

For decades, rice was the main export of the Carolina plantations. But when Pinckney returned to Charleston in 1740 to manage her husband's plantations, she began cultivating indigo from West Indian seeds. After three years of perfecting the exacting fermentation process, Pinckney was selling indigo dye cakes in London. (She also attempted unsuccessfully to develop a silkworm business.)

Other planters bought Pinckney's seeds, and by the Revolutionary War, South Carolina was exporting to London hundreds of thousands of pounds of blue dye annually. (The first public school in Charleston, in fact, was paid for in 1753 by indigo producers.) With the Revolution, however, British indigo subsidies ceased, and by the end of the century, production drastically declined, setting the stage for the rise of cotton.

Despite Eliza Pinckney's prominence, not a single image of her survives. When Eliza Pinckney died of cancer on May 26, 1793, President Washington requested the honor of serving as one of her pallbearers.

IOWA & WISCONSIN

29 STAR FLAG

state | IOWA
president | JAMES K. POLK
material | WOOL
date made | C.1847
admissions date | DECEMBER 28, 1846
flag date | JULY 4, 1847
dimensions | 62" x 78"
period in use | 1 YEAR

The Wisconsin Territory, established in 1836, stretched east from the Missouri River to include Iowa, Minnesota, and Wisconsin.

Two years later, the territory was split in half. Wisconsin Territory receded behind the eastern shores of the Mississippi and St. Croix rivers, Illinois's northern border. The remaining half was renamed Iowa Territory, which itself was split in two in 1846, when Iowa entered the Union.

Months before Iowa's admission to the Union, Elias Howe presented his sewing machine, which executed a lock stitch, at the 1846 National Manufacturers Fair and was awarded a U.S. patent. It was not until after the Civil War, however, that flags were widely made with sewing machines.

3O STAR FLAG

state | WISCONSIN
president | JAMES K. POLK
material | COTTON
date made | C.1847
admissions date | MAY 29, 1848
flag date | JULY 4, 1848
dimensions | 38" x 42"
period in use | 3 YEARS

Minnesota Territory
Oregon Territory
Arkansaw Territory
WISCONSIN 1848
IOWA 1846

This hand-sewn cotton 30-Star Flag managed to survive, even though it was carried on its spear-like pole in the Civil War. Leather washers and handmade nails attached the flag to the pole, which still has its original blue paint.

Preserve, Repair, or Retire?

A tear near the hoist strip

The 29-Star and 30-Star Flags testify both to the fragility of textiles—especially when exposed to weather—and the dilemma of how flags should be preserved, repaired, or retired. Flags in such condition cannot be flown; the slightest breeze, moisture, or even humidity, would assuredly damage the fibers or fabric further, risking complete loss.

The wind's action typically attacks a flag's integrity in several characteristic places. Forces traveling through lines usually begin tears near the grommets or adjacent seams. (Flag makers often added reinforcement patches at these locations.) But since a flag's mechanical motion was most pronounced at the fly end, where the wind often violently whipped the fabric, historic specimens, including the Star-Spangled Banner, often exhibit the most severe fraying along the outer edge.

People sometimes repaired such damage simply by trimming the ends of the stripes to the innermost point of damage and sewing a new hem, altering the original proportions of the flag. Others might reconstitute damaged stripes with patches. Results varied according to the quality of fabric at hand and needle skill.

If a flag was needed for public display, flag etiquette customarily instructed people to "retire" tattered flags by burial or burning as a gesture of respect.

Flags surviving in only fragments, but special or important enough to preserve, such as the woolen 29-Star "Daniel F. Davis" Flag could be carefully mounted to a fine gauze backing, the pieces placed in the best approximation of their original position. (Less fortunate antique flags were sometimes glued to boards, making any future restoration exceedingly difficult, if not impossible.)

A new hem

THE KNOW NOTHING FLAG

President Andrew Jackson's Nullification Crisis provided the rusty bed springs for the unwholesome intermingling of bedfellows—tariffs, sectional politics, abolitionism, nativism, and Manifest Destiny—that would, eventually, produce the Civil War nightmare.

During the 1830s and 40s there was a surge in immigration to America, particularly from Ireland, where the potato famine was displacing millions of starving people. Resentment grew in the United States, as established, native-born Protestant Americans believed the tides of immigration threatened their livelihood and jobs. In 1849, a political movement formed in New York City—although in its early stages it was more a secret society—called the Order of the Star-Spangled Banner. Like the Masonic Order, this society spread as lodges were established in other American cities.

When members were asked about their role in the Order of the Star-Spangled Banner Society, they typically replied, "I know nothing." By 1845, the Order became known as the Know Nothing Party, as it began to support and organize candidates for elected offices. Its platform was essentially anti-immigrant and anti-Catholic, in opposition to the Democratic Party, which welcomed the growing number of votes that immigrants offered. The Know Nothings lobbied for a law that citizenship could only be attained after a person lived in

Starting in 1848, during the construction of the Washington Monument, many nations contributed engraved memorial stones as gifts to America in honor of its first president. The stone contributed by Pope Pius IX was stolen by Know Nothing activists and hurled into the Potomac River. It has never been recovered. In 1982 the Diocese of Spokane, Washington, officially delivered a replacement stone (made of Carrara Marble), a gift from Pope John Paul II and the Vatican City. The monument was not completed until December 1884, when the "pyramidion," made of 262 pieces of marble weighing 300 tons, was lifted in one piece into place. In this illustration, a 38-Star Medallion Flag flies at the monument's summit.

The Know Nothing Party adopted the image of George Washington as its primary symbol. This flag features a carefully sewn portrait of Washington applied on a field of red and white stripes, instead of the more familiar blue canton with white stars. No explanation has been found for why there are seventeen stripes. This is one of the few Know Nothing Flags to survive.

FLAGS THAT MADE HISTORY

One might guess that the stars on this 1848 flag were arranged to suggest "freedom," but the 35 stars were arranged to spell the word "FREE," to declare support for the Free Soil Movement.

Know Nothing Soap was manufactured in Boston in 1854, emphasizing the "uncleanliness" of the foreign-born, Native Americans (Indians), and immigrants. The flag depicted is a 31-Star Great Luminary.

the country for twenty-five years; they wanted to limit immigration and allow elected office only to native-born Americans. They managed to elect one of their members mayor of Philadelphia.

In the early 1850s, the Know Nothings attracted legions of followers. And by 1855, the U.S. Congress had at least forty-five members who were members of the Know Nothing order. But one issue divided the ranks of the Know Nothings— slavery. At the American Party convention in Philadelphia the following year, the party split along sectional lines over the pro-slavery platform. Its highest-ranking political figure was former vice president Millard Fillmore who, after inheriting the presidency from the deceased Zachary Taylor, became the Know Nothing presidential candidate in the election of 1856, running against Democrat James Buchanan and John C. Fremont, the first candidate of the newly formed Republican Party. Fillmore captured eight electoral votes, winning only Maryland. Know Nothings lost most of their seats in Congress. By the following presidential election in 1860, the Know Nothing party disintegrated entirely.

CALIFORNIA

3I
STAR FLAG

state | CALIFORNIA
president | ZACHARY TAYLOR
material | WOOL
date made | C.1851
admissions date | SEPTEMBER 9, 1850
flag date | JULY 4, 1851
dimensions | 47" x 70"
period in use | 7 YEARS

Oregon Territory
Minnesota Territory
Indian Country
Utah Territory
CALIFORNIA 1850
New Mexico Territory

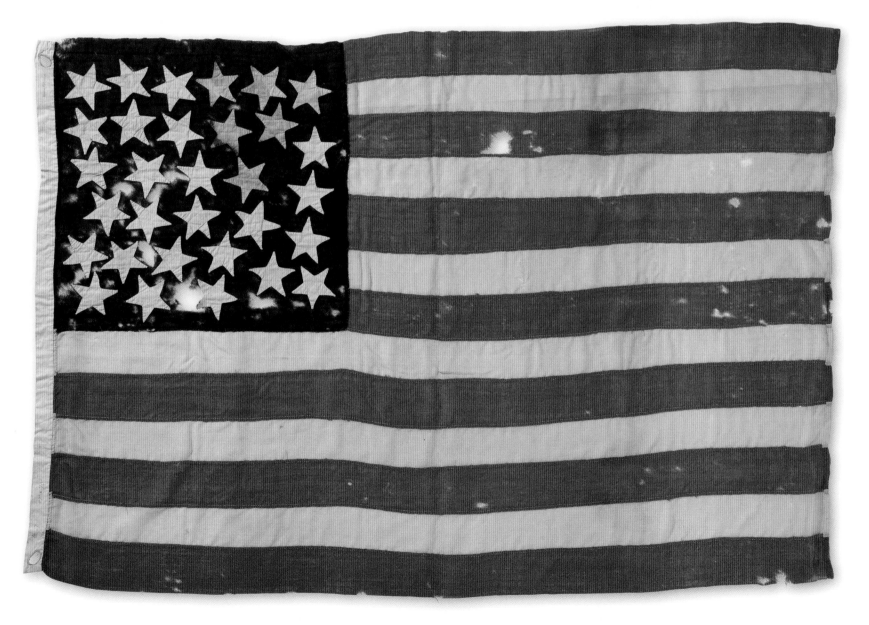

Starting in 1765, the year the Stamp Act riots spun out of control in distant Boston, Spanish missionaries began forays into California. Father Junípero Serra, the most legendary of Franciscan missionary priests, established outposts at San Diego and Monterey, where a cluster of adobes would become the capital of Spanish California. Countering the Spanish move from the south, Russians seeking a foothold in California made it as far as present-day Sonoma County, where they built the timber Fort Ross on cliffs overlooking the Pacific.

The Congressional Declaration of War against Mexico on May 13, 1846, gave President John Polk his opportunity to fulfill his continental ambitions. By mid-September 1847, General Winfield Scott conquered Mexico City. The Treaty of Guadalupe Hidalgo effectively terminated Spanish presence beyond Mexico, apart from the later Gadsden Purchase, which secured possession of the southern terrain of Arizona and New Mexico for the United States (see pages 168–169).

Gold changed everything for California in 1849, when stupefying reports of its quantity and ease of collection caused the population to skyrocket with prospectors rushing to the scene. The Compromise of 1850 admitted California as a state, allowing it to bypass the traditional step of first becoming a territory.

The California Bear Flag was first flown over the town of Sonoma on June 14, 1846. The only known photograph of the flag was taken in 1890. The original flag, which was displayed above the bar of the Society of California Pioneers saloon, burned in the 1906 earthquake and fire.

The 31-Star Flag recognized the admittance of California to the Union. Poetically calling to mind the "new constellation" phrase in the 1777 Flag Resolution (or perhaps even gold dust!), the flag's linen stars were not "arranged" but simply sprinkled onto the canton, giving it an unusual but endearing sparkle. The flag represents the importance of folk and crafts in the cultural life of the nation as it makes no pretense of majesty, but rather speaks of humility and the virtues of basic friendly citizenship.

FLAGS THAT MADE HISTORY

MANIFEST DESTINY, GOLD, AND THE WILD WEST

The American eagle graced John Frémont's personal flag, which he carried on his journeys throughout the West.

In 1841, Jessie Hart Benton, the daughter of Missouri Senator Thomas Hart Benton, married—without her father's approval—the dashing young adventurer John Charles Frémont. This set in motion a set of relationships that would encapsulate the American divisions over slavery, coupled with the relentless expansion west. Senator Benton was a southern aristocrat who possessed plantations and estates. He was also a passionate Democratic partisan, nicknamed "Old Bullion" for his support of hard money. But most of all, he was a champion of Manifest Destiny. Once reconciled with his daughter, Benton sponsored his son-in-law's expeditions to California and Oregon. Frémont's dispatches describing majestic landscapes he and his guide, Kit Carson, explored, such as Lake Tahoe and the Sierra Nevada, captivated the reading public, earning him the title "Pathfinder to the West." For her husband to carry on these expeditions, Jessie Fremont designed a special 26-Star Flag, featuring a light-colored canton framing a bald eagle and two garlands of thirteen stars each.

Manifest Destiny, however, demanded more than sightseeing, so beginning in 1845, Frémont, with encouragement from leaders in Washington, led the takeover of California, hoisting on June 14 (the sixty-eighth anniversary of the Stars and Stripes), a flag for the Republic of California. Around July 4th, 1845, the Stars and Stripes began floating over California's towns and settlements. Four years later, no doubt to the delight of Old Bullion, John and Jessie Frémont were well-placed to parlay the discovery of California gold into a fortune.

Propelled by his national fame and fortune, Frémont became the first Republican to seek the presidency, proclaiming with great passion his intention to crush Southern slavery. But this expedition was one that ended in failure and, ultimately, disaster, when James Buchanan instead became the victor.

MINNESOTA

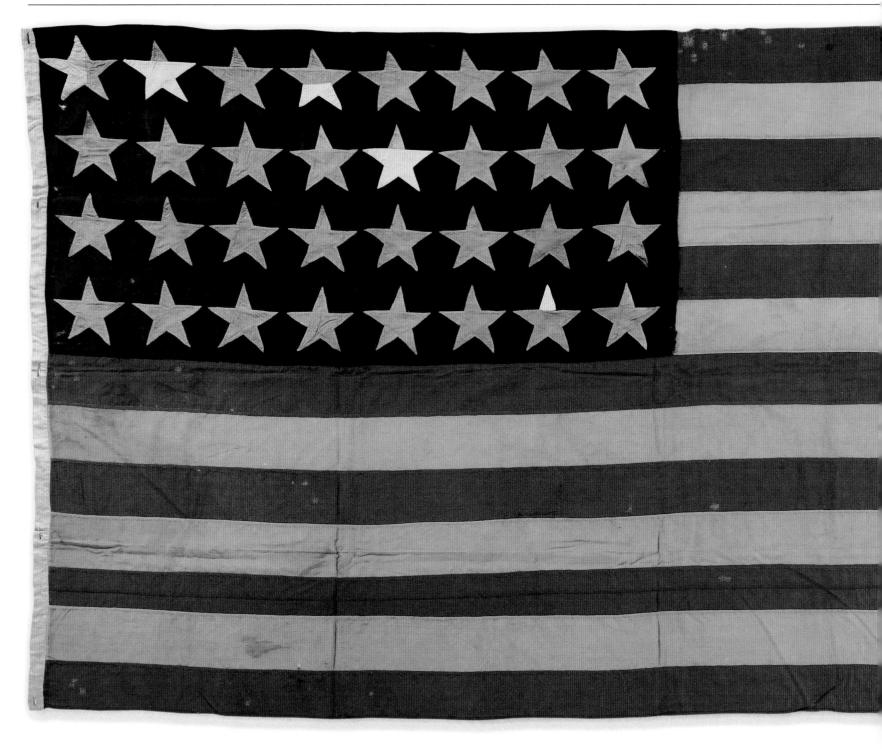

32
STAR FLAG

state | MINNESOTA
president | JAMES BUCHANAN
material | WOOL
date made | C.1858
admissions date | MAY 11, 1858
flag date | JULY 4, 1858
dimensions | 69" x 132"
period in use | 1 YEAR

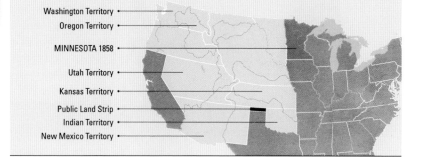

Washington Territory
Oregon Territory
MINNESOTA 1858
Utah Territory
Kansas Territory
Public Land Strip
Indian Territory
New Mexico Territory

Minnesota spent almost a decade as a territory, from 1849 until its statehood in 1858. This distant state played a part in the great drama of sectionalism and slavery on the national stage, as Dred Scott, a slave owned by a military physician, John Emerson, lived for a time at Fort Snelling, at the confluence of the Mississippi and Minnesota rivers.

After the death of his master, Scott and his wife became the property of Emerson's widow. In 1847, Scott appealed to Missouri courts to affirm his freedom. The case went to the U.S. Supreme Court, where Chief Justice Roger Brooke Taney rendered a momentous 6–2 decision on March 6, 1857, upholding that Dred Scott, although having been forced to accompany his master to "free" states, did not have grounds to make himself and his wife free people. The Court's decision, fiercely attacked by many, was one further twist in the downward spiral that had already reached a disastrous low when three years before, the Missouri Compromise was voided by the Kansas-Nebraska Act.

Dred Scott's journey north to Minnesota became emblematic of the struggle away from the South and bondage.

This 32-Star Flag unofficially celebrated Minnesota's entrance into the Union. The entire flag is composed of a two-square rectangle, with the blue canton directly proportional to the whole. (The selection of this geometry meant that the canton would atypically share its "eastern edge" with only six stripes.) The perfectly aligned stars' outstretched arms give emphasis to the stripes' great horizontal sweep, with fingers that almost touch, creating a beautiful blue pattern that rewards attention. Lovingly tended over time, the pure white star repairs, and a deep purple patch on the canton's upper boundary add to its sense of pride.

THE EVOLUTION OF UNCLE SAM

Uncle Sam, a character known to most people as a white-whiskered man in a top hat, blue coat, and striped trousers, has informally represented the U.S. government since he first began appearing in the early 19th century.

The character's origin seems, according to historic record and Uncle Sam's most authoritative "biographer" Alton Ketchum, to be Samuel Wilson, a businessman in Troy, New York, who ran a meat-packing enterprise with his brother Ebenezer. Because mechanical refrigeration was yet unknown, pork and beef, if they were to be preserved for transport, had to be cured in salt and packed, typically, in wooden barrels. The Wilson brothers supplied and inspected such barrels of meat for the U.S. Army during the War of 1812. To identify their product, workers stamped "E.A.–U.S." on the barrels, demarcating the procurement officer, Elbert Anderson, and the United States. Wilson's workers, it is written, joked that U.S. actually meant "Uncle Sam," as their benevolent boss had affectionately come to be known.

By 1814, references to Uncle Sam began appearing in newspapers, including one New York newspaper that stated U.S. troops called their meat rations "Uncle Sam's Beef." Uncle Sam stuck, and soon both the name

{ **By 1876,** Uncle Sam had evolved into the figure we now know: a slender, tall, white-bearded man. This splendid piece of folk art was carved and painted around the Centennial.

{ **Using his own face,** illustrator J. Montgomery Flagg created the most famous Uncle Sam image in 1917, used for World War I recruitment posters.

and the figure became symbolic of the entire federal government, and, depending on the mood of the country, was a figure of admiration and authority, respect and kindliness, or, when his waistline bulged and tax time approached, over-indulgence and monetary burden.

★ ★

Of all the mighty nations
In the east or in the west,
O this glorious Yankee nation
Is the greatest and the best.
We have room for all creation
And our banner is unfurled,
Here's a general invitation
To the people of the world.
Come from every nation,
Come from every way,
Our lands, they are broad enough;
Don't be alarmed,
For Uncle Sam is rich enough
To give us all a farm.

The Hutchinson Family, shown surrounding their patriarch, Jesse Hutchinson, Jr., in the center of this 1880 newspaper illustration, was a popular singing act, whose thirteen siblings toured under various stage names such as the "Hutchinson Family," "Tribe of Jesse," and the "Aeolian Vocalists." One of their songs, performed throughout the United States, and even in England, helped to popularize the personification of Uncle Sam as an ambassador of good will to immigrants. During the Civil War, the family entertained troops and made "The Battle Hymn of the Republic" a special favorite. Their anti-slavery lyrics, while alarming some military officers, pleased President Abraham Lincoln, who declared, "It is just the character of song that I desire the soldiers to hear."

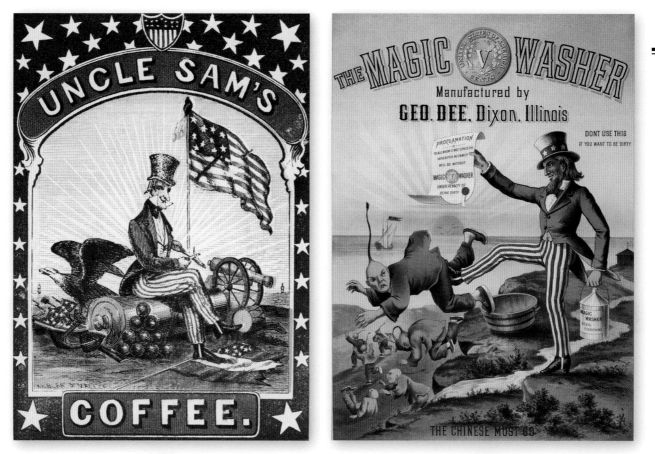

1863

1886

1917

1917

1918

1919

The Songs of Patriotism

The Stars and Stripes has figured prominently in American folk tunes, hymns, and marches. Some compositions even vied with "The Star-Spangled Banner" to be called the national anthem.

One of the earliest songs associated with America was "Yankee Doodle," a simple vernacular jig that first began to be heard in the 1760s. Originally written to mock provincial and slapdash American soldiers—as compared to well-trained and equipped Redcoats—"Yankee Doodle" was soon adapted by each side of the revolution as a point of pride or derision.

{ **John Phillip Sousa** and his band performed "The Stars and Stripes Forever" at the Paris Exposition of 1900.

John Phillip Sousa and his bands became synonymous with American patriotic music. When the young Sousa attempted to run away from home and join a circus, his father enlisted him in the U.S. Marine Corps. He served as head of the U.S. Marine Corps Band from 1880–1892. He wrote his most famous march, "The Stars and Stripes Forever," on Christmas Day in 1896. It is a standard for military bands, and has been designated as the official march of the United States. In November 1909, Sousa's Band performed "The Stars and Stripes Forever" for Thomas Edison, whose Amberol recording is the only recording with Sousa conducting to have survived.

REVOLUTIONARY-ERA TUNES

Francis Hopkinson wrote dozens of patriotic songs, but none succeeded in capturing the public's voice. His son, Joseph Hopkinson, however, wrote the lyrics for "The President's March," composed in 1789 by Philip Phile for Washington's inauguration, and renamed it "Hail, Columbia!," popularly used as an informal American anthem. Today, "Hail, Columbia!" is the official song played to announce the arrival of the vice president.

Variations of "Hail to the Chief" began to appear in musical performances in London around 1810, adapted from Sir Walter Scott's "The Lady of the Lake," making its way across the Atlantic and into theaters by 1812. The first time the song was performed in the presence of a sitting president was on Independence Day 1828, when John Quincy Adams scooped up a symbolic shovel of soil to commence the construction of the Chesapeake & Ohio Canal in Little Falls, Maryland. After "Hail to the Chief" was performed at the inauguration of President James K. Polk, First Lady Julia Tyler, wife of the next chief executive, John Tyler, suggested the song be performed to announce her husband's formal appearances. Not until 1954, however, did the Department of Defense formally establish "Hail to the Chief" as the official anthem of the presidency, to be played by the U.S. Marine Corps Band, known as "The President's Own." (Founded by Congress July 11, 1798, the band was the first formally recognized music ensemble in the United States.)

SONGS OF THE CIVIL WAR

In 1832, Boston minister Samuel Francis Smith wrote lyrics for "America" (also known as "My Country, 'Tis of Thee"), set to the English swells of "God Save the King." A key moment in civil rights history was connected to the song: In 1939, the Daughters of the American Revolution, who built and managed the Constitution Hall auditorium in Washington, D.C., refused to allow the world-renowned American singer Marian Anderson to perform, citing their policy that the auditorium be used "by white artists only, and for no other purpose." When she heard about the racist policy, First Lady Eleanor Roosevelt resigned her DAR membership in protest. The following year, Roosevelt, Secretary of the Interior Howard Ickes, the NAACP, and Howard University organized a special concert for Anderson. On Easter Sunday, Anderson sang on the steps of the

{ **Marian Anderson** singing "My Country, 'Tis of Thee" in front of the Lincoln Memorial.

Lincoln Memorial for a crowd of seventy-five thousand people on the Mall, opening with "America." Four years later, the DAR rescinded their discriminatory policy and invited Anderson to sing. When, in 1955, Anderson became the first black singer to perform for the New York Metropolitan Opera, the audience gave her a ten-minute standing ovation.

The Civil War inspired a robust catalog of hymns, marches, odes, verses, anthems, and folk tunes on both sides of the Mason Dixon Line. The best known of all Civil War songs was "The Battle Hymn of the Republic," written by Julia Ward Howe during a stay at the historic Willard Hotel in Washington, D.C. Howe, the daughter of prominent New Yorkers, was an ardent abolitionist and champion of women's causes, who, in 1870 helped to popularize Mother's Day.

"I Wish I Was in Dixie," although popularly regarded as the Southern anthem during the Civil War, was written in 1859 by a Yankee, Daniel Emmett, a vaudeville performer in New York City. In 1862, Union Brigadier General Daniel Butterfield composed a lullaby, known variously as "Go to Sleep," "Lights Out," or most famously, "Taps." The 24-note melody was played by buglers in both the Northern and Southern armies. Today, it is officially played at military funerals, flag ceremonies, and other official functions, including exercises at the Tomb of the Unknowns.

SONGS OF SERVICE

Each branch of the armed services has its own official song. The oldest song associated with the American military is the "Marine's Hymn," set to music by Jacques Offenbach, and written sometime in the 19th century. Its first line, "From the halls of Montezuma to the Shores of Tripoli," commemorates the Marine Corps service in the Barbary Wars and the Mexican War. Charles A. Zimmerman and Alfred Hart Miles collaborated in 1906 on the music and lyrics for "Anchors Aweigh," the unofficial song of the U.S. Navy. "The Army Goes Rolling Along" was composed by Lieutenant Edmund L. Gruber in 1908, adapted by Sousa into a march in 1917 during World War I, and made the official song of the U.S. Army in 1952. "The U.S. Air Force," written in 1939 by Captain Robert Crawford, was unanimously selected out of hundreds of entries, even one by Irving Berlin, to be the official song of the Air Force. "The Flag is carried by our ships, In times of war and peace," are two lines from "Semper Paratus," the song of the U.S. Coast Guard, composed by Captain Francis Saltus Van Boskerck in 1927.

CELEBRATING AMERICA

After Katharine Lee Bates, an English professor at Wellesley College, visited the World's Columbian Exposition in Chicago in 1893, a train carried her through wheat fields to the Rocky Mountains. "One day some of the other teachers and I decided to go on a trip to 14,000-foot Pikes Peak," she later recounted. "We hired a prairie wagon. Near the top we had to leave the wagon and go

{ **The original sheet music for** "You're a Grand Old Flag" included its composer George Cohan in a tricorn hat.

the rest of the way on mules. I was very tired. But when I saw the view, I felt great joy. All the wonder of America seemed displayed there, with the sea-like expanse." The sites inspired her to write the verses titled "America the Beautiful," later set to music by Samuel Ward. Ray Charles has made a well-known recording of this song.

Music written for Broadway musicals also led to songs of great patriotic importance. George Cohan composed and wrote "You're a Grand Old Flag" in 1906 for his musical, *George Washington, Jr.* Cohan later recounted that the song was inspired by his visit with a Gettysburg veteran who referred to his tattered flag as "She's a grand old rag." Even though Cohan changed "rag" to "flag," fearing the appearance of disrespect, some singers performed and recorded the song with the original line. Cohan contributed another famous song, "Over There," in 1917. James Cagney portrayed Cohan in the Hollywood musical *Yankee Doodle Dandy* in 1942.

Irving Berlin wrote his first version of "God Bless America" in 1918, but did not settle on its final form until 1938, on the eve of World War II. That year, on November 11, Kate Smith sang "God Bless America" for two radio broadcasts (one for the east coast and one for the west), which instantly made the song a hit. (Only Berlin's "White Christmas" surpassed the song's popularity. Both Berlin and Smith contributed the song's proceeds to the Boys and Girls Scouts of America). "God Bless America" was cherished by so many Americans that a movement arose in the 1950s for it to replace "The Star-Spangled Banner" as the national anthem. Legislators considered the change until Kate Smith herself addressed Congress, urging them to preserve "The Star-Spangled Banner" as the nation's song, since it was written to honor Americans in battle.

Symphonic music associated with American patriotism includes Peter Illyich Tchaikovsky's "1812 Overture," which, although composed to commemorate Napoleon's ill-fated invasion of Russia, became a popular

lead-in to fireworks displays on Independence Day. First performed in Moscow in 1882, it was not until 1935 that it was played on July 4th by the Grant Park Orchestra in Chicago. Arthur Fiedler conducted it for the Boston Pops' 1974 Independence Day concert, and orchestras throughout America have played the piece ever since, often with actual cannon fire as prelude to pyrotechnic displays.

Aaron Copland's admiration of American folk melodies greatly inspired his work, which many people regard as classical music that is distinctly American. "Appalachian Spring" made a simple Shaker melody fully symphonic. "Fanfare for the Common Man," a composition of powerful percussion and brass, was composed to inspire audiences during America's entry into World War II. That same year, Copland composed "Lincoln Portrait," music set to narration.

Contemporary songs that have become patriotic standards include "This Land is Your Land," which Woody Guthrie wrote in 1940 as a populist and secular retort to "God Bless America." "We Shall Overcome," based on spirituals, and revised by Pete Seeger, became an anthem of the civil rights movement, used by Dr. Martin Luther King Jr., and quoted by President Lyndon Johnson.

{ **Pikes Peak** and the "purple mountains majesty."

OREGON

33 STAR FLAG

state | OREGON
president | JAMES BUCHANAN
material | WOOL
date made | C.1859
admissions date | FEBRUARY 14, 1859
flag date | JULY 4, 1859
dimensions | 44" x 60"
period in use | 2 YEARS

Washington Territory
Unassigned Territory
OREGON 1859
Nebraska Territory
Utah Territory
Kansas Territory
Public Land Strip
New Mexico Territory

With fervor for Manifest Destiny reaching new heights, a third war with Great Britain became a very real possibility as squabbles over the settlement of Oregon Country, jointly occupied by the Americans and British, became a political firestorm. Devout expansionists loudly promising "54°-40' or Fight!" demanded that the United States take, by force if necessary, all of the west coast, north to Russian-occupied Alaska.

After bitter debate in Congress, including a speech by Senator Thomas Hart Benton (who favored a compromise with the British) that lasted a full three days, Secretary of State James Buchanan signed a treaty on June 15, 1846, establishing the boundary at the 40° parallel, but granting the British all of Vancouver Island. In 1848, Oregon Territory organized most of the land northwest of the Continental Divide. Five years later, in 1853, the Columbia River was chosen as the boundary between Oregon and Washington Territory. Finally, in 1859, James Buchanan, now the president, welcomed Oregon into the Union.

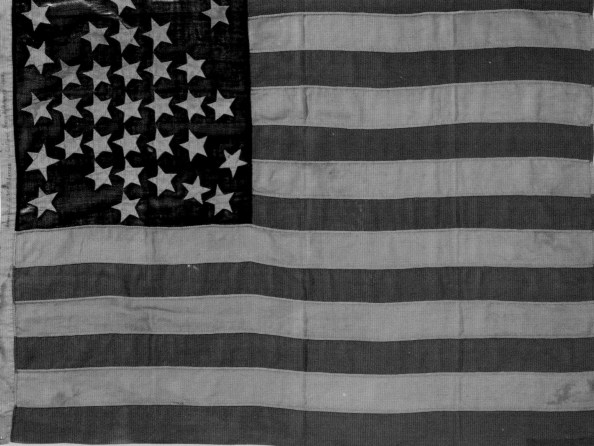

Although the flag was beginning to have a standardized appearance, as of 1859 there were still no guidelines about flag design. This 33-Star Flag, made originally as a 29-Star pattern with four started corners, continued to acquire new stars until the admittance of Oregon.

James K. Polk favored compromise with the British, especially since it provided the United States with Puget Sound. Like Thomas Jefferson, Polk expanded American boundaries vastly, presiding over the entry of five new states, surpassed in this only by President Benjamin Harrison.

FLAGS THAT MADE HISTORY

FLAG OF TRUCE

The Modoc chief Kintpuash, also known as "Captain Jack," led warriors in the Indian Wars to reclaim their ancestral homelands around Tula Lake on the California-Oregon border. Earlier, in 1864, the Modoc had been forced north to a reservation of the Klamaths, an enemy tribe. Unable to see his people "settled" in a hostile place, Captain Jack's struggle led to the outbreak of hostilities at the Battle of the Lost River on November 29, 1872. Greatly outnumbered, the Modoc fled to the lava caves (now the Lava Beds National Monument), where, with fifty fighters, they were able to defend themselves against the U.S. Army for several months. After losing thirty-three of his own men, Major General Edward Canby agreed to peace negotiations under a flag of truce.

The family of Chief Kintpuash, known as Captain Jack, owned this 37-Star clamp-dyed wool flag.

After Captain Jack's execution, his head was sent to the Smithsonian Institution for study, adding to the thousands of Native American skulls and corpses that were already collected. Years later, his descendants succeeded in repatriating the skull for burial. In 1990, a federal law ordered that Native Americans have the right to claim the remains of their tribal peoples.

On April 11, 1873, however, those negotiations violently ended. During one of the meetings, Captain Jack and his men brought out concealed guns and started shooting. One of the U.S. officers, a minister, died on the spot. With his own pistol, Captain Jack shot and killed the unarmed Canby. A third officer, himself seriously wounded, narrowly escaped being scalped because, it is said, he was bald, and the Modocs, eager to escape, had no time to hold the man's smooth head. (This man later testified at trial that th.e U.S. Army had violated the terms of the truce before the killings.)

Three days later, General Jefferson C. Davis responded with one thousand troops; General William Tecumseh Sherman approved by telegraph the extermination of the Modocs, including all women and children. Surrounded and betrayed by one of his own men, Captain Jack gave himself up on the first of June.

The only Native Americans to be tried as war criminals, for violating a "flag of truce," Kintpuash and Schonchin were found guilty by a military tribunal. With crowds in attendance, including schoolchildren who were given a special weeklong holiday, and with their families forced to watch, Kintpuash and Schonchin were hanged at Fort Klamath on October 3. The family and remnants of the Captain Jack's Modoc band were forcibly relocated to Oklahoma.

UPDATING FLAGS

Flag owners often updated flags (instead of making a completely new one) after additional states were admitted to the Union, particularly during periods when new states came in rapid succession. How artfully the new stars were added depended on the flag maker's talent; some placed new stars almost randomly, while others attempted to generate balance and symmetry.

A different number of stars could even appear on a flag's obverse and reverse sides, as if each were meant to commemorate two different periods (see flags below left). While the obverse of this flag has 37 stars, its reverse side has only 36 stars. Made in the late 1860s, the flag recognizes Nevada (36 stars) and Nebraska (37 stars), each side with its own "meteoric" pattern.

In other cases, the flag maker may have added stars as states entered the Union (see flags below right). A digitally corrected image takes this flag back in time to its original design, made in 1845 to commemorate the admission of Texas as the twenty-eighth state (see top right flag below). But as Iowa (1846), Wisconsin (1848), California (1850), and Minnesota (1858) achieved statehood over the next thirteen years, stars were added to the original pattern, turning it into a 32-Star Flag (see bottom right flag below). For some unknown reason, the flag maker stopped adding stars, leaving the lower left corner and left midsection blank—and leaving behind a rather unique-looking flag!

OBVERSE

BEFORE

REVERSE

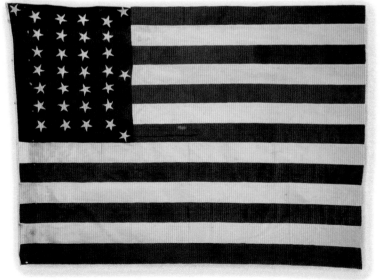

AFTER

FLAGS THAT MADE HISTORY

OLD GLORY

Captain William Driver, a shipmaster from Salem, was given a 24-Star Flag by his mother on his twenty-first birthday. When he unfurled it for the first time on the topmast of his ship *Charles Doggett* in 1831, he announced, "My countrymen, in ancient times when the ocean voyage was looked upon with superstitious dread, it was the custom on the eve of departure to roll the banner in a form like this (a triangle) when ready, and bent like this. A priest stepped forward and, taking the banner in his hand, would sprinkle it with consecrated water and dedicate it to 'God the Father,' 'God the Son,' and 'God the Holy Ghost,' turning a point of the triangle upward as he named each person of the Trinity, thus calling on the Sacred Unity of Creator, Redeemer, and Santifier to bless the national emblem and prosper the voyagers and their friends." When the 24-Star Flag reached the mast's top, Driver cried, "Long live Old Glory mates—Old Glory."

Driver stopped sailing in 1837 and moved to Nashville, Tennessee, where he displayed the flag with regularity on Washington's birthday, St. Patrick's Day (his own birthday), and the Fourth of July. In 1861, Driver's wife and daughter disassembled the tattered flag, repaired its seam, replaced the original stars with a field of thirty-four new stars, and added a small white anchor. (Interestingly, in 1860, there were only thirty-three states. Kansas was not admitted to the Union until January 29, 1861, and the star was not officially added until the following Fourth of July.) In 1861, when Tennessee seceded, Driver remained loyal to the Union but worked in a hospital where he cared for soldiers from both sides. Fearing that Confederates would seize and destroy his famous flag, he had it sewn into his bed cover, making it known, "If you want my flag, you'll have to take it over my dead body."

When Union General William "Bull" Nelson captured Nashville in 1862, his troops tore down the Confederate flag from the Capitol. When they raised a small regimental Stars and Stripes in its place, Driver took soldiers to his home, where he revealed Old Glory by snipping open the bed cover. Under salute, the flag was led under escort to the Capitol where it replaced the smaller flag to cheers on January 25, 1862. It flew only until dawn, too fragile to withstand strong winds, and was returned to Driver's home.

In 1873, Driver gave the flag to his daughter Mary Jane, saying, "This is my ship's flag, 'Old Glory.' I love it as a mother loves her child. Take it and cherish it,

Mary Jane Driver Roland poses with Old Glory in her Mountain View, California, home around 1920. By that time, the flag had become so fragile that the only thing holding the stars in place was the sheeting onto which she had sewn the flag.

for it has been my steadfast friend and protected me in all parts of the world, savage, heathen, and civilized." Driver died on March 3, 1886. In 1922, Driver's daughter gave the flag to President William Harding, who placed it with the Smithsonian Institution, where it is currently preserved by the National Museum of American History.

THE NAME OF OLD GLORY—1896

When, why, and by whom, was our flag The Stars and Stripes first called "Old Glory"?

—DAILY QUERY TO PRESS

I

Old Glory! say, who, By the ships and the crew,
And the long, blended ranks of the Gray and the
Blue,—
Who gave you, Old Glory, the name that you bear
With such pride everywhere,
As you cast yourself free to the rapturous air,
And leap out full-length, as we're wanting you to?—
Who gave you that name, with the ring of the same,
And the honor and fame so becoming to you?
Your stripes stroked in ripples of white and of red,
With your stars at their glittering best overhead—
By day or by night
Their delightfulest light
Laughing down from their little square heaven of blue!
Who gave you the name of Old Glory?—say, who—
Who gave you the name of Old Glory?
*The old banner lifted, and faltering then
In vague lisps and whispers fell silent again.*

II

Old Glory,—speak out! We are asking about
How you happened to "favor" a name, so to say,

That sounds so familiar and careless and gay,
As we cheer it, and shout in our wild, breezy way—
We—the crowd, every man of us, calling you that—
We, Tom, Dick, and Harry—each swinging his hat
And hurrahing "Old Glory!" like you were our kin,
When—Lord!—we all know we're as common as sin!
And yet it just seems like you humor us all
And waft us your thanks, as we hail you and fall
Into line, with you over us, waving us on
Where our glorified, sanctified betters have gone.
And this is the reason we're wanting to know
(And we're wanting it so!
Where our own fathers went we are willing to go)
Who gave you the name of Old Glory —O-ho!—
Who gave you the name of Old Glory?
*The old flag unfurled with a billowy thrill
For an instant; then wistfully sighed and was still.*

III

Old Glory: the story we're wanting to hear
Is what the plain facts of your christening were,—
For your name—just to hear it,
Repeat it, and cheer it, 's a tang to the spirit
As salty as a tear:
And seeing you fly, and the boys marching by,
There's a shout in the throat and a blur in the eye,
And an aching to live for you always—or die,
If, dying, we still keep you waving on high.
And so, by our love
For you, floating above,
And the sears of all wars and the sorrows thereof,
Who gave you the name of Old Glory, and why
Are we thrilled at the name of Old Glory?
*Then the old banner leaped, like a sail in the blast,
And fluttered an audible answer at last.*

—JAMES WHITCOMB RILEY

KANSAS

When on May 30, 1854, Senator Stephen Douglas of Illinois led the passage of the Kansas-Nebraska Act, creating two new territories but in the process dismantling the Missouri Compromise by opening up the west to slavery, the path to dissolution of the Union was all but inevitable. Settlers eager to take advantage of the fertility of Kansas's plains—with profits magnified by slave sweat—swelled the Territory's population. There,

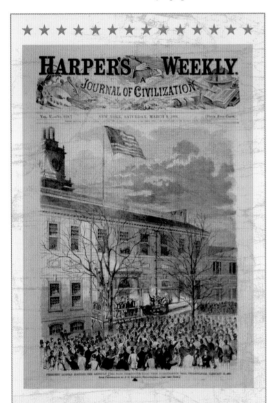

Harper's Weekly was an important and widely read source of news in the mid-19th century, particularly during the Civil War. The newspaper first appeared on January 3, 1857. Its detailed illustrations of battlefields, military officers, personalities, political rallies, and public events were especially enthralling to readers. The newspaper's images were printed from woodcut blocks, since the screen technology for rapidly mass-producing photographic images was not developed until the 1880s. *Harper's Weekly* established the reputations of two of the period's best-known illustrators, Winslow Homer and cartoonist Thomas Nast. *Harper's* images also helped to popularize the symbolism of the American Flag. Seldom was an issue published during the Civil War, in fact, that did not include illustrations of the Stars and Stripes.

clashes between pro- and anti-slave settlers broke out, escalating into massacres and pitched battles and earning the Territory the name "Bleeding Kansas."

Debate in Congress over the entry of Kansas into the Union exacerbated sectional rhetoric. Southerners, confident that Northerners would place money before principle, reminded them of their fibrous contribution to the national economy: "What would happen if no cotton was furnished for three years?" thundered plantation owner Senator James Hammond. "I will not stop to depict what every one can imagine, but this is certain: England would topple headlong and carry the whole civilized world with her, save the South. No, you dare not make war upon cotton. No power on earth dares to make war upon it. Cotton is king."

Abraham Lincoln's election in 1860, however, made war certain. Six states—South Carolina, Mississippi, Florida, Alabama, Georgia, and Louisiana—left the Union within two months of Lincoln's election, and before Kansas, the thirty-fourth state, was admitted on January 29, 1861. Five more states—Texas, Tennessee, North Carolina, Arkansas, and Virginia—seceded in the next months. Debate began over what form the Stars and Stripes would take in response to the waves of Secession.

Some Northerners felt that the Union flag should not include the stars of the secessionist states, and should carry stars only of loyal states. Confederates responded with the creation of the Stars and Bars (see page 116).

Lincoln insisted that no stars be removed. "I would rather be assassinated," he said, "than remove stars from the flag." Removing stars, he argued, would

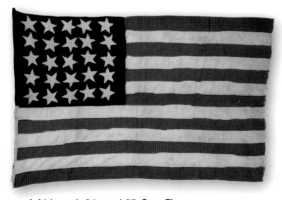

{ **Although 34- and 35-Star Flags** were official banners of the national government through the first years of the Civil War, some flags, such as this 25-Star "Loyalist" flag, were made at this time by Unionists.

recognize the legality of secession and lend legitimacy to the rebellion.

Lincoln's position prevailed. As he made his way from Springfield to Washington to assume power, Lincoln's journey culminated in a Philadelphia rally where he led a special flag-raising ceremony at Independence Hall on February 22, 1861.

The flag he raised above the cheering crowd had thirty-four stars. By and large, Northerners continued to officially fly the 34-Star Flag until West Virginia became the thirty-fifth state in 1863.

❝ *FELLOW-CITIZENS, I am invited and called before you to participate in raising above Independence Hall the flag of our country, with an additional star upon it. I propose now, in advance of performing this very pleasant and complimentary duty, to say a few words. I propose to say that when that flag was originally raised here it had but thirteen stars. I wish to call your attention to the fact that, under the blessing of God, each additional star added to that flag has given additional prosperity and happiness to this country, until it has advanced to its present condition; and its welfare in the future, as well as in the past, is in your hands. Cultivating the spirit that animated our fathers, who gave renown and celebrity to this Hall, cherishing that fraternal feeling which has so long characterized us as a nation, excluding passion, ill-temper, and precipitate action on all occasions, I think we may promise ourselves that not only the new star placed upon that flag shall be permitted to remain there to our permanent prosperity for years to come, but additional ones shall from time to time be placed there, until we shall number, as was anticipated by the great historian, five hundred millions of happy and prosperous people. With these few remarks, I proceed to the very agreeable duty assigned me.* ❞

34 STAR FLAG

state | KANSAS
president | ABRAHAM LINCOLN
material | WOOL
date made | C.1861
admissions date | JANUARY 29, 1861
flag date | JULY 4, 1861
dimensions | 68" x 113"
period in use | 2 YEARS

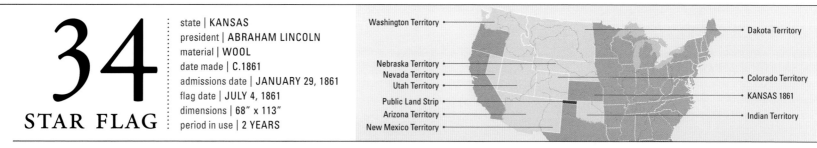

Washington Territory •
Nebraska Territory •
Nevada Territory •
Utah Territory •
Public Land Strip •
Arizona Territory •
New Mexico Territory •

• Dakota Territory
• Colorado Territory
• KANSAS 1861
• Indian Territory

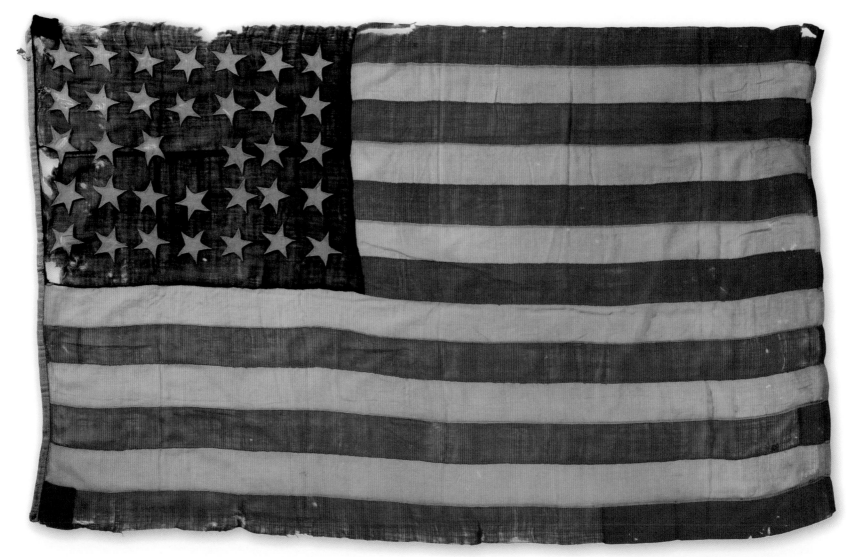

The 34-Star Flag was the last to represent an intact Union. Endowed with vivid red and blue, this flag's pattern suggests unity, its stars forming a phalanx formation to protect the core.

CONFEDERATE FLAGS

There was considerable debate about what should be the official flag of the Confederacy. Many Southerners, including President Jefferson Davis, wanted to keep the Stars and Stripes, since they felt the flag represented the South as much as the North. Others wanted a distinct flag. The compromise, proposed and drawn by Mrs. Napoleon Lockett, the wife of an Alabama plantation owner, was the Stars and Bars. The first official Stars and Bars contained seven stars, and the last official version had eleven. Miss Letitia Tyler, granddaughter of President

John Tyler, raised the first Confederate Flag above the capitol dome during a ceremony in Montgomery, Alabama, on March 5, 1861. While many cheered as the new flag rose on the mast, some Southern men who had fought under the Stars and Stripes in earlier wars wept openly at the sight of Old Glory being lowered.

❝ The flag of the Confederate States of America shall consist of a red field with a white space extending horizontally through the center, and equal in width to one-third the flag. The red space above and below to be the same as the white. The union blue extending down through the white space and stopping at the lower red space. In the center of the union, a circle of white stars corresponding in number with the States of the Confederacy. ❞

– Confederate Flag Proclamation, March 4, 1861, issued in a secret session of the Confederate Congress in Montgomery, Alabama.

{ This very early **Secession Flag** from 1861 has four large four-pointed blue stars denoting the states first to secede from the Union. Unlike the later official Confederate flag, this banner had six stripes—or bars—white at the top and red at the bottom.

FLAGS THAT MADE HISTORY

This silk Confederate Battle Flag, with a field of solid red, incorporated the cross of the martyred St. Andrew, overlaid with a number of stars representing, at various times, the number of states formally a part of or associated with the Confederacy.

FLAGS AND MARTYRS, NORTH AND SOUTH

ELMER EPHRAIM ELLSWORTH

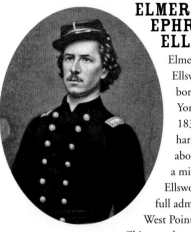

Elmer Ephraim Ellsworth was born in New York on April 11, 1837. Despite harboring dreams about becoming a military officer, Ellsworth never won full admittance to West Point. He went to Chicago where he became a patent lawyer and eventually found work in Abraham Lincoln's Springfield firm. On the side, Ellsworth satisfied his interest in military ritual by establishing a ceremonial precision drill unit—the Zoaves—inspired by the acrobatic soldiers who famously fought in the Crimean War. Ellsworth's flamboyantly uniformed unit dazzled audiences, and soon similar "Zoaves" units began forming in other cities. When Lincoln was elected President, Ellsworth accompanied him as a member of the official delegation on his train journey to Washington, D.C.

When the Civil War officially began, Ellsworth went to New York City where he recruited volunteer firemen to form an actual fighting unit for the Northern cause. Once assembled and equipped, Ellsworth and his men encamped at Washington, D.C. Early one morning, the Zoaves captured the public's attention when they responded to a fire at the historic Willard Hotel. Newspapers lauded their heroic efforts to extinguish the blaze, saving the structure from destruction. Eager to distinguish themselves as among the first to engage the rebels on their own territory, Ellsworth led his men across the Potomac on May 24, 1861, into Alexandria, the day after Virginia's secession. First cutting the city's telegraph lines to disrupt communications, the men proceeded into the city where they caught sight of a rebel flag flying from the Marshall House Inn. Storming the building, Ellsworth personally cut the flag from the upper floor window. But James Jackson, the Inn's owner, stood waiting with a shotgun at the bottom of the stairs. As Ellsworth came down with the Stars and Bars on his arm, Jackson killed him with a single blast. At Ellsworth's side, Francis E. Brownell returned fire, killing Jackson.

Colonel Elmer Ellsworth, it turned out, was the first Union serviceman to be killed in the Civil War.

President Lincoln was shaken by the death of his friend, whose body was ceremonially carried back to the White House by an Honor Guard to lie in state on May 25, 1861. Northern newspapers ran articles making Ellsworth's story of heroism and patriotism a rallying cry for the Union cause. Poems were written, songs composed, and recruitment rallies held in Ellsworth's memory. It is said that Lincoln kept the blood-stained Confederate flag in a White House drawer.

When Francis Brownell was awarded the Medal of Honor in 1877 for his actions in Alexandria, it distinguished the earliest incident in the Civil War to be so honored. The Civil War-era Medal of Honor was designed in 1862, with a ring of 34 stars and oak-leaf clusters to symbolize strength. In all of American history, more than 3,400 Medals of Honor have been awarded.

One of the stars from the Marshall House Confederate flag, taken as a souvenir, was recently discovered and contributed to the New York State Military Museum, where the original Confederate flag is preserved.

Elmer Ellsworth's blood spills onto the Confederate flag as Francis Brownell returns fire, killing James Jackson.

PUBLIC BUILDINGS IN NEW ORLEANS.
No. 301.

UNITED STATES MINT,
On Barracks Street,

Showing the Flag-Staff that Mumford climbed and took down the first U. S. Flag hoisted in New Orleans after the fall, by Commodore Farragut, April 25th, 1862. For this act Mumford was executed, by order of Gen. Butler.

Published by S. T. BLESSING, No. 24 Chartres street, New Orleans, La.

Benjamin Franklin Butler's command policies aroused great passions in the North and South. Hearing of Mumford's execution and Butler's order that any women in New Orleans who insulted Union soldiers be tried and punished as prostitutes, Jefferson Davis ordered that Butler be executed upon capture. In 1865, after an attack led by Butler on a Confederate fort turned into a fiasco, General Ulysses S. Grant and President Lincoln relieved him from duty. Butler returned to Lowell, Massachusetts, where he owned interests in textile mills. He was later elected to the House of Representatives, where he sponsored legislation that required all American flags be made of American fabric.

WILLIAM B. MUMFORD

Less than a year after the death of Elmer Ellsworth, Admiral David Farragut delivered an important Union victory by capturing New Orleans in April, 1862. Benjamin Butler, a Lowell lawyer and textile mill investor, who had earlier positioned himself as the self-annointed Brigadier General of the Massachusetts volunteer regiment, was sent as a military administrator to the captured city, where Faragut had ordered a Stars and Stripes hoisted over the most prominent Federal structure, the U.S. Mint. The flag's presence was intended to affirm the surrender of New Orleans; should it be lowered, Farragut ordered, a battery of howitzers would bombard the city.

On April 26, 1862, William B. Mumford, a Customs House officer, apparently unaware that such an order had been given, broke through a skylight on the Mint's roof and removed the flag. Immediately the offshore guns opened fire, but soon stopped when no return fire materialized. Mumford and his cohorts, it was said, paraded the flag through the streets, tearing it to pieces.

"I find the city under the dominion of the mob," Butler reported to Secretary of War Edwin Stanton. "They have insulted our flag, torn it down with indignity. This outrage will be punished in such a manner as in my judgment will caution both the perpetrators and abettors of the act, so they shall fear the stripes if they do not reverence the stars of our banner."

Mumford was not fortunate enough to get off with only stripes. Instead, Butler ordered him hanged,

The Daily Picuyne reported, "The condemned man, seated on his coffin in a covered army wagon, escorted by a body of troops—horse and foot—left the Customhouse for the place of execution, in the enclosure on the north front of the Mint..."

"having been convicted before a military commission of treason and an overt act thereof, tearing down the United States flag from a public building of the United States." Most in the city did not believe the execution would be carried out, seeing Mumford's act more a piece of harmless street theater than serious crime. Despite tearful pleas from Mumford's family, however, Butler refused to countermand the order, justifying his decision by pointing out that had he been in charge of the Navy instead of Farragut, he would have "reduced the city to ashes" with the removal of the flag.

A *New York Herald* journalist's description of the affair circulated throughout Northern newspapers. On June 7, 1862, the reporter "called on Mumford on the morning of the day of his execution, and found his wife and three children with him, bidding him the long last farewell. He had slept throughout the whole night, and was quite free from nervousness. Mrs. Mumford is a delicate, respectable looking lady, and the children are quite interesting. The oldest is a girl of fourteen years, and the other boys of some six or seven years of age. The interview was of course extremely affecting, and the prisoner, for the first and only time, broke down and groaned piteously. There was no disorder at the execution nor at the funeral, a strong military escort being in attendance."

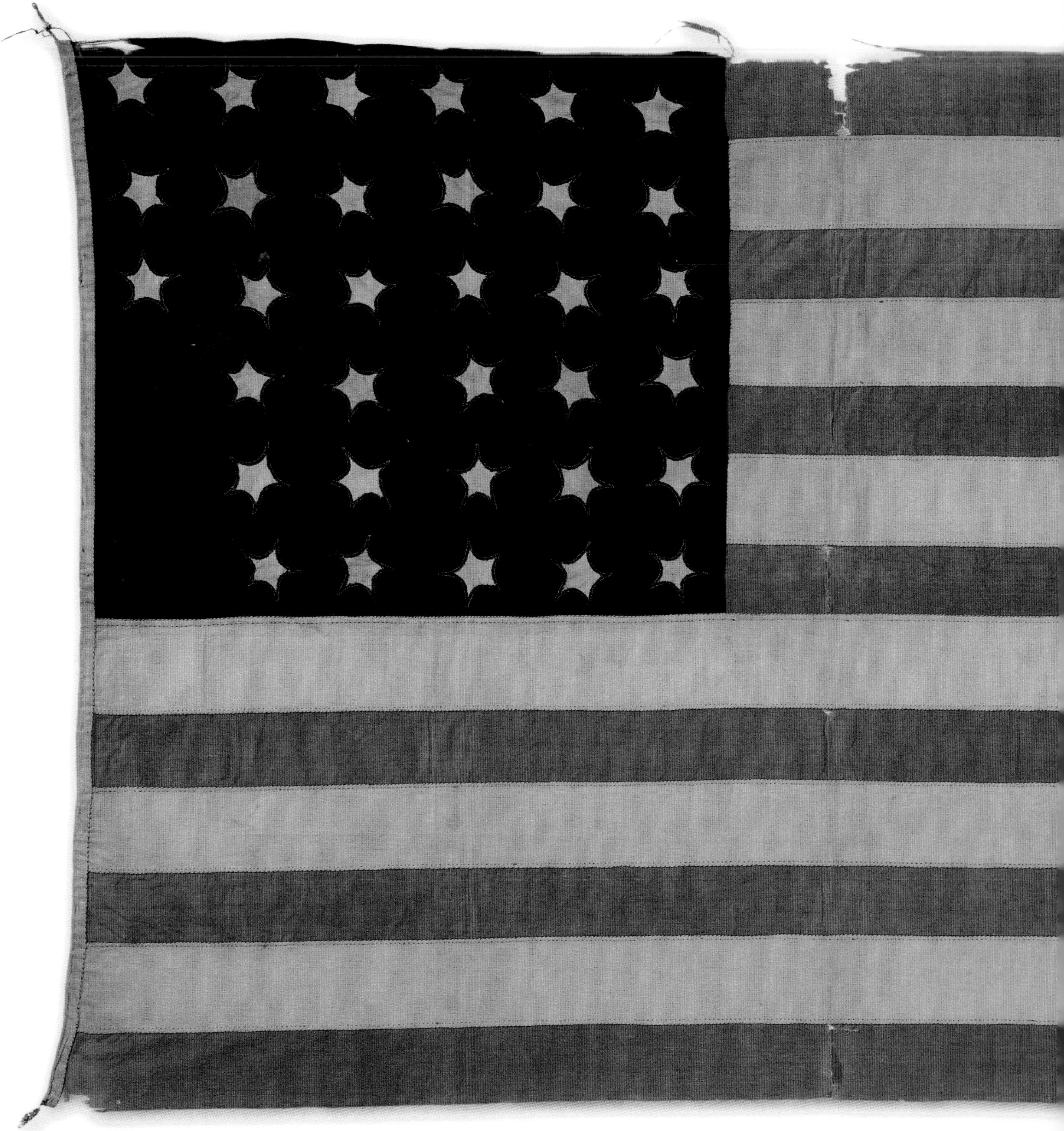

Exquisitely crafted with handmade whip stitches, this 33-Star Flag is documented to have been flown by Union troops at the Battle of Bull Run in 1861. Its condition suggests that this flag was deeply cared for, its patches carefully matched and sewn, its fabric tenderly preserved. The soft cotton fabric's natural dyes have beautifully faded over the decades—a quality that flags later made with artificial dyes would seldom achieve. Curiously, the peek-a-boo stars were cut and attached on the flag's obverse side. Its thirty-three stars are arranged in a manner suggesting the eventual addition of more stars; this might have symbolized resolve for Union victory.

THE MIGHTY STAR

{ **Among the largest** of "Great Luminary" patterned flags to have survived, this star seems to cartwheel across the canton.

When individual stars were arranged to form a large star on the flag, the pattern was variously described as the "Great Luminary" or "Great Star."

In 1818, Peter Wendover and Samuel Reid proposed to have the official U.S. Flag bear the stars in a "Great Star" pattern for use on land and on private ships, and in rows for the navy. Congress did not accept this idea, in fact, Congress purposely did not specify how the stars were to be arranged (see page 30).

The "Great Luminary" pattern became especially popular during the Civil War, since its intermingling of stars suggested unity and the national motto, *E pluribus, unum,* which translates from Latin to, "Out of many, one." (In 1956, the national motto was replaced with "In God We Trust" by an act of Congress. One origin of this new motto is from the final stanza of "The Star-Spangled Banner.")

{ **During the Civil War,** a "Great Luminary" pattern flag was flown over the U.S. Capitol, its dome yet uncompleted.

{ **Four large stars** maintain this canton's corners, while thirty smaller stars are arranged in two medallion star-shapes.

{ **Slight bulges** along the stars' arms give this Great Star the appearance of a giant blossom.

WEST VIRGINIA

35
STAR FLAG

state | WEST VIRGINIA
president | ABRAHAM LINCOLN
material | COTTON
date made | C.1863
admissions date | JUNE 20, 1863
flag date | JULY 4, 1863
dimensions | 20″ x 30″
period in use | 1 YEAR

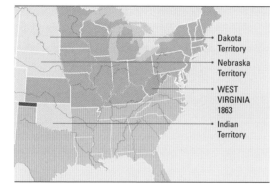

Dakota Territory
Nebraska Territory
WEST VIRGINIA 1863
Indian Territory

West Virginia became the second state, following Maine, to break away from an existing state, precipitated by the refusal of most of its counties to be party to Virginia's secession. In 1861, West Viriginia found Virginia's secession illegal and formed a new state government in Wheeling, even electing two senators to Congress. With its eastern half now fully committed to the Confederacy, the Wheeling Convention put to vote in October 1861 a referendum of independent statehood. Overwhelmingly, nearly 96 percent of its voters opted for independent statehood.

President Lincoln approved West Virginia's Enabling Act at the end of 1862, with the caveat that abolition be written into the state's constitution. And on June 20, 1863, West Virginia became the 35th state.

After the war, however, Virginia ironically sought to invalidate West Virginia's "secession," taking its case all the way to the Supreme Court. In 1871, the Court reaffirmed West Virginia's statehood, leaving Virginia to contend with its shrunken dominion.

Historic Books About the Flag

★ ★ ★ ★ ★ ★ ★ ★ ★ ★ ★ ★ ★ ★ ★ ★ ★ ★ ★

The first book dedicated to the history of the Stars and Stripes was written in 1852 by Schuyler Hamilton. When Senator Daniel Webster asked General Winfield Scott about the origins of the Stars and Stripes, it led Hamilton to research and write *The History of the National Flag of the United States of America.* Hamilton was asked to lecture about the flag on the centenary of the First Flag Resolution on June 14, 1877, at the New York Historical Society.

The second 19th-century book devoted to flag history was written in 1864 by Ferdinand L. Sarmiento. Dedicated to the Union League of Philadelphia, the book was unabashedly anti-Confederacy in its tone.

In 1873, George Henry Preble published *Our Flag.* Regarded as the most diligent researcher and authority of flag history, Preble later expanded the book to the voluminous *History of the Flag of the United States of Americas,* published in 1880.

Schuyler Hamilton's book was the last one checked out of the Library of Congress by Jefferson Davis before he quit the Senate to lead the Confederacy.

THE FLAG RESTORED

{ With a flotilla of ships off shore, a crowd gathered in the ruins of Fort Sumter to restore the Stars and Stripes.

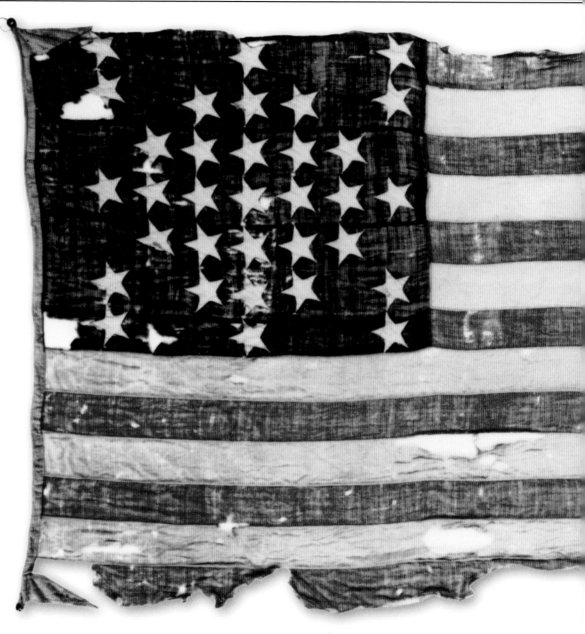

Major Robert Anderson, a retired U.S. Army officer, rejoined the military in April 1865 to perform one final service. Four years before, this Kentucky-born Union loyalist had defended Fort Sumter in Charleston harbor under a barrage of unceasing Confederate bombardment. Surrounded and with dwindling supplies, Anderson finally chose to save the lives of his wounded and shellshocked men by surrendering the smoldering, brick ruin. On April 13, 1861, Anderson lowered Fort Sumter's tattered 33-Star Flag and conceded defeat to one of his fellow West Pointers, General Pierre Gustave Toutant Beauregard. In a display of battlefield etiquette, Beauregard ordered a fifty-gun salute to the bravery of Anderson and the procession of the Stars and Stripes, now an enemy flag. Sumter's fall catapulted the nation into the Civil War.

Four years later, General William Sherman reached the end of his destructive rampage through the conquered South, having set fire to most of Charleston's fabled slave plantations extending up the Ashley River from the ruined city. Robert E. Lee surrendered on April 9, 1865, in Appomattox, Virginia.

With smoke still in the air over the city, federal ships festooned with the Stars and Stripes conveyed notables and dignitaries into Charleston harbor five days later on April 14, 1865. Aboard one of the ships was Major Anderson. Another carried the famous orator, Henry Ward Beecher. President Lincoln, not wanting to unduly flaunt his victory, opted to stay in Washington. They were here to restore the flag to its rightful place above the island fort, and symbolically draw the curtain to America's bloodiest war.

The great national convulsion was over.

> **❝** *We raise our fathers' banner," Ward Beecher intoned on the island fortress, "that it may bring back better blessings than those of old; that it may restore lawful government, and a prosperity purer and more enduring than that which it protected before; that it may win parted friends from their alienation; that it may inspire hope, and inaugurate universal liberty; that it may say to the sword, 'Return to the sheath,' and to the plow and sickle, 'Go forth;' that it may heal all jealousies, unite all policies, inspire a new national life, compact our strength, purify our principles, enoble our national ambitions, and make this people great and strong, not for aggression and quarrelsomeness, but for the peace of the world, giving to us the glorious prerogative of leading all nations to juster laws, to more humane policies, to sincererer friendship, to rational, instituted civil liberty, and to universal Christian brotherhood. Reverently, piously, in hopeful patriotism, we spread this banner on the sky, as of the old bow was planted on the cloud; and with solemn fervor beseech God to look upon it, and make it the memorial of an everlasting covenant and decree that never again on this fair land shall a deluge of blood prevail.* **❞**

The flag that flew over Fort Sumter

While a band played "The Star-Spangled Banner," Major General Robert Anderson raised the same flag that he had lowered four years before.

But the closure was premature. Hours later, one final spasm of the Civil War emanated from the Ford Theatre in Washington, D.C., where John Wilkes Booth aimed his pistol at Abraham Lincoln's head and pulled the trigger.

The last photographs of President Lincoln were taken by Alexander Gardner on April 10, 1865, one day after Lee's surrender and four days before Lincoln's assassination.

Once ashore, William Lloyd Garrison, the editor of the radical abolitionist newspaper, *The Liberator,* was carried on the shoulders of a throng of former slaves to the grave of John Calhoun, who had ardently defended slavery and state's rights. "Slavery," Garrison said to the headstone of his foe, "is now buried deeper than you." People paraded through the streets; preachers invoked healing in the churches. War-weary Charlestonians sought to rebuild their city and economy.

NEVADA & NEBRASKA

36
STAR FLAG

state | NEVADA
president | ABRAHAM LINCOLN
material | SILK
date made | C.1865
admissions date | OCTOBER 31, 1864
flag date | JULY 4, 1865
dimensions | 72" x 72"
period in use | 2 YEARS

This silk military flags (above and right) celebrate the end of Civil War hostilities and the victory of the Federal military. In excellent but very fragile condition, the square-shaped flags are both adorned with braided gold fringe. Silk fabric was smooth and dense enough for stars to be painted in gold, adding to the flags' luster. This 36-Star Flag was simply laid out with even rows of uniform orientation, now beginning to diminish in size, to avoid crowding the canton.

★ ★ ★ ★ ★ ★ ★

Orion Clemens served as territorial secretary and governor of Nevada, appointed by Lincoln as a reward for his loyalty to the Union cause. In Virginia City, where he published the *Territorial Enterprise*, he was joined by his younger brother, Samuel Clemens, aka Mark Twain, who wrote editorials for the paper.

Originally established as part of Utah Territory in 1850, Nevada splintered off as its own territory in 1861. Its path to statehood, achieved in 1864, was fiercely political and tied to the events of the Civil War. The late President Lincoln had benefited from the state's electoral support in his reelection bid against his foe General George McClellan, and the stupefying quantities of silver mined in the Comstock Lode made its admission as a state urgent, in order to bolster the Union treasury.

Nebraska, whose territorial designation in 1854 had helped spark the Civil War, took much longer to become a state, and not without its own controversies. Nebraskans who lived south of the Platte River, hoping to expedite statehood, agitated for annexation to Kansas, their southern neighbor. But Nebraskans in the still sparsely populated lands north of the river resisted the idea, understanding that a loss of the southern population would seriously prolong Nebraska's entry into the Union. To counter the annexation, the Nebraska legislature voted to transfer itself from Omaha to Lancaster, a small town on the southern side, and name it the new capital. But residents of Omaha tried to counter this economically damaging move by renaming Lancaster "Lincoln." They hoped the association with the Great Emancipator would embolden southern-sympathizer legislators to vote *against* the move. It did not. Instead, the move, along with the westward progress of the Union Pacific Railroad, swelled the territory's

37

STAR FLAG

state | NEBRASKA
president | ANDREW JACKSON
material | SILK
date made | C.1868
admissions date | MARCH 1, 1867
flag date | JULY 4, 1867
dimensions | 72" x 72"
period in use | 8 YEARS

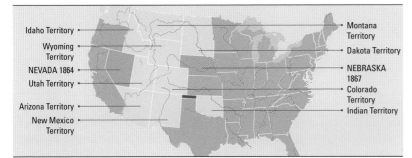

Idaho Territory
Wyoming Territory
NEVADA 1864
Utah Territory
Arizona Territory
New Mexico Territory
Montana Territory
Dakota Territory
NEBRASKA 1867
Colorado Territory
Indian Territory

{ **This 37-Star Flag** is a majestic interpretation of Peter L'Enfant's early elliptical star pattern, but with a double ring, four corners, and two central stars to include all of the states of the transcontinental Union.

The March of Sergeant Gilbert Bates

★ ★

In 1868, three years after the end of the Civil War, Union soldier Sergeant Gilbert H. Bates embarked on a solitary walk from Vicksburg, Mississippi, to Washington, D.C. The walk was inspired by a quirky American movement, "Pedestrianism," most identified with Edward Payson Weston, "Weston the Pedestrian," who exploited the speed of the telegraph, newspaper dispatches, and Americans' passion for wagering. Walking one hundred miles in less than twenty-four hours was his standard challenge, or walking five miles backwards, or even, as his magnum opus in 1869, walking five thousand miles in one hundred days. Never mind that Weston never actually accomplished one of his walks on time, more important was how his "races" captivated newspaper readers everywhere and emptied the pockets of many gamblers.

Sergeant Bates, however, was not interested in velocity but in reciprocity. After arguing with a fellow Wisconsonian about the depth of Southerners' loyalty, Bates wagered that he could walk through the American South, from Vicksburg to Washington, D.C., carrying an unfurled Star-Spangled Banner—and go unharmed. He even suggested that Southerners would welcome, nourish, and comfort him along his journey. Not even the Civil War, Bates believed, could erase the innate love every American had for the Star-Spangled Banner. Mark Twain chimed in, predicting quite a different Southern reception, despite traditions of hospitality, writing in the *Territorial Enterprise*: "This fellow will get more black eyes, down there among those unconstructed rebels, than he can ever carry along with him without breaking his back. I expect to see him coming into Washington some day on one leg and with one eye out and an arm gone. He won't amount to more than an interesting relic by the time he gets here and then he will have to hire out for a sign for the Anatomical Museum. Those fellows down there have no sentiment in them. They won't buy his picture. They will be more likely take his scalp."

As Bates predicted, he found Southerners charitable and full of admiration for the flag he carried. Embarking from Vicksburg, Bates was given a silk Stars and Stripes to replace his own tattered flag. A *New York Times* dispatch reported that cheering Southerners "replenished his basket from their lean larders." At Montgomery, Bates vigorously waved the flag where Jefferson Davis had unfurled the flag of secession. And when he reached Washington, D.C., Bates proudly planted his staff at the Washington Monument, ending his journey. He even repeated his flag march across Scotland and England, demonstrating, with equal success, the restored bonds between Americans and Britons. Later, Buffalo Bill hired him as a part of his Wild West Show.

PART THREE: *1876–2006*

THE 38-STAR FLAG TO THE 50-STAR FLAG

With thirty-seven states in its Union on the Fourth of July 1876, the nation, with a population of over forty-five million—surpassing England and even France—admitted great tides of immigrants through New York City and San Francisco.

It was a time of unbridled production when, for the first time in its history, the United States *exported* more than it *imported*, including steel from Pittsburgh's mills, vast amounts of cotton harvested across millions of acres, and gold and other minerals from the West. Meanwhile, a frenzy of patents, inventions, stock offerings, construction projects, roads, bridges, and schools continued without pause. Alexander Graham Bell was awarded the year's first patent for his telephone. In New York City, thousands gathered in Union Square for pageants and pyrotechnics; the Society of the Cincinnati feasted at

Delmonico's, where a silent toast was made to George Washington, their first president. President Ulysses S. Grant, in the waning months of his eight-year term, stayed at the White House to be present for the Independence Day celebrations in Washington, D.C.

On July 4th, crowds gathered in Independence Square. Governor Rutherford Hayes, who would win the next presidential election by a mere eight to seven electoral votes, shared the stage with Acting Vice President Thomas Ferry. Richard Henry Lee, the grandson of the Virginia Continental delegate who introduced the resolution for independence a century before, read aloud Thomas Jefferson's Declaration. Lee was selected for this honor not only for his familial connection,

{ **Elizabeth Cady Stanton** and Susan B. Anthony, the daughter of a cotton manufacturer, never lived to see full suffrage won in 1920.

{ **Richard Henry Lee's** original handwritten *Declaration of Rights of the Colonies* announced that "all political connection between them and the State of Great Britain is, and ought to be, totally dissolved." The declaration was adopted on July 2, 1776, by the Continental Congress.

but also because he was a Southerner. This Centennial, it was hoped, would broadcast to the world a nation united after the bloodiest Civil War the modern world had seen. Lee read from the actual parchment that had been transported to Philadelphia with the approval of President Grant.

As he read the final lines, four women rose from the audience in a planned protest of the National Woman Suffrage Association. Leading them was Susan B. Anthony, who marched to the podium and handed Vice President Ferry, a supporter of their cause, their own *Declaration of Rights of the Women of the United States*: "And now, at the close of a hundred years, as the hour hand of the great clock that marks the centuries points to 1876, we declare our faith in the principles of self-government; our full equality with man in natural rights . . . We ask of our rulers, at this hour, no special favors, no special privileges, no special legislation. We ask justice, we ask equality, we ask that all of the civil and political rights that belong to citizens of the United States be guaranteed to us and our daughters forever." Suffragists distributed copies to the audience, and then marched to Chestnut Street for a rally and to the First Unitarian Church for speeches.

Amidst the revelry, the day was not without its tragedies. Children shooting guns, errant fireworks, and mishandled powder killed and injured scores. In Philadelphia, Dr. Henry A. Bucher, preparing pyrotechnic rockets in his Moore Street pharmacy, accidentally set off a chemical explosion. The detonation destroyed the brick structure, killing the doctor and his brother, and severely burning their father. One customer in the store perished instantly; another man, entering, was blown into the street and died of his injuries.

That night, when darkness fell over the city, candles appeared in thousands of windows. At Independence Hall, throngs gathered for song and cheers beneath the windows where the first Stars and Stripes was defined, while overhead, novel electric search lights illuminated the Continental Colours, the sky alive with whistles, missiles, fireworks, powder bursts, booms from guns, and clangs of bells hailing America's birthday.

{ **1876's Independence Day**
celebrations focused on the floating
of the Continental Colours.

THE CENTENNIAL EXHIBITION OF 1876

Eager to demonstrate that the United States could host an International Exposition as ambitious as Great Britain's 1851 Crystal Palace Exposition, organizers began as early as 1870 to prepare for a showcase to celebrate the one hundredth anniversary of the Declaration of Independence and the nation's emergence as a power of global significance.

The Centennial Exhibition was awarded to the city of Philadelphia. Various boards of directors, ladies auxiliaries, politicians, developers, boosters, and businessmen began planning a fair on a scale commensurate with American ambition and drive, veritable proof of how liberty provided the basis for many of the greatest advances the world had ever seen.

It was a spectacular success from the day it opened on May 10, 1876, to when it closed on the same day of November. Upwards of ten million people visited the Exhibition; on Pennsylvania Day alone, a quarter of a million people passed through the gates. What they were confronted with were dozens of architectural monuments sheltering acres of everything imaginable— even to begin to take in all that was offered without the freedom of days, or even weeks, was hopeless.

The central theme of the fair was industry and technology, and most of all, America's predominance in just about every industry, whether industrial or agricultural, that produced raw materials and goods for people. Some of the first commercial typewriters were

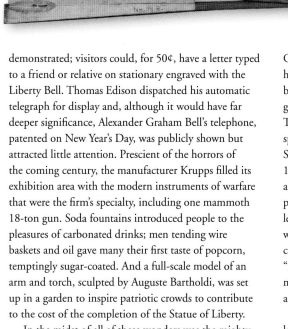

Ladies' fans, in great demand during the hot 1876 summer, were printed with flags and images of the Fairgrounds.

demonstrated; visitors could, for 50¢, have a letter typed to a friend or relative on stationary engraved with the Liberty Bell. Thomas Edison dispatched his automatic telegraph for display and, although it would have far deeper significance, Alexander Graham Bell's telephone, patented on New Year's Day, was publicly shown but attracted little attention. Prescient of the horrors of the coming century, the manufacturer Krupps filled its exhibition area with the modern instruments of warfare that were the firm's specialty, including one mammoth 18-ton gun. Soda fountains introduced people to the pleasures of carbonated drinks; men tending wire baskets and oil gave many their first taste of popcorn, temptingly sugar-coated. And a full-scale model of an arm and torch, sculpted by Auguste Bartholdi, was set up in a garden to inspire patriotic crowds to contribute to the cost of the completion of the Statue of Liberty.

In the midst of all of these wonders was the mighty Double Corliss Steam Engine, built by George Henry

George Pullman purchased the Double Corliss Engine in 1880 for seventy-seven thousand dollars to power his train coach works in Chicago.

Corliss to be the largest of its time, whose 56 tons had "not an ounce of unneeded metal," one reporter breathlessly proclaimed. Pumping up and down, its gigantic pistons provided the power of 2,500 horses. The Corliss even powered an entire printing press that spit out copies of the Exhibition's daily newspaper. So captivating and grandiose was this great feat of the 19th-century engineering mind that the Exhibition was actually "turned on" at its opening ceremonies by it. At precisely 1:22 PM, President Ulysses S. Grant turned the levers, instantly bringing to mechanical life a myriad of wheels, turbines, gears, looms, lights, and pumps in a cacophony of sound accompanied by a choir singing the "Hallelujah Chorus," a symphony orchestra playing a march composed for the occasion by Richard Wagner, and once finished, a one-hundred-gun salute.

To demonstrate this great machine's simplicity and labor-saving power, only one man was required to operate the Corliss. And to give spectators the strongest impression of just how fantastic this machine was, the sole attendant usually sat in a chair, reading a newspaper, dressed in his Sunday best, with no trace of sweat. Only periodically would he look up to confirm the machine's

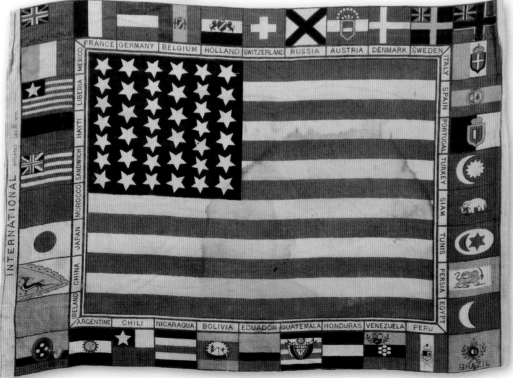

{ The U.S. Government Building included a hanging display, "Origins of the American Flag," including Pine Tree Flags, Union Jacks, and Rattlesnake Flags.

regular rhythm, or less regularly, walk around the perimeter of the stage to answer questions, or ascend the steps to inspect the moving parts.

The Exposition's elaborate displays also impressed visitors with just how far America's textile industry had come in a mere century from the days of homespun. The Singer Sewing Machine Company, demonstrating its dominance in this new era of technical marvel, built its own pavilion and sponsored each of its employees to board trains from New York City to the fairgrounds. Active silk colonies taught people how filament was gathered, spun, and woven into fabric. Massachusetts and New Hampshire mills proudly displayed all manner of fabrics. English, Irish, and Scottish cases proudly displayed their finest threads, linens, laces, and tartans. And the U.S. Bunting company presented flags, banners, streamers, pennants, and decorative bunting.

{ A cotton 39-Star Flag, printed as a Centennial souvenir, proclaimed America's emergence as a world power, a bridge to East and West.

COLORADO

38

STAR FLAG

....

state | COLORADO
president | ULYSSES S. GRANT
material | WOOL
date made | C.1877–1889
admissions date | AUGUST 1, 1876
flag date | JULY 4, 1877
dimensions | 72″ x 141″
period in use | 13 YEARS

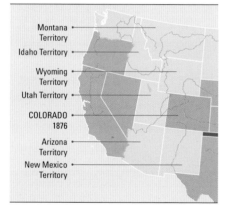

Montana Territory
Idaho Territory
Wyoming Territory
Utah Territory
COLORADO 1876
Arizona Territory
New Mexico Territory

The Colorado Territory was created in 1861; its north, east, south, and western parts were drawn from the territories of Nebraska, Kansas, New Mexico, and Utah, respectively. Colorado attracted the nation's attention when gold was discovered in the Rockies, sparking a new rush in 1859—these prospectors were known as "Fifty-Niners."

The Colorado War, fought in the midst of the Civil War, pitted U.S. soldiers against several Indian tribes. The Sand Creek Massacre became an infamous episode when Colonel John Chivington, hoping to burnish his political future, attacked a Cheyenne and Arapaho village, which had signaled a truce under an American flag. All of the

This well-balanced and thoughtfully composed 38-Star Flag perfectly summarizes the State of the Union in late 1876. Four stars indicate the four corners of the United States, stretching between Oregon and Florida, California and Maine. A double ellipse, with the inner ring composed of thirteen stars, embraces a prominent star recognizing Colorado.

A Stars and Stripes flies over the Farwell Mill at Camp Independence, founded after the July 4, 1879, discovery of a large lode of gold. When the brutal winter of 1899 descended on Independence, miners who were left stranded without supplies abandoned the town by crafting skis from the wooden buildings and racing to Aspen. Independence was left a ghost town.

village's nine hundred inhabitants were killed. Congressional investigations ensued. When testimony confirmed that women and children were slain, Pennsylvania Senator Charles Buckalew asked, "How cut?" "With knives; scalped," a witness testified, "their brains knocked out." Such unsettling accounts served to complicate Colorado's petition for statehood, made already complex by Reconstruction politics. President Andrew Johnson vetoed Colorado's statehood bills twice, in 1866 and 1867, deepening congressional Republican resentment that exploded when he became the first president to be impeached and tried. (He was acquitted by a single vote in the Senate.)

The exhaustion of the gold depressed Colorado's population, but soon new settlers flooded in on railroads. President Ulysses S. Grant finally signed its statehood bill on August 1, 1876.

FLAGS IN THE AGE OF THE MACHINE

Machine technology and mass production coincided with the government's and military's increasing demand for flags. More and more, the military outlined specifications for fabric quality, color, and sizes that machines could readily fulfill.

At the same time, many events and phenomenas brought flags closer to home. The Civil War, westward expansion, the Centennial, and a sense of mature nationhood encouraged by literature, art, music, more illustrated newspapers and magazines, and global travel all worked together to impress the fibers of the Stars and Stripes deeper into the American consciousness.

No longer was the Stars and Stripes simply a symbol of nationhood or maritime signal, but rather a symbol of individual and communal identity, one that Americans embraced with greater and greater feeling and devotion. It was now commonplace for ordinary Americans to fly Stars and Stripes in their homes, schools, and businesses.

A portrait of William Perkin in his laboratory with a piece of synthetically dyed cloth. In 1906, he was invited to Columbia University to celebrate the fiftieth anniversary of his discovery. The trip included a visit to the White House.

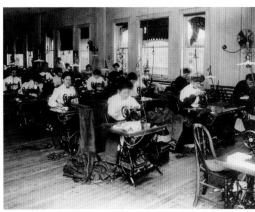

Teams of women use sewing machines to make flags at the Brooklyn Navy Yard in 1909. Ships were first built there in the 1780s, later came frigates, ironclads, battleships, and aircraft carriers, including the *Fulton II*, U.S.S. *Monitor*, U.S.S. *Maine*, and U.S.S. *Saratoga*. During World War II, 70,000 men and women worked there; in 1966, the Brooklyn Navy Yard was decommissioned and closed.

ARTIFICIAL COLORS

The first steps toward creating artificial colors, ending millennia of painstaking manipulation of natural sources for fabric dye, began in 1834 when a German physician, Friedlieb Runge (1795–1867)—who was the first to identify and isolate caffeine from coffee beans in 1819—created small amounts of bluish dye from aniline, a by-product of coal tar, a dense black sludge of organic compounds that was left over from the distillation of coal. Despite its use as a preservative for ship's hulls and railroad ties, so much coal tar was created that inventors sought ways to transform the black goop into chemical gold.

William Perkin (1838–1907), an eighteen-year-old aspiring chemist in London, continued his mentor August Wilhelm von Hofmann's quest to create quinine—a palliative for malaria only found in the South American Cinchona tree—from coal tar. Working in his makeshift home laboratory in 1856, Perkin failed to produce quinine but, inadvertently mixing some of his chemicals, noticed a powder that produced deep purple stains on silk. Unwittingly, he had stumbled on the first aniline dye, mauve. By the end of the decade, a fashion craze for "Perkin's Purple" had swept over the continent, helped along when Queen Victoria wore a mauve gown to her daughter's wedding, and Perkin, who shrewdly predicted its financial potential, built a dye factory in Scotland and made a fortune.

Perkin's discovery ignited decades of fierce competition among British, French, and German chemists. Colors resulting from their rivalry added, one by one, a spectrum of artificial colors and shades—including black, one of the most elusive textile "colors." Hofmann was among the first experimenters to discover magenta. Carl Graebe and Carl Lieberman struck upon alizarin in 1868. Artificial brown came in 1873, from the laboratories of Groissant and Bretonniere. Five years later, Adolf von Baeyer synthesized indigo. In 1897, Heumann brought synthetic blue to the scene on a commercial scale.

A banner advertises one of America's largest flag manufacturers, Annin & Company.

THE SEWING MACHINE

Creating a machine to replicate the intricate actions of fingers and hands, and choreograph the movement of needle and thread proved to be a daunting challenge for 19th-century inventors. Conceptualizing how such a machine could work was difficult enough—making one that reliably executed tight stitches was even harder. Threads had to be held in tension tight enough to stitch, but not so tight as to break. Fabric had to be led through evenly for a clean stitch; somehow needles and threads had to pass through the fabric and be sent back through in reverse. And it had to be powered.

The challenge—and the great financial potential such a device promised—made for intense competition, resulting in a flurry of models, patents, espionage, infringement lawsuits, fortunes, and broken dreams.

Rudimentary sewing machines were in use as early as the 1830s, such as Barthelemy Thimonnier's French model that executed a chain stitch. According to historian Grace Rogers Cooper, however, this invention incited a mob of tailors, "fearing that the invention would rob them of their livelihood," who apparently smashed Thimonnier's contraptions and hounded him out of Paris.

Several American inventors followed suit. In 1842 John J. Greenough was awarded the first ever American sewing machine patent. His machine was able to make a running stitch and a back stitch in leather goods. The next year, Benjamin W. Bean won a patent for a machine that could sew fabric. Months later, George H. Corliss peddled yet another patented machine but without luck. James Roger's equally unsuccessful machine in 1844 was followed, two years later, by a

By the 1893 Columbian Exposition, Singer's sewing machines were a symbol of domesticity, and the company's success was made iconographic in the Singer Building, which was the world's tallest skyscraper in 1908.

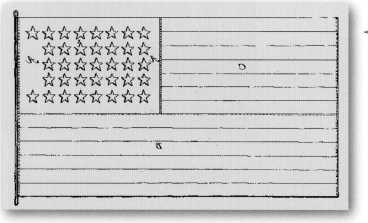

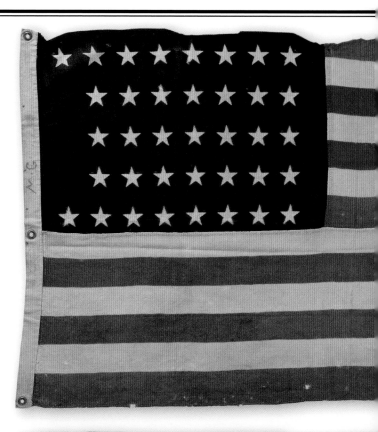

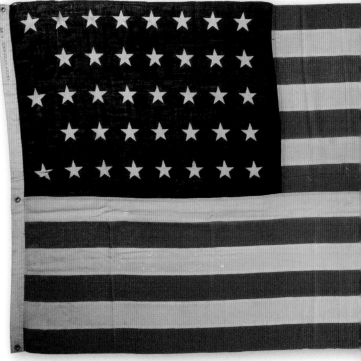

A patent drawing of a 37-Star Flag, mass-produced through the clamp dye process.

{ A 37-Star Flag of Middlesex Company wool made by U.S. Bunting after 1867.

machine by Elias Howe. Howe's machine proved to be successful, not so much for its design, but for the fact that he was able to protect his patented ideas and later license them to other inventors and manufacturers.

In 1853 an inventor named Isaac Merritt Singer entered the fray in a fashion that would prove to be a trademark of his personality. Loud, boisterous, tireless, with an insatiable appetite for life and women (he married in significantly overlapping intervals), and quick to seize opportunities, Singer produced a lock stitch machine that ignited a fierce battle among attorneys and judges, and sewing machine inventors and companies. Elias Howe was his staunchest opponent.

But true to the maxim that the inventor himself does not matter as much as the person who capitalizes on the invention, Singer and his company soon rose to the top. By 1876, the Singer Sewing Machine Company was a model of American entreprenurial success. By the Centennial, the company was selling as many sewing machines as all of its competitors combined.

THE CLAMP DYE PROCESS

Edward Brierley was the first to adapt ancient clamp-dye methods to dye fabric, earning him a U.S. patent in 1849. His clamps each consisted of a cage of metal strips lined with rubber. After a sheet of fabric was stretched out in the frame, screws, tightened under great pressure, compressed sections of the fabric between the rubber strips. The whole assembly was then lowered into a dye bath. Areas of fabric under compression did not admit the color, creating stripes. For fancier plaid patterns, the fabric could, after drying, be shifted and dyed again.

John Holt adapted the same technique in 1870, with his own patent, to make American flags. Two pieces of fabric (one for the top half of the flag, another for the bottom half) were individually dyed with crimson stripes, and the canton, with its own clamp apparatus with star-shaped rubber plugs, was dunked in an indigo dye bath. American Ensign and U.S. Bunting utilized the clamp process to manufacture nearly identical flags.

{ Stripes flow from a machine at the Annin Flag Company in 1943, supplying the huge demand for colors during World War II.

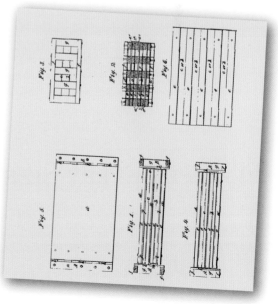

{ Patent applications detailed the construction of the clamp apparatus.

{ When the 38-Star Flag was introduced in 1877, the manufacturer, American Ensign, simply had to add an extra star to the clamp apparatus.

Large flags, such as this wool 48-Star, require special care and extra people to help display and fold them. When working with any antique or delicate textiles, it is important to wear archival gloves.

FLAGS IN EVERY SIZE AND SHAPE

Throughout American history, flags have been made in all kinds of sizes and shapes for many different uses, military and civilian. The development of the sewing machine, coupled with the ability to produce stronger fabrics, allowed even bigger flags to be made, while, conversely, printing technology permitted tiny parade flags to be manufactured with great speed.

The government has always been a large consumer of flags, since the Stars and Stripes flies, of course, at all U.S. government buildings, military installations, on all vessels, and during ceremonies. The original, everyday flag to fly at installations was the Post Flag (sometimes known as a Camp Flag). During inclement weather, the smaller Storm Flag was used. Garrison Flags, the largest of military flags, were used for special occasions. (The Star-Spangled Banner is a garrison-sized flag.) The Cavalry Flag, first defined in 1834 (also known as a Guidon), was swallowtail in shape.

Oftentimes, the upper part of the fork on this flag was red, and the lower part was white.

Parade Flags were typically printed on cotton or linen and attached to a stick. Typical parade flags were 8 x 12 inches, but some could be as small as 2 x 3 inches. While military or naval regulations often specified acceptable proportions and sizes for flags, it was not until the 20th century that national rules for flag dimensions were formulated.

President Woodrow Wilson
Camp Sherman, Ohio
21,000 people

Statue of Liberty
Camp Dodge, Iowa
18,000 people

{ **After World War I**, Arthur Mole and John D. Thomas, photographers from Chicago, traveled to military bases where they organized great crowds of military personnel into formations of patriotic symbols. After organizing the men and women, who were dressed in the appropriate shades of clothing, some standing at attention, others lying down, they took photos from a tower.

Liberty Bell
Camp Dix, New Jersey
25,000 people

Machine Gun Insignia
Camp Hancock, Georgia
22,500 people

Great Seal Shield
Camp Custer, Michigan
30,000 people

{ **Soldiers at Fort Hood**, Texas, work together to keep a large 48-Star Flag (similar to the one on the opposite page) from coming into contact with the ground as it is being hoisted on the camp's flag pole. Flags even larger than garrisons were made for special events, such as a 1909 Independence Day celebration in Pittsburgh, when a flag, 80 x 160 feet, was hoisted above Grant Street.

★ ★

{ **Colonel Fisk** lies in his flag-draped coffin after being shot and killed in 1872 by Edward Stokes—a violent end to a feud over a show girl. The murder ended, according to *Harper's Weekly*, "a career of brilliant crime and audacious indecorum."

Colonel James "Jim" Fisk, who started out as a circus attendant and pencil salesman, became one of the 19th-century's most corrupt rascals, whose exploits included the use of his steamships to smuggle Civil War cotton; the fraudulent takeover of the Erie Railroad; and a gold price-rigging scheme that led to the financial panic of 1869, a crisis that required the direct intervention—some suspected his own involvement—of President Ulysses S. Grant and the Federal Treasury to stabilize the national economy. Fisk was shielded from prosecution by his crony Boss Tweed.

In 1870, Fisk purchased for himself the position of colonel of the New York Ninth Regiment, to satisfy, apparently, his intense need for erecting a military persona for himself. Next, he visited the Greenwich Village flag shop of Sally Ann McFadden, which was established in 1834. Fisk ordered McFadden to make him a flag, larger than any other, for his training encampment at Long

Beach. "She told him the biggest flag then in existence was that in the rotunda of the Capitol at Washington, in every stripe of which was enough silk to make a dress for every woman who had contributed to the flag." Fisk insisted that his should be bigger, ignoring McFadden's warning that such a flag could not be flown. The six hundred dollar order was placed. Five weeks later, McFadden and her girls sewed the final pieces together in the street, 110 x 50 feet.

Fisk invited McFadden, her assistants, and a crowd of spectators to witness the unfurling. Fisk's men hauled the enormous banner up the pole, but true to McFadden's prediction, its weight was too great for the wind. Making matters worse, the next day a mighty storm violently tangled the flag's vast square yardage in the halyards. Unable to relieve the immense force of the wind and weight, the pole itself snapped, and everything was swept into the sea.

NORTH DAKOTA & SOUTH DAKOTA

39
STAR FLAG

state | NORTH DAKOTA
president | BENJAMIN HARRISON
material | WOOL
date made | C.1889
admissions date | NOVEMBER 2, 1889
flag date | UNOFFICIAL
dimensions | 72" x 72"
period in use | N/A

A flag flies on Mt. Rushmore's summit. Work began on October 4, 1927, and was completed on October 31, 1941. Sculpted by Gutzon Borglum, his son Lincoln, and teams of daring carvers, the monument was planned to celebrate America's Sesquicentennial, but construction took longer than hoped. George Washington was completed on July 4, 1934, followed by Theodore Roosevelt, Abraham Lincoln, and Thomas Jefferson, who had to be carved twice, the first attempt having failed. A bill to add Susan B. Anthony was rejected in Congress.

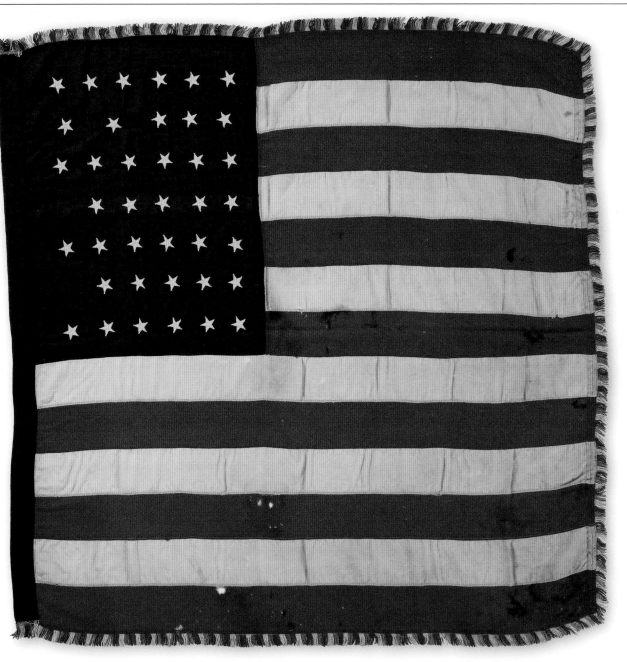

The 39-Star and 40-Star Flags representing the Dakotas could not be more unlike. With its unique tricolor fringe, the square flag for North Dakota has a blue hoist strip and small stars arranged in uneven-numbered rows.

40
STAR FLAG

state | SOUTH DAKOTA
president | BENJAMIN HARRISON
material | WOOL
date made | C.1889
admissions date | NOVEMBER 2, 1889
flag date | UNOFFICIAL
dimensions | 60" x 129"
period in use | N/A

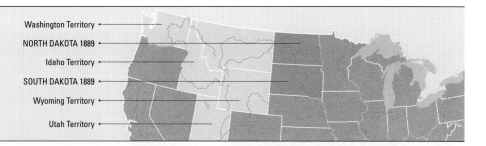

Washington Territory
NORTH DAKOTA 1889
Idaho Territory
SOUTH DAKOTA 1889
Wyoming Territory
Utah Territory

Admitted to the Union on the same day, November 2, 1889, North and South Dakota might have been admitted as a single state had it not been for the political imperative of gaining four Senators instead of two.

Organized as the Dakota Territory in 1861 (and including parts of Minnesota, Wyoming, and Idaho), the Dakotas' statehood brought the last remaining pieces of Jefferson's Louisiana Purchase into the Union.

Eager to sidestep the appearance of favoritism, Secretary of State James G. Blaine (who served in that post under three presidents), diplomatically shuffled the admission papers for North and South Dakota before they were signed by President Benjamin Harrison, cloaking forever the actual order of admission. Traditionally, North Dakota's rank as the thirty-ninth state is recognized by mere alphabetical hierarchy.

Its 40-Star sister chooses bloated "puffy" stars that stuff the canton, with a no-nonsense series of five rows of eight stars each. Each of the flags's stars are skewed slightly toward the upper left corner of the canton.

MONTANA

General George Custer, who captured public attention for his Civil War service (it was he who accepted the first Confederate flag of truce), was immortalized in the 19th-century consciousness for his mythic demise. On June 25, 1876, Custer and his cavalry engaged the Lakota and Cheyenne at Little Big Horn. Isolated on what came to be known as Last Stand Hill, the ensuing battle took the lives of Custer himself and every one of his soldiers, save one Sioux scout. News, however, of the great defeat did not reach New York until the Centennial July 4th, from an account by a correspondent from the *Helena Herald*. Shocked readers were presented with the account: "The Indians poured a murderous fire from all directions. Gen. Custer, his two brothers, his nephew, and brother-in-law were all killed, and not one of his detachment escaped. Two hundred and seven men were buried in one place."

41
STAR FLAG

state | MONTANA
president | BENJAMIN HARRISON
material | WOOL
date made | C.1889
admissions date | NOVEMBER 8, 1889
flag date | UNOFFICIAL
dimensions | 72" x 124"
period in use | N/A

Washington Territory
MONTANA 1889
Idaho Territory
Wyoming Territory
Utah Territory
Public Land Strip
Arizona Territory
New Mexico Territory

Sidney Edgerton, the first governor of the Montana Territory, was a schoolteacher, lawyer, prosecutor, Free-Soiler, Congressman, Territory of Idaho judge, and a colonel of the Ohio militia known as the Squirrel Hunters, so named because the volunteers, drawn from 60 counties-worth of farm boys, "never had to shoot at the same squirrel twice." They defended Cincinnati from Confederate invasion.

O n May 20, 1862, President Abraham Lincoln signed the Homestead Act, which encouraged westward migration, allowing any citizen "who is the head of a family, or who has arrived at the age of twenty-one years" and "who has never borne arms against the United States Government" to stake a claim on a one quarter section of the public domain, equivalent to one hundred sixty acres. The new law, which made land ownership possible for ordinary Americans, opened up the West to increased settlement. A great patchwork quilt of family-owned farms and ranches unfolded across the landscape.

Two years later, on May 26, 1864, the Montana Territory was organized from the northeastern section of the Idaho Territory, straddling the Continental Divide. Along with the flurry of states admitted between 1889 and 1891, Montana's statehood was made official on November 8, 1889.

This unofficial 41-Star Flag of late 19th-century vintage has a most peculiar arrangement of stars. No other flag like it is known to exist. Its stars appear as though an arrangement of 8-6-8-6-8 had suddenly been obliged to accommodate an extra row of five stars. One might guess the flag was first made as a 36-Star, but the identical materials and stitching suggest it was made all at one time by a carefree flag maker.

PARADE FLAGS

This **13-Star** Parade Flag with a medallion pattern was likely made in 1876 to celebrate the Centennial.

This **especially** fancy 48-Star Parade Flag has a stitched fringe.

Parade Flags were made in great abundance for Americans to wave during holiday celebrations, ship launches, troop embarkations, bond rallies, political conventions, and processions through small-town Main Streets or great avenues in the grandest of cities. Most Parade Flags were mass-produced by simple printing methods on inexpensive sheets of cotton, linen, silk, rayon, or paper. After printing, the flags were trimmed and attached to sticks.

Like their full-size counterparts, Parade Flags were made with an array of star configurations, numbers, and patterns. Some were glazed or waxed for rain protection, others had fringes, while still others could roll up and disappear into a cane.

These four 36-Star Parade Flags from the 1860s were simply printed with blocks of red and white.

This **nicely proportioned** and printed 45-Star Flag with staggered rows was made at the turn of the century.

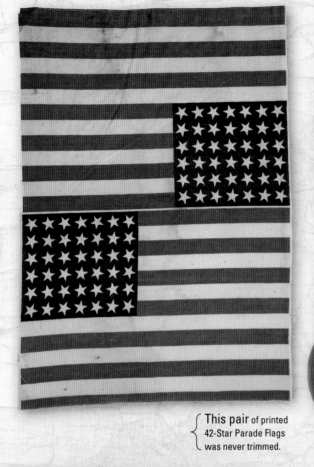

{ This pair of printed 42-Star Parade Flags was never trimmed.

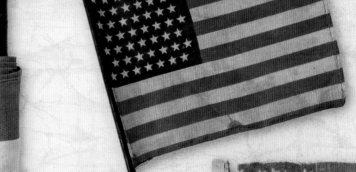

{ A Main Street parade in distant Nome, Alaska, in 1918.

{ This 49-Star Parade Flag includes a fancy pointed pole.

{ Each 44-Star Parade Flag in this triplet has its own arrangement.

{ This 19th-century Parade Flag conveniently rolls up to fit inside a cane.

{ Scribbling on this 33-Star Parade Flag dates from the Civil War.

WASHINGTON

42
STAR FLAG

state | WASHINGTON
president | BENJAMIN HARRISON
material | COTTON
date made | C.1889
admissions date | NOVEMBER 11, 1889
flag date | UNOFFICIAL
dimensions | 17" x 23"
period in use | N/A

WASHINGTON 1889
North Dakota
Montana
Idaho Territory
South Dakota
Wyoming Territory
Utah Territory

Despite the great scarcity of people living in the northern section of Oregon Territory, settlers began organizing for autonomy from faraway Portland in 1851. The original petition for statehood proposed Columbia for its name, but when it reached the House floor for Congressional debate, Representative Richard Stanton of Kentucky suddenly proposed it be called Washington.

"I shall never object to that name," Joseph Lane, the territorial representative said, hoping to win acceptance through acquiescence. When it was awarded territorial status in 1853, with the Columbia River and 46° latitude used as the dividing line from Oregon, the region was home to, at best, only four thousand Americans.

Washington was not just the only state named for a president, but settlers had already named a county each for President Franklin Pierce and Vice President William King, hoping to garner support for statehood.

The territory receded within its current boundaries in 1859 and 1863, as the other northwest territories and states were resolved (the northern border is shared with the Canadian province of British Columbia). With Washington's admission to statehood on November 11, 1889, the Pacific Northwest finally settled into place.

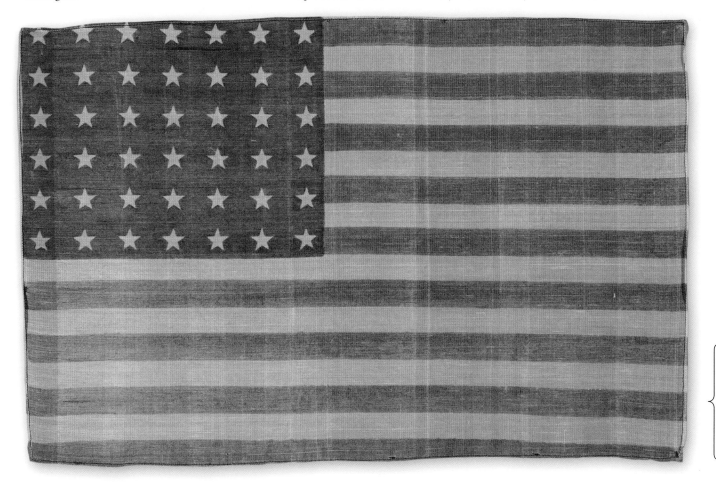

This 42-Star Parade Flag has four extra stripes, possibly the result of trimming the printed sheet incorrectly. Its rows are run evenly, unlike these 42-Star Parade Flags (far left), whose stars are staggered.

TICKER TAPE PARADES

The first ticker tape parade, which occurred during the great festivities opening the Statue of Liberty on October 28, 1886, was not planned. Because the celebration's parade was planned for a Thursday, many workers, including ones on Wall Street, were not given a holiday. When parts of the parade finally reached Wall Street, after having started uptown and passed through Madison Square, where it was reviewed by President Grover Cleveland, office boys high in the windows began spontaneously throwing ticker tape into the street. Soon others joined in and the air was soon filled with ribbons of paper—a unique new kind of parade was invented.

Not all New Yorkers were thrilled with the growing popularity of ticker tape parades. "Fortunately so far no serious disaster has been caused by it," warned "An Old Native New Yorker" to the *New York Times* in 1904, "but it does not require much imagination to picture the possibility of a spirited horse being frightened by a bit of tape flashing unexpectedly across his eyes, and a single plunge into the dense crowd usually pressing close to the edge of the sidewalk would be a pretty serious matter." The gentleman also denounced the litter resulting from each parade.

But such complaints did not suppress the public's great enthusiasm for the ticker tape parade, and it remained a favorite way for New Yorkers to welcome visitors and celebrate greatness. Kings and queens, visiting prime ministers and presidents, athletic heroes and Olympians, astronauts and explorers, and soldiers and veterans have been given the honor of parading through the "Canyon of Heroes," including Amelia Earhart, Richard Byrd (honored the most times with three parades), President Eisenhower, Charles de Gaulle, General Douglas MacArthur, Queen Elizabeth II, the Yankees and the Mets, Pope John Paul II, and the freed American hostages.

Ticker tape, slender strips of paper, were printed with stock prices transmitted over telegraph wires.

At the appropriate moment, three men high on the Statue of Liberty released ropes that had secured an enormous French flag over her face. Horns blasted from thousands of ships— clanging bells, cannon fire, pyrotechnics, and cheering millions joined in.

The New York Times DESCRIBED THE STATUE OF LIBERTY FESTIVITIES:

"Liberty! A hundred Fourths of July broke loose yesterday to exult her name, and despite the calendar rolled themselves into a delirious and glorious one. At daybreak the city stirred nimbly and flung a million colors to the heavy air, for the cloud king had covered the heavens herself and moored upon the waters; but she plumed herself and showered scarlet, and snow, and azure, and gold, defying the skies to darken her festival. Then streamed the people; convergent rivers of life hurrying and sweeping through a thousand channels to the path of the pageant; there edifying, or gathered, or running counter to the onward tide, till the great thoroughfares overflowed and billows of humanity surged crosswise and splashed sprays of small boys to every ledge and cornice and accessible foothold till the very lamp posts were crowded and the doomed telegraph poles cracked with their

Forty-two years later, another ticker tape parade would celebrate the even greater Apollo 11 voyage to the moon and back.

IDAHO

43 STAR FLAG

state | IDAHO
president | BENJAMIN HARRISON
material | WOOL
date made | C.1890
admissions date | JULY 3, 1890
flag date | JULY 4, 1890
dimensions | 54" x 102"
period in use | 1 YEAR

Montana
IDAHO 1890
Wyoming Territory
Utah Territory

> President Benjamin Harrison signed six statehood bills, the most of any chief executive. Harrison was the grandson of another president, William Henry Harrison, whose own father signed the Declaration of Independence.

The Idaho Territory was yet another creation of President Abraham Lincoln, who approved it on March 4, 1863. Legislators agreed that the Continental Divide (the line separating east- and west-spilling waterways) would indicate the border between Idaho and Montana. The team commissioned to survey the divide, however, deviated from their course (in Montana's favor) up the Bitterroot Range.

As Idaho Territory organized for statehood, settlers in the panhandle pressed for a state of their own but were placated when the state's land-grant university was established in Moscow, a northern town. (Separatists in the north attempted to break off again, in 1905, as the state of Lincoln.)

In November 1889, four states were admitted to the Union in rapid succession: North Dakota, South Dakota, Montana, and Washington. On July 3, 1890, the eve of Independence Day, Idaho became the forty-third state. According to tradition, the new 43-Star Flag was introduced the next day.

Most Americans knew that Congress was going to admit Wyoming as the forty-fourth state on July 10—six days after Independence Day. Anticipating that the 43-Star Flag would be shortly out-of-date, most flag makers jumped ahead to the 44-Star Flag.

The 43-Star Flag is one the rarest and most difficult to find; another name for it is the "Seven-Day Flag." Very few authentic 43-Star Flags were made, and even fewer survive. Machine-sewn of wool parts, this canton includes the forty-third star in the top row, nudging it slightly out of step with the others.

WYOMING

44 STAR FLAG

state | WYOMING
president | BENJAMIN HARRISON
material | SILK
date made | C.1890
admissions date | JULY 10, 1890
flag date | JULY 4, 1891
dimensions | 72" x 72"
period in use | 5 YEARS

Idaho Territory
WYOMING 1890
Utah Territory
Arizona Territory
New Mexico Territory

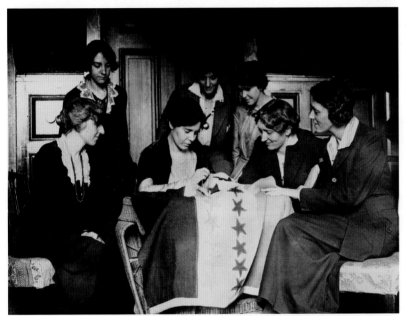

Suffragists shouldered decades of political and social struggle to win the universal right to vote in 1920, with the passage of the 19th Amendment. Days before Tennessee ratified the Amendment, reaching the necessary thirty-six votes, Alice Paul—president of the National Women's Party—sewed the last star on the Suffrage Flag (silk, with gold, white, and purple bands), which was then draped from their Washington headquarters to celebrate their long overdue victory.

The Wyoming Territory formed on July 25, 1868, from lands in the Dakota, Utah, and Idaho territories. It was the first place in the United States—indeed the first government in the world—to grant women the right to vote.

Esther Hobart McQuigg Slack Morris (1814–1902) is considered the mother of the suffrage movement in Wyoming. Born in New York but orphaned when she was eleven years old, Morris was raised by a seamstress and milliner. As a young, headstrong, and independent-minded woman, she joined the emerging Abolitionist movement, working to end slavery in the South. After the Civil War, Morris and her husband went to Wyoming Territory when they heard there was gold ore and prospecting opportunities. Once settled, she began pressuring her representative to the territory's legislature to introduce a bill granting women the right to vote, believing Wyoming's reputation would be enhanced by such a forward-thinking policy.

In 1869, the bill was passed and signed into law, upon the urging of Governor John Campbell's wife and the scores of women holding a candlelight vigil outside his office. Esther Morris became the first woman to serve as Justice of the Peace in the United States—a considerably important and dangerous post on the wild frontier. Wyoming also inaugurated the first female governor, Nellie Tayloe Ross, who was elected the same day as Miriam Ferguson was voted governor of Texas. Ross was later named the first Director of the U.S. Mint by Franklin Roosevelt.

Because the Wyoming Territory granted suffrage, Congress initially rejected its application for statehood. Politicians were fearful of the precedent it would set for states that outlawed women from polling places. "We will remain out of the Union for a hundred years rather than come without our women," Wyoming stated in Congress. And on July 10, 1890, President Harrison signed the bill to make Wyoming the forty-fourth State.

William Henry Jackson's photographs, created for stereoscope view, of Yellowstone's majestic landscapes helped convince Congress and President Ulysses S. Grant to cancel planned auctions of the land and instead create the world's first national park in 1872.

A banner of great optimism and celebration, this resplendent 44-Star Flag of silk, tassel, and fringe displays a triple medallion with a center and four corner stars. The stars are hand-painted gold. Each ring, starting from the inner circle of six stars, increases by seven to the outer ring.

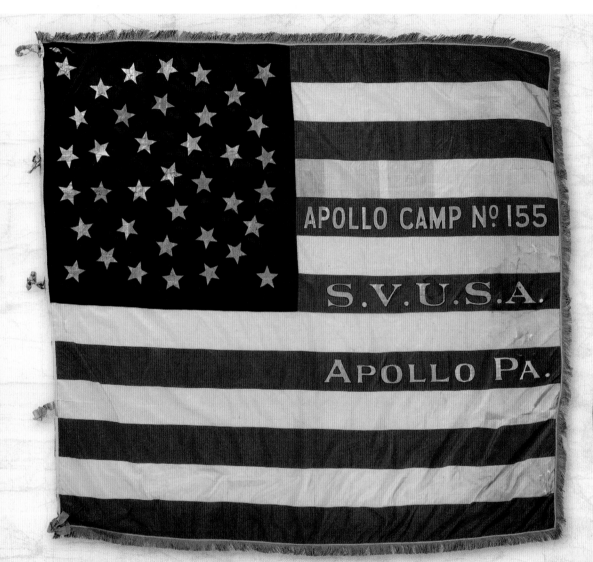

PATRIOTIC GROUP FLAGS

Starting with the Society of the Cincinnati, patriotic groups have flourished in the United States. Veterans associations, fraternities and sororities, ethnic and civic groups, and charitable and religious organizations often incorporated the Stars and Stripes into their image. Groups organized parades to promote patriotism, raised funds and bonds for troops, commemorated familial lines of colonists and revolutionaries, supported civic and neighborhood development, and sustained bonds made in military service. The Grand Army of the Republic, started in 1866, brought Union veterans together as advocates for pensions and care for disabled soldiers, support for widows and orphans, and remembrance of those who lost their lives in the Civil War. The Veterans of Foreign Wars grew to be the largest group of all, arising out of the Spanish-American War and uniting members through many subsequent wars.

This flag, which was named after General Joseph Hooker, flew at the Grand Army of the Republic in Dayton, Kentucky. The Civil War general was defeated by Robert E. Lee at Chancellorsville, Virginia.

Flags were often printed with an organization's name and location for display at a headquarters or use in parades. The silk 38-Star Flag was made for the Apollo, Pennsylvania, post of the Sons of Veterans of the United States of America. A pair of early 19th-century epaulets (left) commemorate George Washington.

General Joseph Hooker was known for allowing a group of women to follow his troops during the war, entertaining the men in the evening, leading to the false tradition that his name was the origin of the word "hooker."

THE PLEDGE OF ALLEGIANCE

The Youth's Companion, a popular 19th-century children's monthly that helped popularize poets and authors such as Emily Dickinson and Jack London, was first published in 1827. Its zenith of popularity—with a circulation upwards of one half-million copies—coincided with the 1893 Chicago Columbian Exposition. This World's Fair's spectacular success capped off the period's renewed interest in Christopher Columbus, a popular symbol for immigrants and Catholics who fought against widespread bigotry.

In 1888, *The Youth's Companion,* which coordinated children's events at the Exposition, began a campaign to increase recognition of Columbus Day, along with a drive to sell Stars and Stripes to schools for teachers to display in the nation's classrooms. Francis Bellamy, a Boston minister and socialist activist, became an editor of *The Youth's Companion* in 1891. "*The Youth's Companion* Flag Pledge," which he claimed to write,

was printed for the first time on September 8, 1892. This pledge was to be part of the program for the Columbus Day celebration in schools across the nation.

A year later, Bellamy and James Upham had an idea to promote the building of Liberty Poles on promontories of every democratic republic. Each pole would fly the host nation's flag, within a border of white, symbolizing the peaceful fruits of representative democracy. The first was built between the Twin Lights at Navesink, due south of the entrance to New York Bay, so that immigrants would see the Stars and Stripes held aloft by "liberty" upon arrival in their new land.

{ **The Pledge** was recited at the raising of the Liberty Pole at the Navesink Twin Lights.

Other poles were scheduled to appear at the Golden Gate Bridge, in France on the English Channel, and in Brazil and Switzerland, among other places. Bellamy and Upham were invited to the unfurling of the Liberty Pole flag in Navesink, where they led guests in "*The Youth's Companion* Pledge." With President Benjamin Harrison's assent, the Pledge grew in popularity as a morning salute by millions of schoolchildren.

Bellamy commented on his careful choosing of words for the Pledge, "It began as an intensive communing with salient points of our national history, from the Declaration of Independence onwards; with the makings of the Constitution . . . with the meaning of the Civil War; with the aspiration of the people . . ."

Beginning in 1892, slight changes have been made to the original verse's twenty-two words. While some questioned the legality of requiring schoolchildren to voice an oath to the United States, it was the addition of two words—"under God"—that sparked many legal challenges over the Pledge's constitutionality, most arguing it as a violation of the Establishment Clause, which separates Church and State. The debate, and subsequent law suits, continues today.

Reliability

I will be honest in word and in act. I will not lie, sneak, or pretend. I will not do wrong in the hope of not being found out. I will not take without permission what does not belong to me. I will do promptly what I have promised to do.

National Institution for Moral Instruction, Washington, D.C.

{ **A pair of flags** with photos of a schoolgirl (left) and schoolboy (opposite), C. 1910, each with personal oaths written on the white stripes.

Clean Play

I will not cheat nor will I play for keeps. I will treat my opponent with courtesy. If I play in a group game, I will play, not for my own glory, but for the success of my team and the fun of the game. I will be a good loser or a generous winner

Contributed by National Institution for Moral Instruction, Washington, D.C.

"*I pledge allegiance to my Flag and the Republic for which it stands, one nation indivisible, with liberty and justice for all.*"

ORIGINAL PLEDGE OF ALLEGIANCE
BY FRANCIS BELLAMY

Added by Bellamy in 1892.
Changed by the American Legion on Flag Day, 1923.

I pledge allegiance to my flag the flag of the United States of America, and to the Republic for which it stands, one Nation under God, indivisible, with liberty and justice for all.

Inserted by the National
Flag Conference in 1924.

President Dwight Eisenhower approves religious addition
in 1954, as advocated by the Knights of Columbus.

UTAH

45 STAR FLAG

state | UTAH
president | GROVER CLEVELAND
material | WOOL AND COTTON
date made | C.1896
admissions date | JANUARY 4, 1896
flag date | JULY 4, 1896
dimensions | 37" x 67"
period in use | 12 YEARS

UTAH 1896 •
Arizona Territory •
Oklahoma Territory •
New Mexico Territory •

This cotton flag's stars have nearly disappeared into the faded canton. The 45-Star Flag is the final Stars and Stripes of the 19th century.

Utah's "journey" to statehood was both literal and figurative. It remained a territory for half a century, its genesis as a state originating as a Christian sect in New York that propelled itself across the continent, arriving at the Great Salt Lake on July 24, 1847.

When Utah first applied as the state of Deseret in 1849, Congress rejected the application and instead outlined the federally governed Utah Territory (encompassing all of Nevada and parts of Colorado and Wyoming) as a section of the Missouri Compromise legislation. But with a rapidly multiplying Mormon community thriving in the central part of the territory, and the completion of the transcontinental railroad at Promontory Summit on May 10, 1869, the territory's periphery regions, with non-Mormon settlers, had greater success in achieving statehood, despite much smaller populations.

Americans' adamant condemnation of plural marriage, and the fierce partisan competition in territorial politics, doomed Utah's bids for statehood again and again. "As for Utah," one editorialist declared in 1890, "although much the most populous of the territories, having more than two hundred thousand inhabitants, possibly more than two hundred thirty thousand, she has yet to do her first work in destroying polygamy before aspiring to the sisterhood of States." Utah, firmly in the hands of the Republicans, finally won statehood in 1896; one of its first senators, George Q. Cannon, was the son of a Mormon Church elder who had five wives.

A gigantic 45-Star Flag was stretched across the facade of the Mormons' Great Temple in celebration of statehood in 1896.

The "Wedding of the Rails" at high noon, on May 10, 1869, brought the "Jupiter" and the "119" locomotives nose to nose at Promontory Point, Utah, and was hailed as yet another physical and symbolic unifying moment for the nation.

OKLAHOMA

46 STAR FLAG

state | OKLAHOMA
president | THEODORE ROOSEVELT
material | WOOL
date made | C.1908
admissions date | NOVEMBER 16, 1907
flag date | JULY 4, 1908
dimensions | 46" x 79"
period in use | 4 YEARS

OKLAHOMA
1907

This hand-sewn 46-Star Flag, with a hoist sleeve and original rope, testifies to the beautiful ways textiles and dyes can age. Wool parts make up the canton and stripes. Shrinking and stretching over time, caused by the action of water and air, contorted the once-rectangular flag into a trapezoid. The tug and pull of seams crinkled the edges of the stars. Deep and rich, the blue sits astride the red and white stripes that have turned sunset gold. Its cotton stars, struggling to find some order for a number that allows few divisions, are arranged in six staggered rows, generally following the recommendations of Admiral Dewey's flag commission (see page 168), although this flag maker chose to let the stars dance around a bit more freely.

Oklahoma was the last bastion into which many Native American tribes were driven by the Indian Relocation Act and along the Trail of Tears, with the guarantee that it would forever be Indian Territory, preserved in the heart of the nation. But the promise of great bounty from the Territory's fertile lands trumped once again any promise of sovereignty, and soon a plan was hatched to allow homesteaders to storm the state and grab land to call their own.

On April 22, 1889, the Land Rush began. Settlers, known as "Boomers," lined up on the Texas or Arkansas borders and, when the sun reached its zenith at noon, stampeded across the border to stake claims. ("Sooners" were settlers who had illegally crossed earlier to claim prime sites.) The Santa Fe Railroad, which had already cut through the Indian Territory,

carried carloads of men and women to blank town sites, scratched out with building plots. "The coaches were so crowded," one reporter observed, "that many men were compelled to squeeze through the windows in order to get a fair start at the head of the crowd. Almost before the train had come to a standstill the cars were emptied. In their haste and eagerness, men fell over each other in heaps, others stumbled and fell headlong, while many ran forward so blindly and impetuously that it was not until they had passed the best of the town lots that they came to a realization of their actions."

One town, Guthrie, was established that very day. Settlers who woke the next morning were suddenly members of a ten-thousand-person community, albeit a dusty city whose dwellings were covered wagons and tents. Eighteen years later, having drawn tens of thousands of settlers, landlocked Oklahoma became a state.

This photograph shows an 1889 traffic jam of men, horses, wagons, and carts during the Oklahoma Land Rush free-for-all. A generation later, the dust would soak up all of the fertile land's moisture, sending many "Okies" west on an exodus of their own.

NEW MEXICO

47 STAR FLAG

state | NEW MEXICO
president | WILLIAM HOWARD TAFT
material | WOOL
date made | C.1912
admissions date | JANUARY 6, 1912
flag date | UNOFFICIAL
dimensions | 96" x 132"
period in use | N/A

NEW MEXICO
1912

Wrested from Mexico in 1848 and denoted a Territory on September 9, 1850, New Mexico had a longer path to statehood than any other official territory, taking sixty-two years total.

Under the influence of the Catholic diocese of Santa Fe, New Mexico flirted with pro-slavery policies, but by the Civil War the Territory had committed itself to the Union. Texas Confederates, however, hoping to claim all of the Southwest for their cause, invaded New Mexico. Ill-equipped to defend the city, the governor fled Sante Fe. "You can imagine . . . what I felt," said one nun who remained to defend her convent, "on seeing all our troops leave [with] that banner under whose shadow I had been reared."

The Confederate raiders easily captured the city, where they hoisted their "piratical banner." Historian Paul Horgan, in his biography of Bishop Juan Bautista Lamy, described how Colorado volunteers, led by Colonel John Chivington, swept down from the north and dislodged the Texans from the Territory. On April 20, 1861, the Stars and Stripes was hoisted above the Plaza.

{ **This machine-stitched** wool 47-Star Flag, even though it was unofficial, embodies the regularity and orderliness proscribed by President Taft's Executive Order.

{ **The Stars and Stripes** fly above a fortification near Santa Fe in 1862.

ARIZONA

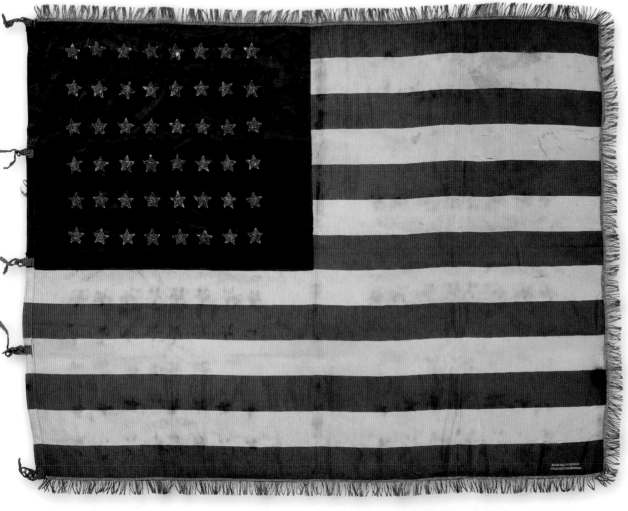

This satin and sequin 48-Star banner has red silk tie ribbons, gold fringe, and is embroidered with the name "Principessa Jolanda."

After the Mexican War, southern portions of Arizona and New Mexico were left in limbo, claimed by both sides. In 1853, President Franklin Pierce dispatched James Gadsden to Mexico where, with ten million dollars, he secured the land for the United States. As early as 1857, rumors began circulating that settlers in the Gadsden Purchase were organizing to separate from New Mexico as the Arizona Territory. Other rumors hinted that southern California might even split away and allow slave states access to the Pacific.

In his State of the Union message to Congress in 1857, with Kansas in crisis and Utah spinning out of federal control, President James Buchanan pledged to safeguard American interests in the Gadsden Purchase. But a bid by the Arizona Colonization Company failed to win support for its territorial ambition. Nonetheless, in 1860, Arizona organized a legislature, and on April 11, 1861, voted themselves out of the Union, joining the Confederacy.

With an announcement on February 18, 1863, that Arizona "has been swept clean of the rebels," President Abraham Lincoln moved quickly and proclaimed a federally sanctioned Arizona Territory. Forty-nine years later, in 1912, Arizona became the forty-eighth state, completing the continental United States.

48

STAR FLAG

state | ARIZONA
president | WILLIAM HOWARD TAFT
material | SILK
date made | C.1912
admissions date | FEBRUARY 14, 1912
flag date | JULY 4, 1912
dimensions | 36" x 60"
period in use | 47 YEARS

ARIZONA 1912

Gadsden Purchase

EXECUTIVE ORDER OF 1912

When Oklahoma became the forty-sixth state in 1907, and as the nation's military and government agencies became more complex, the first steps were undertaken to regulate how the flag of the United States should be designed. Admiral George Dewey was entrusted by the War Department to lead a committee, whose recommendation was for the stars to be arranged in six staggered rows of seven or eight stars each.

But the admission of New Mexico invalidated their design, and once again the committee met to suggest an agreeable way to lay out the 48-Star Flag. Six rows of eight stars each, arranged evenly, seemed the logical choice. Each star would be oriented identically, with one point up. All flags made for the government or military would also adhere to a set of proportions and sizes. President William Howard Taft concurred and signed an Executive Order on June 24, 1912.

The Flag Act coincided with the growing desire of Americans to preserve important historic flags. For instance, on March 6, 1912, flags that were flown on Commodore Oliver Hazard Perry's ship during the War of 1812 battle on Lake Erie were hung in the House chamber, where its members voted unanimously to provide thirty thousand dollars for the neglected textiles, owned by the Naval Academy. Restoration work, they estimated, would require one hundred needlewomen working one hundred days.

Admiral of the Navy
George Dewey (1837–1917), the highest ranking naval officer in history, won national acclaim for his victory in Manila during the Spanish-American War, leading to the establishment of the Philippines as a U.S. protectorate in 1898.

This 48-Star Flag was made according to the specifications of the Flag Act of 1912. The official flag for forty-seven years, the 48-Star Flag's longevity was surpassed by the 50-Star Flag in 2007.

After losing his ship *Lawrence* on Lake Erie, Commodore Perry carried its main flag, and an ensign bearing the famous words "Don't Give Up The Ship," in a rowboat to another vessel in his fleet, the *Niagara*. His younger brother, Commodore Matthew Perry, became famous for his voyages to Japan.

President William Howard Taft spoke at the Manassas Court House in Virginia on November 10, 1911, to commemorate the Civil War battles fought there fifty years before. In 1921, Taft became the only president to serve on the U.S. Supreme Court, nominated by President Warren Harding and unanimously confirmed by the Senate as Chief Justice.

NATIONAL AND PATRIOTIC HOLIDAYS

THE FOURTH OF JULY

Although the Declaration of Independence was approved by Congress on July 2, 1776, and its famous parchment copy was signed by delegates over a period of weeks beginning in August, it was July 4th that became the day Americans identified, from the beginning, with their bid for freedom and independence.

The first Fourth of July was celebrated with dinners, toasts, artillery

{ A young American gathers her supplies to celebrate the Fourth in 1906.

share Independence Day and celebrate unity, nationhood, and liberty (see page 74). During World War I, Fourth of July celebrations were a time to demonstrate patriotism and support for the troops. On July 5, 1916, the *New York Times* reported that the previous day's observances were "the biggest as well as the 'sanest' Fourth of July celebration this city has ever seen. Americanism was its dominant note and the flag almost wholly supplanted the firecracker as the exponent of patriotic fervor."

FLAG DAY

On June 14, 1917, one hundred fifty years after the Continental Congress passed the first flag legislation, President Woodrow Wilson led the first formal nationwide observance of Flag Day. Although the day had been informally observed by schoolchildren, local governments, and patriotic organizations in the 19th century, it was not until the surge of patriotism and recruitment efforts leading up to World War I that Wilson encouraged the entire country to recognize the Flag's birthday. (On August 3, 1949, President Harry S. Truman signed an Act of Congress designating every June 14 as National Flag Day.)

A silk ribbon emblazoned with a Bald Eagle and a Stars and Stripes commemorated the especially poignant Fourth of July following the end of the Civil War and Abraham Lincoln's death.

To inspire national unity following Pearl Harbor on the Fourth of July 1942, hundreds of magazines devoted their covers to the Stars and Stripes.

salutes, and pyrotechnics in 1777. Throughout the first years of the Republic, however, Independence Day—first called that in 1791—became a focus of partisan rancor. Federalists fervently celebrated the anniversary, while Democrat-Republicans preferred less jubilant celebrations, if none at all.

But the July 4th deaths of Thomas Jefferson and John Adams—bitter political opponents who reconciled with each other in old age—helped inspire Americans to

President Woodrow Wilson leads a Preparedness Parade with a 48-Star Flag.

Addressing the nation with the spectre of war rising, President Wilson delivered the following speech on the grounds of the Washington Monument:

{ **Five parade flags** designed for mounting on a bicycle frame or an automobile hood.

❝ *My fellow citizens, we meet to celebrate Flag Day because this Flag which we honor under which we serve is the emblem of our unity, our power, our thought and purpose as a Nation. It has no other character than that which we give it from generation to generation. The choices are ours. It floats in majestic silence above the hosts that execute these choices, whether in peace or in war.*

And yet, though silent, it speaks to us—speaks to us of the past, of the men and women who went before us and of the records they wrote upon it. We celebrate the day of its birth, and from its birth until now it has witnessed a great history, has floated on high the symbol of great events, of a great plan of life, worked out by a great people. We are about to carry it into battle, to lift it where it will draw the fire of our enemies. We are about to bid thousands, hundreds of thousands, it may be millions of our men— the young, the strong, the capable men of the

Nation—to go forth and die beneath it on the fields of blood far away—for what?

For some unaccustomed thing? For something for which it has never sought the fire before? American armies were never before sent across the seas. Why are they sent now? For some new purpose, for which this great Flag has never been carried before, or for some old, familiar, heroic purpose for which it has seen men, its own men, die on every battlefield upon which Americans have borne arms since the Revolution?

These are questions which must be answered. We are Americans. We in turn serve America, and can serve her with no private purpose. We must use her Flag as she has always used it. We are accountable at the bar of history and must plead in utter frankness what purpose it is we seek to serve. ❞

As Wilson made his speech on that first Flag Day in 1917, General John Pershing was landing in France at the head of the American Expeditionary Force.

Other National Holidays

★ ★ ★ ★ ★ ★ ★ ★ ★ ★ ★ ★ ★ ★ ★

Thanksgiving
Observed: Third Thursday of November
Established: 1939

Washington's Birthday (Presidents' Day)
Observed: Third Monday of February
Established: 1880–1885

Labor Day
Observed: First Monday in September
Established: June 28, 1894

Memorial Day (Decoration Day)
Observed: Last Monday of May
Established: 1880s

Independence Day (Fourth of July)
July 4

Veterans Day (Armistice Day)
Observed: November 11
Established: 1919

Columbus Day
Commemorates: October 12, 1492
Observed: Second Monday in October
Established: 1937

Birthday of Martin Luther King, Jr.
January 15, established on November 2, 1983

{ **Berkeley Plantation,** built in the 17th century and the home to the Harrison lineage of statesmen and presidents, is believed to be the first place where Thanksgiving was formally held. "Taps" was also composed at this estate on the James River.

FLAGS THAT MADE HISTORY

{ **Printed paper banners** like this one welcomed people to United Service Organizations (U.S.O.) parties, bond rallies, and recruitment drives.

WORLD WAR II FLAGS

Perhaps no image in American history can compete with the resonance of the flag being raised on Mount Suribachi on Iwo Jima after a fearsome invasion and battle. Associated Press photographer Joe Rosenthal captured the image on February 23, 1945, as five U.S. Marines and one Navy corpsman elevated the Stars and Stripes, planting its pipe in a mound of jagged rocks and debris, buffeted by the wind. When it was published, the photograph was printed in hundreds of newspapers and magazines and captured the hearts of the nation. Rosenthal was awarded the Pulitzer Prize, and the surviving men captured on the black and white film returned to the United States, as ordered by President Franklin Roosevelt, to participate in bond rallies to raise desperately needed funds.

{ **When the Japanese** formally surrendered to General Douglas MacArthur and Admiral Chester Nimitz on the USS *Missouri*, two American flags were displayed on deck. One was a standard 48-Star Flag; the other was the flag that Commodore Perry flew on his frigate when he arrived in Japan in 1853.

{ **Families with sons or daughters** in service during WWII displayed Living Service Flags, like this one, in home windows. Each blue star represented a family member in service during times of war. In the event of death, a gold star would be superimposed, leaving a blue border.

The Marine Corps War Memorial rendered the two-dimensional image (far left) into 100 tons of three-dimensional bronze, sculpted by Felix W. de Weldon. The Memorial was dedicated on November 10, 1954, by President Dwight D. Eisenhower.

{ **This cotton 48-Star** Flag of World War II vintage mixed gold and red stripes.

{ **A cotton banner** emblazoned with a proud eagle welcomes troops home.

FLAGS THAT MADE HISTORY

48-Star Flags were used throughout World War II, as Alaska was still a territory and Hawaii was not yet a state when Pearl Harbor was attacked by the Japanese. This 48-Star Flag was rolled and bound tightly with twine and sent to Toulon in 1944, for parades celebrating the liberation of France. The flag has never been unrolled.

Toulon
Aug 1944

Parisians celebrate the liberation of their city—in August, 1944, by U.S. troops— with an American flag and a French flag.

49
STAR FLAG

state | ALASKA
president | DWIGHT D. EISENHOWER
material | SILK
date made | C.1959
admissions date | JANUARY 3, 1959
flag date | JULY 4, 1959
dimensions | 8" x 11"
period in use | 1 YEAR

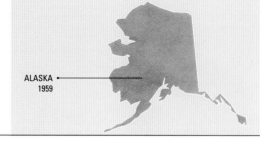

ALASKA
1959

ALASKA

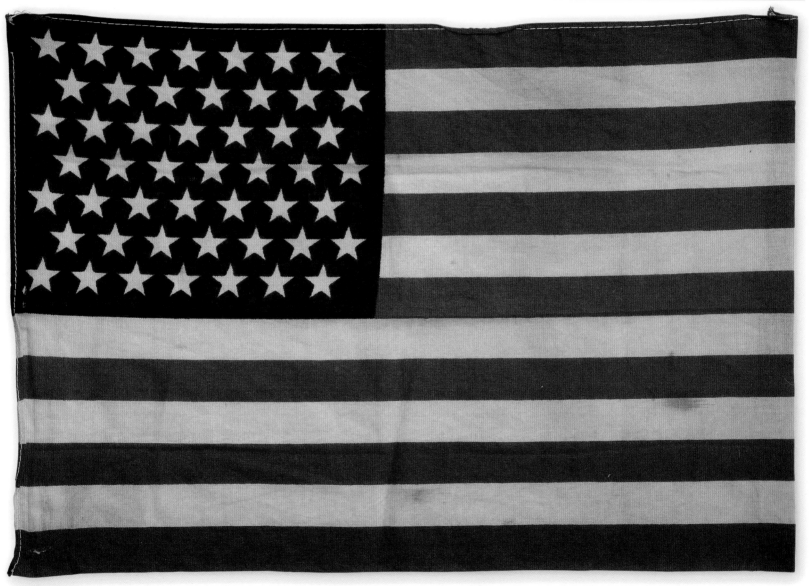

Seven staggered rows of seven stars were chosen as the most rational and vibrant design for the 49-Star Flag. When President Eisenhower signed Alaska into the Union, the flag that had been present in the Oval Office was sent to Philadelphia, where it was hoisted above Independence Hall on the Fourth of July.

This painting of **William Seward** by Emmanuel Leutze, most famous for his depiction of Washington crossing the Delaware, was sent as a gift to the Secretary by prominent New York businessmen who speculated on great profits to be had in the Alaskan wilderness.

The **Stars and Stripes** and a moose head adorn the U.S. Marshal's Office in distant Seward, Alaska, at the head of the Iditarod Trail, where many gold prospectors landed.

Secretary of State William Seward oversaw the purchase of Alaska for President Andrew Johnson from Russia on April 9, 1867. Many Americans questioned such an extravagant purchase—$7.2 million for over 350 million acres—of such a remote and frozen expanse. "King Andy and his man Billy," one cartoon trumpeted, "lay in a great stock of Russian ice in order to cool down the Congressional majority."

The Department of Alaska was variously administered by the Treasury, the Army, and the Navy until 1884, when it became the District of Alaska. In 1896, news of Klondike gold drew adventurers and prospectors to Alaska, boosting the population to support the designation of the Territory of Alaska in 1912.

In 1927, Benny Benson, a thirteen-year-old student in Seward, Alaska, won a contest to design the Territory of Alaska Flag. Recalling the First Flag Act, his unanimously chosen design featured an actual constellation of stars. "The blue field," he explained, "is for the Alaska sky and the forget-me-not, an Alaskan flower. The North Star is for the future state of Alaska, the most northerly in the union. The Dipper is for the Great Bear—symbolizing strength."

After World War II (when Japan briefly occupied Alaskan islands until routed by American fighters), President Dwight D. Eisenhower signed the Alaska Statehood Bill on January 3, 1959.

Standardizing the Flag and Its Display

★ ★ ★ ★ ★ ★ ★ ★ ★ ★ ★ ★ ★ ★ ★ ★ ★

On the same day of Alaska's admission, President Eisenhower signed an Executive Order that spelled out more precisely than ever before how the Stars and Stripes should be designed. The design was approved by a committee headed by Cabinet secretaries with help from the Heraldic Branch of the Quartermaster General office. By the end of the summer, however, the 49-Star Flag would have less than a year to fly, as Eisenhower shepherded Hawaii into the Union.

An Executive Order signed on August 21, 1959, accepted the design of the nation's current 50-Star Flag, including eleven different sizes of flags. The same committee that had decided on the 49-Star Flag, when presented with a design devised by a seventeen-year-old Ohio student, Robert Heft, by his Congressman, accepted the logic of his 50-star arrangement.

Nine staggered rows of either six or seven stars pleased President Eisenhower as well, and the 50-Star Flag became official.

President Dwight Eisenhower inspects a 49-Star Flag presented to him in the Oval Office.

HAWAII

The only state composed entirely of islands, the Kingdom of Hawaii attracted American interest in the early 19th century, when explorers and missionaries sailed the Pacific. American and European settlers, who consolidated power through their profits from sugar and pineapple plantations, forced an overthrow of the kingdom in 1893, bolstered by the presence of U.S. Marines, and established the Republic of Hawaii, with Sanford Dole, cousin of the pineapple magnate, named its president.

On July 6, 1898, President William McKinley, whose victory in the Spanish American War led to an expansion of American territory, approved the annexation of the Territory of Hawaii, to be governed by Dole until 1903. After Amelia Earhart brought great attention to Hawaii by her solo flight from Wheeler Field in Honolulu to Oakland, California, in only 18¼ hours in 1935, Hawaiians first pursued statehood. But Southern legislators, adamant not to admit a state with a racial minority in the majority, stripped away necessary votes. Six years later, however, the events of Pearl Harbor cemented Hawaii in the hearts and minds of Americans, and its statehood was finally accepted in 1959.

A Stars and Stripes flies over the capsized USS *Oklahoma* following the attack on Pearl Harbor. In 1958, President Eisenhower authorized the USS *Arizona* Memorial, a structure that rests atop the partially sunken U.S. Naval vessel. An American flag flies high as the focal point of the memorial, in remembrance of all those who lost their lives during the December 7, 1941 attacks.

50 STAR FLAG

state | HAWAII
president | DWIGHT D. EISENHOWER
material | WOOL
date made | C.1960
admissions date | AUGUST 21, 1959
flag date | JULY 4, 1960
dimensions | 96" x 144"
period in use | 47 + YEARS

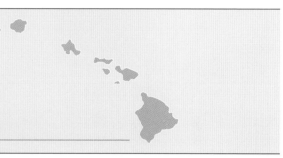

HAWAII 1959 ←

{ The flag of the Republic of Hawaii, which incorporated the British Union Jack, was struck from the Iolani Palace and replaced with a 45-Star Flag in 1898.

{ This 50-Star Flag was made according to the rules of President Eisenhower's Executive Order (see page 177).

FLAG ETIQUETTE

How one should properly display, care for, and treat the American flag is known as flag etiquette. While there are no laws that explicitly govern flag etiquette, the guidelines for flag etiquette have been developed as the Flag Code of the United States of America, first adopted in 1923, and periodically amended with authorization from the president.

Some of its key guidelines include the following:

"No disrespect should be shown to the flag of the United States of America; the flag should not be dipped to any person or thing. Regimental colors, State flags, and organization or institutional flags are to be dipped as a mark of honor.

"The flag should never be used as wearing apparel, bedding, or drapery. It should never be festooned, drawn back, nor up, in folds, but always allowed to fall free. Bunting of blue, white, and red, always arranged with the blue above, the white in the middle, and the red below, should be used for covering a speaker's desk, draping the front of the platform, and for decoration in general. The flag should never be used as a covering for a ceiling.

"No part of the flag should ever be used as a costume or athletic uniform. However, a flag patch may be affixed to the uniform of military personnel, firemen, policemen, and members of patriotic organizations. The flag represents a living country and is itself considered a living thing. Therefore, the lapel flag pin being a replica, should be worn on the left lapel near the heart. The flag should never be fastened, displayed, used, or stored in such a manner as to permit it to be easily torn, soiled, or damaged in any way.

"The flag should never have placed upon it, nor on any part of it, nor attached to it any mark, insignia, letter, word, figure, design, picture, or drawing of any nature.

"The flag should never be used as a receptacle for receiving, holding, carrying, or delivering anything. The flag should never be used for advertising purposes in any manner whatsoever. It should not be embroidered on such articles as cushions or handkerchiefs and the like, printed or otherwise impressed on paper napkins or boxes or anything that is designed for temporary use and discard. Advertising signs should not be fastened to a staff or halyard from which the flag is flown.

"The flag, when it is in such condition that it is no longer a fitting emblem for display, should be destroyed in a dignified way, preferably by burning."

HOISTING, LOWERING, OR PASSING OF FLAG

"During the ceremony of hoisting or lowering the flag, or when the flag is passing in a parade or in review, all present except those in uniform should face the flag and stand at attention with the right hand over the heart. Those present in uniform should render the military salute. When not in uniform, men should remove their headdress with their right hand and hold it at the left shoulder, the hand being over the heart. Aliens should stand at attention. The salute to the flag in a moving column should be rendered as the flag passes."

FOLDING THE FLAG

"Although there is no civilian rule regarding the proper way to fold a flag, the military custom of folding a flag in a triangular shape is now commonly accepted as the preferred way to fold a flag. Many historic flags are stored flat or rolled on tubes to prevent creasing. When historic flags are folded, they should be unfolded and re-folded periodically to prevent sharp creases from forming and damaging the textiles."

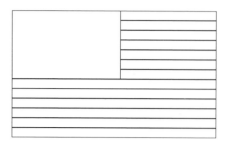
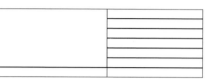

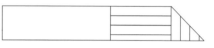

1) **Fold lower half** up onto the canton. 2) Fold lengthwise again, with the canton facing out. 3) Fold upper corner into a 45° triangle. 4) Repeat the triangular fold. Tuck the remaining end of the flag into the fold.

When flown from a vertical mast, the canton must always be in the upper left corner. Flags should be flown upside down as a signal of distress.

FLAGS AT HALF-MAST

"Flags flown at half-mast or half-staff are a symbol of respect following the death of a person of national importance or an important foreign dignitary. The decision to fly flags at half-mast can be authorized only by the president (for nationwide observance) or a governor (for statewide observance.) No private citizen should fly flags at half-mast to honor or indicate personal loss.

"The correct method of setting a flag at half-mast is to hoist it to the top of its mast, pause, and then lower the flag to the mid-point of the mast. At the end of the day, the flag should be raised to the top of the mast before being lowered and folded. (On Memorial Day, flags are flown at half-mast until noon, and then at full height until sunset.)

"When the flag is used to cover a casket, the union should be at the head and over the left shoulder. The flag should not be lowered into the grave or allowed to touch the ground."

HALF-MAST DURATIONS

30 days **President or former President**
10 days **Vice President**
    Supreme Court Chief Justice
    Speaker of the House
Period between death and burial
    Supreme Court Justice
    Cabinet Secretary
    Former Vice President
    Governor
Day of death and following day
    Member of Congress

DISPLAYING THE FLAG

"It is customary to display the flag only from sunrise to sunset on buildings and on stationary flagstaffs in the open. However, when a patriotic effect is desired, the flag may be displayed 24 hours a day if properly illuminated during the hours of darkness. Flags should be raised briskly and lowered ceremoniously.

"The flag should be displayed daily on or near the main entrance of every public institution, near every polling place on election days, and during school days in or near every schoolhouse.

"The flag, when carried in a procession with another flag or flags, should be either on the marching right; that is, the flag's own right, or, if there is a line of other flags, in front of the center of that line. The flag should not be displayed on a parade float except from a staff. The flag should not be draped over a vehicle, train car, or a boat. When the flag is displayed on a car, the staff shall be fixed firmly to the chassis or clamped to the right fender.

"No other flag or pennant should be placed above or, if on the same level, to the right of the U.S. flag, except during church services conducted by naval chaplains at sea, when the church pennant may be flown above the flag. No person shall display the flag of the United Nations or any other national or international flag equal, above, or in a position of superior prominence or honor to, or in place of, the U.S. flag at any place within the United States or any territory or possession thereof, except at the U.N. headquarters, where its flag is given prominence over all national flags."

"The U.S. flag, when it is displayed with another flag against a wall from crossed staffs, should be on the right, the flag's own right, and its staff should be in front of the staff of the other flag. The U.S. flag should be at the center and at the highest point of the group when a number of flags of states or localities or pennants of societies are grouped and displayed from staffs.

"When flags of states, cities, or localities, or pennants of societies are flown on the same halyard as the U.S. flag, the latter should always be at the peak. When the flags are flown from adjacent staffs, the U.S. flag should be hoisted first and lowered last. When flags of two or more nations are displayed, they are to be flown from separate staffs of the same height. The flags should be of approximately equal size. International usage forbids the display of the flag of one nation above that of another nation in time of peace."

If a flag is flown vertically from a pole extending from a structure, suspended over a street, or displayed in a room, the canton should appear, from the viewer's perspective, in the upper left hand corner.

When visible from both sides, the flag's canton should be oriented to the north or east.

GLOSSARY

TEXTILE TERMS

Textile terms are often confusing, since definitions and translations change throughout history. Terms are also often used interchangeably to denote different things; for instance, "ply," when used as a noun or verb, has several different meanings. Some basic textile terms are fundamental to the history of antique American flags, and follow here.

drape
The aesthetic quality of the manner in which fabric hangs or furls.

fabric (cloth)
The end-product of the spinning and weaving process.

fibers
Strands or filaments that are used to make yarns and eventually fabric. Fibers can generally be divided into three types: plant or cellulose, such as cotton or linen; animal or protein, such as wool or silk; or synthetic, such as rayon or nylon.

loom
A machine or device for weaving yarn into fabric. Hand looms can range from very small to large free-standing contraptions operated by hands and feet, or completely automated machines. However complex, the loom's fundamental purpose is to hold warp yarns in tension so that weft yarns can be interwoven to create fabric.

needlework
The skill of hand-stitching textiles or embroidering.

pick
A length of weft yarn.

ply
As a noun, an individual yarn in a "plied" yarn. (In fabric, a ply also denotes a single thickness in a layer of fabric.) As a verb, to ply is to twist single yarns together to form, for instance, a 2-ply yarn.

rope
A braided, or plaited, length of fibers that form a strong linear textile.

seam
Stitching that joins pieces of fabric.

selvedge
A tightly woven border that runs along the warp and prevents the fabric from unravelling or fraying.

spinning wheel
A hand-, foot-, or machine-powered device used to spin threads.

staple
A term that denotes the length of fibrous materials.

stitch
A loop, or link, of thread made by drawing a needle through fabric. Stitches generally fall into two categories: ones made by hand and ones made by machine.

thread
Strong, tightly twisted yarn used for sewing.

twist
The manner, direction, and tightness of yarn spinning. Yarns either have a clockwise (Z) twist or a counter-clockwise (S) twist. (Yarns are also defined by the number of plys that are twisted together.)

warp
Yarns that are held in tension longitudinally on a loom. (Warp yarns are also known as *filling*, or, in silk production, *organzine*.)

weft
Yarns woven over and under warp yarns during the weaving process. *Tram* are silk weft yarns.

yarn
Spun lengths of wool, cotton, linen, or silk fibers, prepared for weaving, knitting, and sewing. Lengths of yarn are woven on a loom to form fabric.

DYE TERMS

affinity
The capacity of a certain kind of fiber to accept and retain a dye.

dyestuff
A substance, either natural or synthetic, that is used to color fibers and fabric. Natural dyestuffs are derived from animals or botanical and mineral sources, while synthetic dyes are fabricated through chemical processes.

fastness
The ability of a fabric and its dye to maintain its original color and intensity. *Lightfastness* measures fading due to exposure to light; *washfastness* indicates a fabric color's ability to withstand moisture and washing.

fixing
The washing, heating, or oxidizing step in the dyeing process that sets the dye.

fugitive
The opposite of fastness. The propensity of a dye to quickly fade because of insufficient bonding to the textile substrate.

mordant
A chemical substance that facilitates or enhances the chemical bonding of a dye to a substrate.

substrate
The fiber or fabric which receives the dye.

BIBLIOGRAPHY

Butler, Benjamin F. *Butler's Book*. Boston: A.M. Thayer & Co., 1892.

Canby, George, and Lloyd Balderston. *The Evolution of the American Flag*. Philadelphia: Ferris and Leach, 1909.

Cooper, Grace Rogers. *Thirteen-Star Flags*. Washington, DC: Smithsonian Press, 1973.

Corcoran, Michael. *For Which it Stands*. New York: Simon & Schuster, 2002.

Cresswell, Donald H. *The American Revolution in Drawings and Prints*. Library of Congress, 1975.

Dawson, Henry. *Mass Violence in America: The Sons of Liberty in New York*. Arno Press, 1969.

Drake, Joseph Rodman. *The American Flag: An Anecdotal Biography of the American Flag*. New York: James Gregory, 1861.

Ecker, Grace Dunlop. *A Portrait of Old Georgetown*. Richmond: Dietz Press, 1951.

Fallows, Samuel. *Story of the American Flag*. Boston: Educational Publishing Company, 1903.

Fischer, David Hackett. *Liberty and Freedom*. New York: Oxford University Press, 2004.

Furlong, Rear Admiral William Rea and Commodore Byron McCandless. *So Proudly We Hail*. Washington, DC: Smithsonian Institution Press, 1981.

Garfield, Simon. *Mauve, How one Man Invented a Color that Changed the World*. New York: W.W. Norton & Company, 2000.

Glick, Carl and Ollie Rogers. *The Story of Our Flag*. New York: G. P. Putnam's Sons, 1964.

Grant, Nancy S. *Old Glory*. New York: Crescent Books, 1992.

Greenfield, Amy Butler. *A Perfect Red, Empire, Espionage and the Quest for the Color of Desire*. New York: Harper Perennial, 2005.

Gross, Linda P. and Theresa R. Snyder. *Philadelphia's 1876 Centennial Exposition*. Arcadia, 2005.

Gue, Rev. George W. *Our Country's Flag*. Davenport, Iowa: Egbert, Fidlar, & Chambers Publishers, 1890.

Guthrie, Addie. *The Story of Our Flag*. Chicago: A. G. Weaver, 1898.

Hamilton, Schuyler. *The History of the National Flag of the United States of America*. Philadelphia: Lippincott, Granbo and Co, 1853.

Hendricks, J. Edwin. *Charles Thomson*. Farleigh Dickinson, 1979.

Hindle, Brooke. *David Rittenhouse*. Princeton University Press, 1964.

Holzman, Robert S. *Stormy Ben Butler*. New York: The Macmillan Company, 1954.

Horner, Harlan Hoyt. *The American Flag*. Albany: State of New York, 1910.

Ide, Emily Katharine. *The History and Significance of the American Flag*. Cambridge, Massachusetts: Huntington Art Press, 1916.

Kagan, Hilde Heun. *American Heritage Pictorial Atlas of United States History*. McGraw Hill, 1966.

Kerrick, Harrison Summers. *The Flag of the United States—Your Flag and Mine*. Columbus, Ohio: The Champlin Printing Co. 1925.

Ketchum, Alton. *Uncle Sam: The Man and the Legend*. New York: Hill & Wang, 1959.

King, Henry C. *Geared to the Stars: The Evolution of Planetariums, Orreries, and Astronomical Clocks*. Toronto: University of Toronto Press, 1978.

Maberry, Robert. *Texas Flags*. College Station, Texas: A&M University Press, 2001.

Malone, Dumas. *Jefferson and His Time: The Sage of Monticello*. Boston: Little Brown, 1981.

Mastai, Boleslaw and Maria-Louise D'Otrange. *The Stars and the Stripes*. New York: Knopf, 1973.

Montgomery, Florence. *Textiles in America*. New York: W.W. Norton & Company, 1984.

Muller, Charles G. *The Darkest Day: 1814*. Philadelphia: J.B. Lippincott Company, 1963.

Orisz, Joel L. *The Eagle that Is Forgotten*. Wolfeboro: Bowers and Merena Galleries, 1988.

Nieto-Galan, Agusti. *Colouring Textiles, A History of Natural Dyestuffs in Industrial Europe*. Dordrecht: Kluwer Academic Publishers, 2001.

Pastoreau, Michel. *The Devil's Cloth: A History of Stripes*. New York: Washington Square Press, 1991.

Pettit, Florence Harvey. *America's Printed & Painted Fabrics 1600–1900*. New York: Hastongs House, 1970.

Pettit, Forence Harvey. *America's Indigo Blues, Resist-Printed and Dyed Textiles of the Eighteenth Century*. Hastings House, 1974.

Pitch, Anthony S. *The Burning of Washington, the British Invasion of 1814*. Annapolis: Naval Institute Press, 1998.

Preble, George Henry, Rear Admiral, U.S.N. *History of the Flag of the United States of America* Boston: A. Williams and Company, 1880.

Purvis, Thomas L. *Revolutionary America: 1763–1800*. New York: Facts on File, 1995.

Quaife, Milo, Melvin J. Weig and Roy E. Appleman. *The History of the United States Flag*. Philadelphia: Harper and Row, 1961.

Robinson, Stuart. *A History of Dyed Textiles*. Cambridge: M.I.T. Press, 1969.

Schermerhorn, Frank Earle. *American and French Flags of the Revolution, 1775–1783*. Philadelphia: Pennsylvania Society of Sons of the Revolution, 1948.

Sedeen, Margaret. *Star-Spangled Banner*. Washington, DC: National Geographic, 1993.

Sellers, Charles Coleman. *Mr. Peale's Museum*. New York: W. W. Norton & Company, 1980.

Sheads, Scott. *Fort McHenry*. Mount Pleasant, SC: Nautical & Aviation Publishing, 1995.

Sifton, Paul G. *Historiographer to the United States: The Revolutionary Letterbook of Pierre Eugene du Simitiere*. New York: Vantage Press, 1987.

Smith, Francis Scott Key. *A Sketch of Francis Scott Key, with a Glimpse of his Ancestors*. Washington, DC: c.1908.

Tabbert, Mark A. *American Freemasons*. New York: New York University Press, 2005.

INDEX

ACKNOWLEDGMENTS

When we embarked on this journey four years ago, we had little idea how many people would graciously offer their ideas and enthusiasm. Many thanks first go to the team at DK, particularly Carl Raymond, Anja Schmidt, Dirk Kaufman, Jessica Park, and Chrissy McIntyre, whose enthusiasm and hard work were abundant and focused from the very beginning.

We began to conceptualize this book in New York City, while watching people react to the windows of Bergdorf-Goodman on 5th Avenue, where many flags from our collection were displayed over a week to commemorate the first anniversary of 9/11. People found them so compelling, which convinced us that a book might bring the same reaction. We thank Ron Frasch, Bergdorf Goodman's CEO, Linda Fargo, and David Hoey, for his window-design magic.

We know vivid photographs are essential to give readers a sense of each flag's character, a task that Jacob Termansen and Pia Marie Molbech have ably accomplished.

Laura M. McGuire, our research assistant, contributed mightily to the project with her sharp eye and critical insight. Authors Steven Harrigan, H.W. Brands, Henry Moeller, S. Rabbit Goody, Amy Butler Greenfield, Robert Maberry, Jr., David Hackett Fischer, and Alfred Young all provided feedback and ideas.

Many scholars, archivists, and curators offered their expertise. These include: Marilyn Zoidis, formerly Curator, Star-Spangled Banner Project at the Smithsonian's National Museum of American History, now Senior Curator of the Kentucky Historical Society; Louis E. Jordan III, Director of Special Collections at the University of Notre Dame; Scott S. Sheads at the Fort McHenry National Monument; Jacqueline DeGroff at Drexel University; Andy Masich, President and CEO of the Historical Society of Western Pennsylvania; Ross Kronenbitter at the Heinz History Center; Linda Eaton at the Winterthur Museum & Country Estate; Jack Gumbrecht at The Historical Society of Pennsylvania; Lisa Acker Moulder at the Betsy Ross House; Anna Berkes of Monticello; Valerie-Anne Lutz at the American Philosophical Society; Calle Raspuzzi at the Bennington Museum; Christine Messing of George Washington's Mount Vernon Estate & Gardens; Candace Adelson at the Tennessee State Museum; Esther Méthé of The Textile Museum; Karen Herbaugh and Clare Sheridan at the American Textile History Museum; George Hicks, former Executive Director of the National Civil War Museum; Joyce Doody, Executive Director, and Clark Rogers of the National Flag Foundation; Fonda Ghiardi-Thomsen, textile analysis and preservation expert; and J. Kenneth Kohn, American Flag expert, consultant and friend. Finally, John Pollack at the University of Pennsylvania, Laurel Masten Cantor at Princeton University, Thomas Hughes, and Bill Mills all provided information about David Rittenhouse and his orreries.

In Pennsylvania, Ray Werner for "kneading" the idea of the book and providing unending encouragement; Retired Major Graham Morgan, a true patriot and one of our heroes; Mike Blackwood and everyone at Gateway Health Plan; Catherine Bene of WGCB, PBS affiliate. Lest we forget the inspiration of friends: John Bremyer, a Kansan, who proudly ushered Perry's Flag to the USS *Missouri* for the Japanese surrender; Retired Corporal Joseph Fennimore of Florida and Retired Lieutenant Colonel Sam Lombardo of Pennsylvania, who fabricated American Flags amidst the German battlefields during WWII; and Sergio Boldrin, Venetian mask maker and patriotic friend of America.

In Texas, many thanks to Willard & Corde Hanzlik, Diana Keller, Mary Margaret Farabee, Jason Gouliard, Linda Moore; Alex Caragonne and Margie Shackelford; Laura and Bobby Cadwallader; Eden and Hal Box; Heather McKinney, George Elliman, Vance Muse, Jeffrey Chusid, Pankaj Gupta and Christine Mueller; Kevin Milstead, Ann Bahan, Samantha Randall, and Jim Yarbrough; Kevin and Elaine Harrington; and Donlyn Lyndon and Alice Wingwall, mentors and friends.

Finally, and closest to home, this book would not have happened without the unending support of our family: wife and mother, Patricia; sister Karla and brothers Craig, Christopher, and Kent. Also, Kane, Kyle, Kenzie, Cassidy, Katie, CJ, Owen, and Ella, who are the next generation of family patriots.

ILLUSTRATION CREDITS

Alamy: Mary Evans Picture Library 91tr; The Print Collector 98br; Stock Montage, Inc. 169tr

American Antiquarian Society: 43

American Ornithology; or, The Natural History of the birds of the United States/Alexander Wilson (Philadelphia: Bradford & Inskeep, 1808–1814), Special Collections, Univ. of Virginia Library: 25

American Philosophical Society: 45r

AP Wideworld Photos: 144bl, 172,173bl, 175tr

Architect of the Capitol: 21tr

Art Resource: The New York Public Library/Art Resource 128bl, 143bl; Scala/Art Resource 96bl

Aspen Historical Society: 137tr

Autry National Center: 102bl, 111bl

Beinecke Rare Book and Manuscript Library: 18

Bennington Museum, Bennington, Vermont: 51bl

The Colonial Williamsburg Foundation: 20tl

Courtesy The Bostonian Society/Old State House: 38bl

Chicago History Museum: 31br

Collections of Seward House, Auburn, NY: 177bl

Corbis-Bettman: 23tr, 33tr, 52, 53, 55tl, 58r

Duke University Rare Book, Manuscript and Special Collections Library: 83br

Eisenhower Library/National Archives: 177br

The Free Library of Philadelphia/Print and Picture Collection: 135tr

Getty Images: 108tr, 153l, 170c

The Historical Society of Washington, D.C.: 63tr

Library Company of Philadelphia: 26tr, 39tr

Library of Congress Prints and Photographs Division: 13tr, 21bl, 22, 23, 24tr, 27tl, 27c, 27br, 28br, 29tr, 30tl, 30tr, 31bl, 35, 38tr, 44, 49br, 54, 55tr, 55br, 56, 57, 60, 67, 69, 75, 79tl, 84t, 86br, 87, 88tr, 89tr, 94tl, 96r, 97c. 100tl, 101bl, 105, 106tr, 106bc, 107, 108bl, 109.110br, 118tl, 118br, 118bl, 119br, 123tl, 126tl, 127br, 132tr, 133, 134bl, 139tl, 140tl, 141tr, 143tl, 143tc, 143tr, 143cl, 143c, 143cr, 146l, 147br, 149tr, 152bl, 154bl, 157, 158, 165, 168tl, 169br, 170tr, 170br, 171br, 177tc, 178bl, 178br

Louisiana State Museum: 119tc, 119tr

Missouri Botanical Garden: 95tr

Monticello/Thomas Jefferson Foundation, Inc.: 74

NASA: 153br

National Archives: 26bl, 27tr, 90bl, 132bl, 163br

Courtesy of the New York State Military Museum & Veterans Research Center: 118tr

Princeton University Archives: 41

The Royal Society: 95tl

Science Photo Library/Photo Researchers: 138bl

The Society of California Pioneers: 102tr

Courtesy of the Society of the Cincinnati: 28tl

Tennessee State Library & Archives: 113br

Texas State Library and Archives Commission: 85br

State Museum of PA, PA Historical and Museum Commission: 49tl

The State Preservation Board, Austin, TX: 78bl

U.S. Department of the Interior: 126–127

U.S. Patent Office: 90tl, 140bl, 141br

Reproduced from the original held by the Department of Special Collections of the University Libraries of Notre Dame: 37tl, 42bl, 51tr

J. Willard Marriott Library, University of Utah: 163tr